"DON'T PROVOKE HIM."

Connie felt violated. She wanted to scream and shout and throw things at Wayne and hurt him— even though her face was already swollen, her cheeks purple and yellow, and her arms black and blue.

But her brother's advice echoed in Connie's ears.

Wayne was no longer on the edge, however. His violent moment had dissipated as quickly as it had erupted, like so many times before. To him this was just another spat. Soon he and Connie would make up and everything would be normal again.

Connie felt trapped. In just a few savage minutes she had gone from worrying how she would ever survive without Wayne to the near certainty that she would never survive *with* him.

PRISONERS OF FEAR

GERA-LIND KOLARIK

AVON BOOKS ◆ NEW YORK

PRISONERS OF FEAR is a journalistic account of the life of Connie Krauser Chaney, her marriage to Wayne Chaney, and the stalking which led to her murder on March 17, 1992, in Mount Prospect, Illinois. The events recounted in this book are true, although some of the names have been changed. The scenes and dialogue have been reconstructed based on diaries and letters written by Wayne and Connie Chaney, tape-recorded formal interviews, police department records, court records and transcripts, and published news stories. Quoted court testimony has been taken verbatim from trial transcripts.

AVON BOOKS
A division of
The Hearst Corporation
1350 Avenue of the Americas
New York, New York 10019

Copyright © 1995 by Gera-Lind Kolarik
Published by arrangement with the author
Library of Congress Catalog Card Number: 95-94145
ISBN: 0-380-77345-7

First Avon Books Printing: September 1995

RA   10 9 8 7 6 5 4 3 2 1

Acknowledgments

In the past year, stories involving stalking by spouses and domestic violence have been extremely topical. To investigate and objectively re-create the lives of two people leading up to a tragic conclusion is difficult, and finding information and people to talk to is not easy.

Special thanks to Liz Mitchell, book editor of *Today's Chicago Woman,* who first called me with this story idea and impressed upon me the importance of writing a book like this from both sides.

I thank psychotherapist Kate Couris, of Partners in Psychiatry, in Des Plaines, Illinois, whose work with the victim program STAR was helpful to me in my interviewing of people involved in the case.

For Connie and Wayne's family members and friends, a book like this is painful as well as healing. Special thanks to Chris and Al Musetti, Jane, Tom, and John Krauser, Steve and Ken Chaney, Tammy Braithwaite, Jo Anne Hicken, Loretta Wagner, Jackie and Joan Mudd, Cathy Sullivan, Diane Tarver, Susan Melton, Kathy Hoshell, Letty Pacheco, Cheryl Answorth, Jill Jozwik, Donna Rubenstein, Ken Thrasher, and David Walters.

Many agencies became involved in the criminal case of Connie and Wayne Chaney and their representatives spoke openly to me about not only their roles, but also their feelings. I am grateful to Judge Sheila O'Brien, attorneys Dennis Born, James Kissel, Karen McNulty, Mark McNabola, John Galarnyk, John Collins, Lee Howard, and Wayne Shapiro. I thank also private investigator Jeff Mills, director of Life Span (in Des Plaines) Leslie Landis, counselor Vicky Poklop, and coroner of Kane County, Illinois, Mary Lou Kearns.

Many police departments played a major role in helping me to investigate and obtain documents in this case. Were it not for the help of Commander Al Freitage of the Des Plaines Police, many people would never have granted me interviews. Special thanks to Des Plaines officers and detectives: James Prandini, Randy Atkin, Robert Weirick, James Ryan, Ron Sharin, Mike Lambeau, Robert Schultz, Terry McAllister, Bill Spyrison, Larry Zumbrock, Kevin O'Connell, Angela Burton, Tim Veit, and Norman Klopp.

I also thank former Cook County Sheriff police captain Frank Braum, along with Mark Caridei, Paul Cagle, Robert Arrigo, and Commander Len Marak.

Special thanks to my photographer and good friend Sharon White, whose ideas made the photos, and to Wein James and Dariel Eklund, who spent hundreds of hours transcribing my many interviews. Without you both I may never have finished this book.

Author's Note

For twenty years I have worked in Chicago as a journalist for a wire service, newspaper, and two television stations. During that time I have covered dozens of stories involving domestic violence.

Though domestic violence cases are covered constantly in the news, few journalists have had the opportunity not only to report but also to experience the fears and emotions of the men and women involved in these stories. I have, and perhaps this is the first book to ever truly tell both sides of the story.

The writing of *Prisoners of Fear* has evoked far more emotions in me than any other story or TV miniseries with which I have dealt. The diaries, letters, and tape recordings of Wayne Chaney, and the personal diaries and letters of Connie Krauser Chaney, provide all of us with a rare window into Connie and Wayne's true feelings over a three-year period. Wayne's diaries, descriptive and filled with narration, reveal conversations he had, not just with Connie, but with others who were touched by their tragic lives. Having such access is a journalist's dream. But, because of what happened to Connie, Wayne, and Max William Chaney, it is a nightmare as well.

Upon publication of this book, Max William Chaney, the young son of Connie and Wayne, will be six years old. Members of the Krauser and Chaney families have offered their cooperation for the sake of helping Max to one day understand who his parents were, and why they are unable to be with him. It is Max who is the real victim of this story. Perhaps, when Max reads this book, he will come to understand that both his parents did what they believed to be "best for Max"—that they did, in fact, love him deeply.

Through the Freedom of Information Act I was able to obtain criminal data both from trial and police reports. I have recreated dialogue in this book from the above, as well as from personal letters, diaries, and tape recordings made available through family members and friends. Those whose names have been changed are marked with an asterisk upon first introduction. Scenes reconstructed from physical evidence have been verified by police and medical experts as reasonable accounts of what has happened.

While reading through court transcripts in this case, I was amazed to learn how little the divorce courts and criminal courts communicate. If judges would act immediately when there is an alleged violation of protective orders, rather than allowing the accused a thirty-day period in which to respond, and if men and women in such cases were immediately to be ordered psychiatric evaluation and counseling rather than being placed on a three-month waiting list to receive services, cases such as Connie Krauser Chaney's might be prevented.

But the purpose of this book is not to glorify or condemn any one person. It is to provide insight into the fears and feelings of people involved in domestic violence cases, and to examine what far too often, tragically, results in death.

If there is anything good to be said about the Connie Krauser Chaney case, it is that the case has been instrumental in the passage of the stalking laws in Illinois, which have prevented violence in many cases.

The author will donate a percentage of the proceeds from the publication of this book to counseling programs aimed at domestic violence. Groups that deal with domestic violence counseling are crucial for support and help to men and women like Wayne and Connie. It is my hope that Connie and Wayne Chaney's story will encourage others to find the help they need in programs that deal with their pain of separation, so that tragic results may be prevented.

I'm grateful that I am one of the fortunate ones to be able to have the opportunity to tell you all good-bye. Each and everyone of you here has touched my life in one way or another. We all have memories of each other, some good and some not so good. I will always cherish our memories. I had some wonderful times. I want you all to know that they're wonderful because of you. It is a sad fact that someone could steal another's life, yet it is really up to God to make that final decision.

I want to break a minute to ask you all to take care of my baby. Nobody could touch a person's life like a child, the whole world looks different through a child's eyes. Please teach him to be confident, caring and moral. To know that he can accomplish whatever he wants. Protect him and love him. He was my life.

>—Connie Krauser Chaney,
>   *a farewell letter to her friends and family,*
>   *July 13, 1991*

*This book is dedicated to
Max William Chaney*

Contents

Prologue

Wayne Chaney sat in his brown Ford Galaxy, parked a few houses from the apartment building where his wife's new lover lived. He had come by earlier to check it out. Now he knew where the door was, where the stairs were. He was waiting for Connie, his wife, to come to her lover. And when she did, he was going to shoot both of them, then he would take their three-year-old son, Max, and raise him properly, just as he had promised his grandfather.

Wayne, a stockily-built man in his twenties, was armed with two revolvers and two shotguns. He was ready. He had already packed another car with sleeping bags, camping supplies, fishing gear, and cooking utensils. He'd parked the car at a friend's house, and he would use it to get away. The brown Galaxy he had bought for this mission alone, and he had never told anyone about it.

He sat in his car, the revolver tucked into the belt of his faded jeans, with his t-shirt pulled over it. He knew he could wait for as long as it took. He also had to know who this Patrick Carlson* guy was. The image of Connie having sex with some other man was as painful as a tumor growing in his gut.

He thought about the promise he had made to his grandfather two years earlier. William Martin Jackson, "Gramps," had been Wayne's mentor, the one person who had always given Wayne unconditional love. "Raise Max right," Gramps had said on their last visit, and Wayne had promised that he

---

*Asterisk denotes changed name.

would. It had become an obsession with him. "Raise Max right." The words often ran through his head like a mantra.

And Max was not being raised right, Wayne thought now. Connie was sleeping with a man who was not Max's father. Wayne was allowed to see Max only on certain days at times that Connie agreed to. No, this was not raising Max right. He wanted to do the things with Max that Gramps had done with him: hunting, fishing, learning to love the land. But how could he with another man living with Connie and Max.

Now, sitting in the car, Wayne began to cry. In his mind he could see Gramps at the kitchen table, bouncing Max on his knee, just as he had once bounced Wayne on his knee.

"He has the Jackson eyes and the Jackson grip," Gramps had said. "He looks the way you did, Wayne."

As Gramps was leaving that day he had turned to Wayne and said, "Take good care of this boy. Promise me that you will raise him right. A part of me is in him." The old man had kissed Max then, and handed the child back to Wayne.

"I promise," Wayne had said. "I'll raise him right."

A few days later Gramps had died.

And now, as Wayne sat in the car and waited for Connie and his son to arrive, he knew that keeping his promise to Gramps was all that mattered. His life with Connie was over. She had left him and filed for divorce. Now their love had turned bitter, and they fought over petty things just to jab at each other. He had sold his boat for three hundred dollars. He had sold the mobile home for four thousand dollars. In one day he had moved everything he owned out of his home and into his truck. He had thrown things away, he had given things away. Every item that he packed had been loaded with stinging memories of Connie and Max, and he had cried throughout. Most of all he had cried when he came upon the toys still left in Max's play area. Neighbors and friends had helped, but nothing had eased his pain.

Now, as he waited outside the apartment building, he felt like such a fool for sending Connie tapes and letters, trying to win her back. He wanted to let her know how much he was hurting, let her hear his feelings in his voice. Wayne felt that she must be feeling the same pain. But she had probably laughed at him. She and her lover. And then he became angry.

Every time a car came down the block Wayne felt his body tense. This could be it. He was fed up. She'd been playing games with him, and all the time sleeping with some guy named Patrick. He would take his son.

Wayne dozed off a few times, but woke up suddenly, alert. By midnight Connie had not shown up. Maybe the private detective he had hired had been wrong. Maybe this apartment was not the lover's. Maybe this was the wrong address. As he became more sleepy, his rage began to subside. It could wait, he thought. Yes, she could wait a while longer and it would be all the sweeter. He pulled the pistol out of his waistband and put it back inside its carrying case, and zipped it up. He turned on the ignition and headed back to Des Plaines. He would rest before he would try again.

1

Childhood Years

December 24, 1976
Des Plaines, Illinois

All her life Connie Krauser remembered fondly the Christmas seasons of her childhood. Each year when yuletide came to Des Plaines, Connie's mother hung a huge evergreen and holly wreath on the front door. A magnificent Christmas tree was erected next to the fireplace in the living room by the large patio window and everybody took a hand in the decorating. The smell of baking cookies filled the air. Eggnog was poured, drinks were served, neighbors were greeted. Currier and Ives could hardly have painted a more wholesome picture than that of the Krausers celebrating the holiday.

Connie's mother, Cynthia, was a petite woman with a solid and dependable look about her, and she smiled almost always. Efficient and organized, she was a regular supermom who could drop one girl off at the school science fair, fill in for another mother at the Cub Scout meeting, pick up a baseball glove at the K-Mart, drop her son off at the ball field, and still have a hot supper on the table by five o'clock, and then take all the kids and all their friends to the beach the next day. To Cynthia a day off from work didn't mean a day of soaking in a hot tub filled with bubble bath; it meant a day with her children.

When the Christmas season of 1976 rolled around, Connie's mother, then forty-eight, was still healthy and active, the undisputed queen of the Krauser household. The Krausers lived in a two-story house that smelled of lemon-scented furniture polish. Cynthia had filled her home with the antique redwood furniture that she adored, and she cared for the house as if it were a fifth child. Nothing made Cynthia happier than having all her family together on Christmas Eve.

She had three girls. Connie's sister, Christine, was the oldest, and the one who looked the most like Cynthia. By 1976 Christine was living on her own in Chicago and planning, like her mother, to wear nursing whites. Then there was Jane, six years younger than Christine. Jane looked more like her father, thin and tall, with short, jet-black hair. Less social than the others, she was inclined to bury her face in a novel, or close the door to her room and just sew for hours. And then there was Connie Rose, who, despite a typical and often painful shyness, could sometimes be as troublesome as Dennis the Menace.

Even so, Connie was Cynthia's baby, and her favorite. Connie's hazel eyes shone through her brown oval glasses, although she thought they made her eyes seem as big as a frog's. Connie was dressed that Christmas Eve in a lovely long red velvet dress, tied with a white ribbon at her waist. A large red bow pulled back her shoulder-length brown hair. She was accompanied by her dachshund, Peppy.

Tom, Cynthia's only boy, was seventeen then, a good-looking kid with wavy blond hair. He had an apparently average physique, but he was an accomplished wrestler, a star on the varsity team, and two times tough enough to make life unpleasant for anybody who treated his sisters poorly. Tom especially doted on Connie. The girl had quite a bit of tomboy in her, and, in the absence of a brother, that suited Tom just fine. He taught Connie how to wrestle and how to toss a football. "Spin it with the fingertips," he would shout, and nobody was prouder than Tom when Connie was able to launch a perfect spiral pass.

Christmas Eve was special to the family also because it was one time when they could be sure that Dad would be home. John Krauser, a tall and slender man who was quiet and introverted like Jane, worked for an airline in Chicago. But he was also an inveterate tinkerer who did electronics and TV repairs from his house. Both jobs kept him busy.

Connie had learned that much of the time when her father was in the house, he wasn't exactly "home," and sometimes she thought it would be easier to get one of her mother's redwood chairs to talk to her than to wring a few words from her father. But tonight John Krauser was with his family in body and spirit, lining his bottles of brandy and rum and eggnog and wine along the small counter in the kitchen. He would be the bartender; it was a Christmas tradition. He would greet the neighbors and fill their glasses with Christmas cheer. John and the girls had also laid out trays of home-made cookies and finger sandwiches. It promised to be a marvelous Christmas Eve.

Donna Chaney arrived early that night, along with her second youngest son, Wayne. The Chaneys, however, were not there as guests, even though they lived only three blocks away. Donna was a local Avon lady, and Cynthia would buy perfumes and soaps from her to give as gifts. Wayne, a tall, husky boy with long sandy hair, was four years older than Connie. He had come along to help his mother deliver the order.

As Wayne and his mother arrived, Connie was girlishly sliding across the newly buffed kitchen floor. When Wayne saw her he came into the kitchen. "Do you want to race?" he asked.

"Yeah, sure," she said. She grabbed a fresh-baked peanut butter cookie and stuffed it into her mouth. Then the two of them ran from the front hallway to the kitchen, stopping suddenly so they could slide across the floor. Wayne's height and weight made him faster.

"Two out of three," Connie shouted.

Back to the hallway they went. Then they ran. And when they hit the kitchen floor this time Connie spun out of control, and slid directly into a wall where some decorative holiday plates were hung. The impact sent one of the plates flying. Wayne reached out suddenly, grabbing the plate just before it shattered against Connie's head. Then he rammed into Connie and another plate went flying, this one smashing to pieces on the floor.

Cynthia rushed into the kitchen. "What on earth are you two doing?" she asked. Wayne and Connie, still stunned, were surrounded by the pieces of the shattered plate. Next Wayne's mother came into the room.

"Wayne Chaney!" she said. She shook her head, embarrassed by her son's behavior. She turned to Cynthia. "I'll pay for the plate," she promised. She grabbed her son by the arm. "He'll pay for it from his snow shoveling jobs."

Wayne, also embarrassed by the incident, rose slowly. He handed Cynthia the plate he had rescued. "I'm sorry, Mrs. Krauser," he said. "It was my fault. I wanted to race with Connie."

Connie picked up her glasses and looked at Wayne. The accident was her fault more than his, yet he had taken the blame to protect her. She didn't know why he would do that, but she knew that he had also saved her from a pretty good bump on the head. It was a moment she would remember for a long time.

Too shy to utter anything to Wayne, she smiled at him to say thank you. He smiled back as his mother pushed him towards the door.

The first of Connie's friends to arrive that night was Tammy, who had been her best friend since kindergarten. The two girls were as close as twins and everybody knew that when you saw Connie, you wouldn't have long to wait before you would see Tammy, with her long red pigtails bouncing off her shoulders and her freckled face. When Tammy arrived on Christmas Eve, Connie felt more secure, less dopey. Sometimes she felt as if Tammy were another part of her, and that without Tammy she was not complete. She knew that someday she would feel that way about a boy, but for now Tammy was the best.

Cynthia put the girls to work distributing the Christmas presents that she and John had bought for the neighbors. Men got aftershave and tie clips. And the small, delicately wrapped packages for the ladies contained perfume, mostly Donna Chaney's Avon products.

"Donna Chaney's perfumes might be here, but she won't be," Connie whispered to her friends. The girls giggled at the gossip, as Connie told Tammy about the plate incident with Wayne.

The Chaneys were always excluded from the Krausers' holiday celebration, mainly because the three Chaney boys were roughnecks, a bit too loud, and liable to break things.

The guests kept coming. John Krauser always seemed to

find another tray of cookies in the kitchen for them. Dishes of salad and homemade casseroles were laid out on the open dining room table. It was a happy time, a time for retelling the stories of the year that was ending. Connie's mother recalled those sunny August days at the beach with the kids, and the smell of a Saturday morning "farmer's breakfast" cooked over an open grill at the nearby forest preserve. "Eggs!" she exclaimed. "And bacon! And potatoes!" as if she were announcing the Cubs' starting lineup. Just the sound of it made Connie reach for more cookies.

It was, all in all, the kind of family Christmas we all yearn for, a singular moment of assembled friends, burning logs, and laughter that echoes through the hallways. Connie was happy that night. She lived in the embrace of a kind and forgiving world.

The importance of this particular Christmas would come only with memory. Shadows were gathering around the girl, but she was happily unaware of them. Her beloved Tommy would be leaving for Georgia Tech in the fall on a wrestling scholarship. Her sister Chris would soon begin nurse's training and be pulled even farther from the center of Connie's life. And Connie didn't know that already, after twenty-two years of marriage and almost as many as a dad, John Krauser had decided that he would leave the family. She didn't know that she would be forced to do a lot of growing up in the coming months, that this Christmas Eve in 1976 she'd received her last few hours of sweetness and innocence.

September, 1978

After John Krauser filed for divorce and moved in with another woman, Cynthia Krauser did not condemn her husband. Instead, she blamed herself for the marriage going bad.

"It's my fault," she told Connie one afternoon after school. "I was always busy with work, with the family. I didn't leave enough time for John."

Cynthia, devastated by the breakup of her family, turned to alcohol. In the months that followed Connie watched helplessly as her mother freefell from the caring, loving person who would do anything for her kids, to a mother on whom

Connie could not count for the simplest things, such as a hot breakfast.

One by one, Connie's protectors—her father, Tom, Chris—disappeared from the house. Most of the time, even Jane wasn't home. The once-immaculate house became filthy and cluttered. The dog, neglected, ran wild. Clothes were unwashed. Meals were uncooked. Unopened mail littered the tables. It became agonizingly clear to Connie that she no longer mattered. Only one thing was important to her mother: the bottle.

Her friends—Tammy, Jackie, and Cathy—stayed close to Connie, trying to comfort her. Often they would invite Connie over for dinner, and these were bittersweet evenings when Connie could laugh with someone else's family, and pretend that her life had not turned horrible. But in the midst of things there would be a family comment, an endearing remark, even a friendly scolding, that would fill her with longing for the security of family that had been so suddenly taken from her.

Several horrid incidents would stay with Connie for the rest of her life. One night her mother, drunk, crashed her El Dorado through the back wall of the garage and had to be taken to the hospital. Another time Connie discovered her mother had thrown all of Connie's clothes into a garbage can. When Connie asked her why, Cynthia replied, "I didn't want you to leave me."

Connie became enraged. She charged at her mother, clamped her hands around Cynthia's small arms, and shook her violently. "I hate you," Connie screamed. "I hate you. I hate you. You're a drunk, that's all you are, a drunk."

Soon after that incident, Cynthia fell asleep on the couch with a lit cigarette. Connie and Tammy found her surrounded by flames. They saved Cynthia that time with a garden hose, and again got her to a hospital. Cynthia went on a rehab program for a short time, but soon it looked once again as if she were bent on self-destruction.

Not two months later, Connie and Jane discovered their mother, again unconscious, sprawled out on the bedroom floor by her redwood dresser. Cynthia was taken to the hospital and placed in intensive care, but this time her luck had run out. She had fallen and smashed her head. There had been a lot of internal bleeding, the doctors explained. This time Cynthia did not come back.

2

The Lost Years

October, 1979

When Connie Krauser was fourteen she was a freshman at Maine West high school, and she was miserable. Her mother's death had left her lonely and alienated. The house had been sold. The antiques and the beloved redwood furniture had been hauled away. And, most painfully, Connie had been separated from her friends. She and Jane had moved in with their father and his girlfriend on the other side of town. The arrangement made Connie heartsick. She felt that no one really wanted her.

So she turned inward. She drank. She smoked marijuana. For acceptance she turned to kids who gathered after school every day at Axe Head Lake in Des Plaines. The lake, and surrounding park, was a popular party spot.

Most afternoons Connie would slip into ripped, faded jeans and a baggy sweatshirt, hitch a ride over to the lake, and listen to music. There she found that hanging out with the kids, tossing a Frisbee, smoking joints, and drinking beer made it easy to forget how sad she was. There she felt she belonged. And there, on a cold and crisp October afternoon in 1979, Connie began her fateful relationship with Wayne Chaney.

Wayne, who was dating Connie's best friend at the time, was four years older than Connie. Then a small-time drug dealer and occasional burglar, Wayne would pull up in his

10

1969 red Ford Mustang and sell marijuana, cocaine, acid, and speed to his friends. He didn't make much money at it, but his role as drug supplier gave him the social status that he craved.

Connie had known him from afar for years ever since Wayne's mother sold Cynthia Christmas perfume. Though Connie didn't know Wayne well, she had said hello to him a few times at the lake. He was eighteen, strong and stocky, and whenever she saw him he always wore the same outfit. She thought of it as his uniform: blue jeans, jacket, t-shirt, and combat boots. His brown shaggy hair hung down to his shoulders and often he would go a day or two without shaving so that his beard would hide his babylike features and make his face look thinner.

If she had avoided Wayne at all, it was probably because her brother Tom hated Wayne.

"The Chaney brothers are all wild," Tom used to say. "They're bad news."

Wayne, in fact, was everything that Tom wasn't. Wayne was hot tempered, wild, and undisciplined. By the time she started hanging out at Axe Head, Connie had cut her wavy blond hair short, and dyed it brown. She had replaced the ugly oval glasses of her childhood with contact lenses, and though her taste for beer had given her a small paunch, she still attracted boys, especially older ones. These were not the type of boys to buy flowers and candy; mostly, they drove Connie around town and bought marijuana and beer.

Her date for this particular day was an older boy named Lester Gould, a tall and lanky sandy-haired fellow who didn't say a whole lot, but he had been good about getting beer and drugs.

By sunset many of the kids were stoned on beer and marijuana, and the empties were piling up in paper bags. The sex play was heating up among the teenagers. Some kids French kissed openly, as others pressed their bodies against each other while leaning on parked cars. And some headed into the woods.

Lester became aroused as he looked at Connie. They stood in the parking lot, near a field of grass, and he leaned over and kissed her neck, letting his tongue flicker down to her shoulders. Connie was uncomfortable. She was shy, and she wasn't particularly attracted to this boy. Now he moved his lips to the other side of her neck and kissed her there. She wriggled away from him, but he'd been drinking and was not attuned to subtleties. He kissed her again on the neck and ran his fingers gently along her sides, barely tickling her under the breasts.

"Please, don't," she said.

"Come on, be a sport," Lester said. He quickly threw his arms around her and pulled her toward him. Now Lester kissed her on the mouth. Connie tried to squirm away, but he had her firmly in his grip. She pulled harder and finally broke his embrace. Then he grabbed her by the waist. She lost her balance and fell back. "Come on," he said, yanking her arm.

"No," she said.

"Come on, don't be a jerk, Connie." He began dragging her toward the grass, and Connie got scared.

"No," she said. "You're drunk."

Lester was stronger than he looked. He picked her up, slung her against his hip, and now hauled her toward the grass. She pounded him with her fists. The other kids started jeering and laughing, rooting for Connie, but they were not taking the attack seriously. Some of the girls threw beer cans at Lester.

"Hey, asshole," one of them shouted, "leave Connie alone."

Connie, remembering some of the wrestling tricks that Tommy had taught her, twisted her body and somehow managed to push her feet against him, breaking his hold. She and Lester tumbled to the ground. "Way to go, Connie," someone shouted. Kids applauded. But Lester, embarrassed, was not giving up. He grabbed her again and continued toward the grass.

Wayne Chaney, standing off to one side by his Mustang and drinking beer, had seen enough. He didn't think it was funny. He put his beer can down on the pavement and walked briskly towards Connie and the boy. "Hey, asshole," Wayne shouted. "Can't you hear? Connie says leave her alone." He ripped Lester's arm away from Connie.

Wayne had massive hands, and he just leaned down and grabbed the collar of Lester's t-shirt. With one quick move he picked the boy up and tossed him through the air. Lester landed with a thump.

But the fight wasn't over. Lester rose quickly to his feet and took a fierce swing at Wayne. Wayne charged at him, grabbed him in a bear hug, and squeezed the breath out of him.

"Okay, okay," Lester cried.

Wayne dropped him to the ground, gave the kid an icy stare, and said, "Connie's a friend of mine. Don't ever mess with her. You understand?"

"Sure," Lester said, and he took off.

Wayne then turned to Connie who, still shaken, was on her knees in the grass.

"You okay?" he asked.

"Yes," she said. "Thanks."

Wayne offered his hand and Connie took it. He helped her to her feet. His hand was strong, reassuring, and when she looked into his eyes she no longer saw the hot-tempered kid who dealt drugs and drove too fast. She saw her protector instead.

The next day when Connie left school Wayne was waiting in the parking lot with some other boys, but he left them to walk over to her.

"I'd like to drive you home," he said. "Or to the lake, if I can. Lester might be there, so I thought I ought to go with you."

Connie was impressed by Wayne's thoughtfulness. This was not the boy she'd known as a kid. She followed him to his car, and he gallantly held the door for her.

"Thank you," she said, "but I'm not sure where I want to go."

"How about a hamburger?" Wayne said.

"Great," she said. He revved his engine and peeled out of the parking lot. He cranked up a tape of Led Zepplin's "In Through the Out Door" and pointed to a cooler of beer in the back seat. Connie felt good. She liked the speed of the car, the loud music, the beer.

They pulled into a burger joint and ate hamburgers in the car, washing them down with beer. Wayne seemed awkward at first, as if he had to struggle to think of things to talk about. He showed Connie his collection of tapes. They talked about music. She told him about the house being sold. She talked about her mother, remembering that Wayne had come to the funeral, and had offered his sympathies.

When they got to the lake that day, Lester was there. He glared at the couple as they climbed out of Wayne's car. He tried to talk to Connie as they walked by.

"Connie doesn't want to talk to you," Wayne said. He gave Lester a threatening look, put his arm around Connie's shoulder, and led her away. Connie turned to Wayne. She liked the feel of his hand on her shoulder. Their eyes met and she felt for a moment as if she had communicated with this young man in a way that was special. Later she would describe it to her girlfriends as the moment when she became charmed by Wayne Chaney.

In the days that followed Connie learned quite a lot about Wayne. They stood in the parking lot, leaning against his Mustang, and he talked to her about himself as few boys had.

He told her that he had dropped out of Maine West when he was sixteen because he was always being accused of stealing or being involved with drugs.

"I punched a kid in the classroom," Wayne said.

"How come?"

"He told the cops that I broke into his van and stole his stereo and his jacket."

"Did you?"

"Naw. But the cops questioned me about it. Made me nervous. So I went to school the next day and cornered the kid. I told him I didn't steal his stuff, then I punched him and ran out."

Since dropping out of school Wayne had worked in the family garage, fixing used cars and broken appliances. He had also worked as a machinist and had done a short stint in an auto parts store.

"I got fired from that job," he told Connie. "Someone told the owner I was driving their truck recklessly. I lost my temper and threatened to slash the guy's tires. But I didn't really do it."

Wayne told her that at home he got along well enough with his mother, a hard-working church-goer who spent much of her time mediating intrafamily battles. The battles were often between Wayne and his father. Tom Chaney felt that a boy out of school ought to be working, which Wayne often was. But Wayne also liked to go fishing and partying, and that did not sit well with Tom, who saw Wayne as a shirker. So battles would break out and Donna would be the one to settle them, but not before hurtful things had been said and fists had been thrown.

As Wayne saw it, his father, a tool designer, was a hot-tempered man who ran his family like an army unit. The tension between Wayne and his father had been hot since Wayne's twelfth birthday. Wayne always believed that his father was angry with him for quitting the Cub Scouts at age twelve, and that he wasn't as intelligent as his father wanted him to be. Wayne had his father's temper and they would often scream at each other. During his teens, Wayne admitted, he once even pushed his father through a wall.

Wayne was close to his brothers, Ken and Steve, however. Ken, five years older than Wayne, was constantly in trouble with the law. At one point he was sentenced to two years in prison on drug charges. Steve, the youngest, did not seem to share his brothers' penchant for mischief.

The person Wayne Chaney cared most deeply about at this time, he told Connie, was his grandfather. When things were bad at home Wayne would often head over to Gramps's and spend days there. ''Gramps understands me,'' he told Connie. And as the days passed and this short-tempered young man shared more and more of his life with her, Connie began to think, I understand him, too, and she started to consider Wayne both her protector and friend.

February 28, 1980

It was four-thirty on a cold wintry morning in Chicago as Wayne Chaney pulled his Mustang over to the side of the highway across from the O'Hare office complex, near the airport. He and his friend, Dan Roberts*, got out of the car and began walking on the freshly fallen snow. It was still dark, and few cars traveled the toll road. Too goddamn cold, Wayne thought, rubbing his hands together as he walked. He wore a yellow windbreaker, a blue jeans jacket, and a sweater, but still he was cold. He and Dan made their way across the quiet toll road to the office complex. In the deep pockets of his windbreaker Wayne felt the nylon stocking and the length of chain he would need for the robbery that they were going to pull.

For almost a year Wayne had been working for a Latino man who owned a landscaping firm. Wayne, who was capable of working hard for his money, reseeded and planted lawns, replanted trees, raked leaves, plowed snow. His dream was to have his own landscaping operation and his chance had come when his boss ran into financial problems and offered to sell the business to Wayne. The only problem was Wayne had no money with which to buy it. He had tried to borrow the money from the one person he felt he could turn to, his grandfather, but the loan was not forthcoming.

But there were other ways of getting money. Wayne and Dan had often thought up quick ways to get money, most of which were illegal. This time, they decided on a robbery. Their victim would be an older man who owned a local restaurant. The man, Wayne knew, left his home near the office complex every morning at four-thirty to open the restaurant, and he always carried enough cash to start the day. They had heard that he carried a large amount of money, close to five thousand dollars in bills and change. Taking it from him would be simple, Wayne reasoned. And nobody had to get hurt.

Wayne's accomplice in the crime was like a brother to him. This was hardly their first mischief together. Wayne and Dan had sat endlessly in area diners and planned robberies and muggings and con jobs that never were executed, and hatched schemes that sometimes were. Mostly, they ended up just hustling new players at Chicago pool rooms. But tonight was supposed to be something bigger.

They left tracks in the fresh deep snow as they made their way across the highway, through backyards, and across driveways at Craig Drive, an upper-income residential area. When they got to the intended victim's house, Dan, dressed in blue jeans and a dark blue coat, found a spot off the lawn, where he could watch both the house and the street. He was the lookout.

Wayne, his heart beating with excitement now, pulled a curled-up coat hanger out of his jeans pocket. Carefully he straightened out the wire and slipped it into the door of the victim's 1972 blue Cutlass. Slowly, carefully, he edged the wire up along the seal between the door and the doorpost. It made a scraping noise and he stopped and looked around. Dan signaled that everything was cool. Wayne began to move the wire again, finally reaching the lock button at the top of the door and popping it open. In the quiet of the early morning he opened the door carefully and climbed into the car. He hunkered down behind the driver's seat, and laid himself out on the floor so that he could not be seen when the driver got into the car. From the pockets of his windbreaker he pulled out the nylon stocking, slipped it over his head, and pulled it down over his face. He couldn't resist the urge to look at himself in the rearview mirror. His features were distorted and grotesque under the stocking. It amused him. He lay down again in the back of the car, and pulled out the twelve-inch length of link chain that he had bought at the hardware store. He would have to put the chain around the man's neck to make him hand over the money. But it shouldn't require too much force, just enough to scare the hell out of the guy, Wayne thought.

After he had been lying there quietly for several minutes, waiting for the moment, he heard Dan cry out.

"Shit, the cops," Dan shouted.

Then Wayne heard Dan running across the driveway. "Stop!" a man shouted. Then another set of steps tore past. This time he could see a beam of light, a flashlight, bobbing up and down. Wayne stayed put. He listened for more cops. He waited. He yanked the nylon stocking off his head and stuffed it, along with the chain, under the front seat of the car. If he was going to get caught, he at least wasn't going to be found with this.

Finally, when he was sure the coast was clear, he climbed out of the car. "Goddamn it to hell," he said out loud, kicking at the car. "Shit, shit." He began to make his way back through the yards to the highway, reasonably certain that if Dan did get caught he wouldn't spill his guts.

When Wayne got to the parking lot of the office complex he ran out of luck. A police cruiser came at him from around the side of the building. The car came to a sudden halt and a young officer jumped out, gun in hand.

"Okay, you," he shouted at Wayne. "Put your hands up in the air."

"What for?" Wayne said. "I'm just walking to my car." But he put his hands over his head anyway, and laced his fingers together. He knew the drill from past encounters with cops.

"Fine," the officer said. "Then you wouldn't mind coming into the station and answering a few questions, would you?"

"Ah man, shit," Wayne said.

Wayne was cuffed and brought into the police station where he met Michael Lambeau—tall, soft spoken, and a twelve-year veteran police investigator. He took Wayne into an interrogation room, sat down, lit a cigarette.

"Janitor in one of the buildings saw your car on the side of the highway, and called the police," Lambeau said. "Officer traced the footprints. Any special reason why you're parking along the highway in the middle of the night?"

Lambeau eyed Wayne carefully as he spoke. The investigator was wary of teenaged suspects, and with good reason. A few years earlier he'd been questioning a teenager when the kid pulled out what appeared to be a pen. But it was a pen gun and the kid managed to get off a .25-caliber bullet, which would have gone into Lambeau's head if he hadn't knocked the kid's arm aside as he fired.

Wayne told Lambeau that he had been walking back to his car because a friend had just dropped him off at a nearby shopping center.

"Why did you leave your car on the tollway?" Lambeau asked. "Why didn't you leave it at the shopping center? Your car could be yanked from the tollway."

Wayne thought about it. Finally, he decided there was no sense in making up some bullshit story that no cop would ever believe. "Look, he said, "you have nothing to charge me with. Except maybe parking on a toll road. What is that, a life sentence in Illinois?"

Lambeau took a puff of his cigarette and blew the white smoke into the air. "You're right, Wayne, I've got nothing to charge you with. But I will find out what you were doing out there. It may take a few days, but I will find out. Trust me."

Lambeau stood, walked across the interrogation room, and

unlocked the door. "You can leave as soon as your prints clear," he said.

As it happened Lambeau was right. Wayne had, apparently, shot off his mouth about the robbery, and Lambeau, through informants, was able to find out who the intended victim was. Lambeau had the restaurant owner's car searched. He found the nylon stocking and the chain and placed them in a sealed plastic evidence bag.

April 30, 1980

At around 1:00 a.m. Wayne and Dan parked Dan's 1972 Oldsmobile Cutlass four blocks from the Diversey Chemical Company plant in Des Plaines. It was a balmy night and though Wayne Chaney had his blue windbreaker, he wasn't wearing it. He was carrying it. Wrapped inside the windbreaker was a sixty-foot length of rope, a crowbar, three screwdrivers, a weight bar, a glass cutter, and a hammer. As Wayne and Don walked cautiously along the sidewalk, trading guesses about how much money they would score tonight, they put on their work gloves. Stuffed in the rear pocket of their jeans were nylon stockings that they would slip over their heads on the way out of the factory, just in case they were seen. But in fact they were already being seen.

Two months after Wayne and Dan's aborted robbery of the restaurant owner, Officer Lambeau and Investigator Bob Schultz were investigating a string of business burglaries in Des Plaines when they got a tip that Wayne and Dan Roberts were planning a burglary at the chemical company.

This was the news Lambeau had been waiting for, and by midnight of April thirtieth, Lambeau and Schultz, along with two other detectives, in unmarked squad cars, had parked near the railroad tracks that ran along the back of the plant. Schultz, a fifteen-year veteran, knew the Chaney family. One of his daughters had gone to school with Wayne.

Schultz, Lambeau, and the others watched through binoculars with some amusement as Wayne and Dave arrived and moved stealthily to the back of the building. In the dim light that came from the nearby streets they could see Wayne pull the length of rope out of the windbreaker and fashion a lasso

from it. The plan was to loop it around an air vent that jutted
out from the roof, climb up, then drop down into the building
through a sun window. Wayne coolly twirled his lasso and
tossed it up towards the air vent. He missed.

Again, he twirled and let the rope fly. He missed again.

Then he twirled the rope a third time, this time letting it
spin a little longer before he took aim. He let the rope fly.
He missed.

"I don't believe this. It's like a comedy act," Lambeau
said. He handed Schultz the binoculars. Schultz giggled.
Wayne was on his sixth try.

After a few more tries, the burglars gave up on this particular approach and, instead, walked around to the side of the
building. Schultz picked up the walkie-talkie and called for
the other unmarked squad car to watch for them on the other
side. Then he called in for another squad car to stand by.

At the side of the building Wayne and Dan found a large
industrial dumpster. Wayne pulled himself up on it and then,
banging his head on the low-hanging gutter, he struggled onto
the roof. Dan followed. When they got to the sun window,
it was boarded up with plywood.

"Shit," Dan said.

"No problem," Wayne told him. He pulled out his crowbar, and shoved it under the plywood. With one swift yank
he busted the board loose from the window. It snapped free
with a noise that sounded like a shot in the quiet night. The
two men crouched low, waited in silence until they were sure
that nobody had heard the noise. Then Wayne tied his rope
to another air vent on the roof and he and Dan, feeling like
accomplished cat burglars, slowly lowered themselves into
the factory.

Tonight's big prize was not to be some safe full of money,
or a factory payroll. Wayne and Dan were strictly small time
and what they were after was the nickels and dimes that
had accumulated in the company's vending machines and the
dollars that had piled up in the change-making machine.
Wayne knew the layout of the factory because he had come
there earlier, applying for a job. Now, by the light of a flashlight, the two young men made their way to the lunchroom.

Once there they worked by flashlight. Dan shoved his
screwdrivers into the change machine and battled it until he

had the lock pried open. Then he scooped up the one- and five-dollar bills and shoved them into a small plastic bag. Next, he shoved the crowbar into the side of the sandwich vending machine. It wouldn't budge. Wayne tried it. But the machine was too strong.

"Come on, let's go man," Dan said. He shook the money bag. "We got enough." They slipped the nylon stockings over their heads. Wayne and Dan were feeling pretty confident as they went back to the rope that dangled down from the skylight window. They had a bag of money and an escape route. But going up was not to be as easy as coming down had been. With a bag of money and the jacket full of tools, Wayne's own weight was too much for him to pull up the rope. After a couple of tries he got disgusted and rushed upstairs to a door that led to the roof. He threw it open, knowing it would trigger an alarm. The alarm shrieked as the young men ran onto the roof. Wayne was not worried. He was sure that he and Dan would be long gone by the time the cops arrived.

By this time the police cars had already moved in to surround the building. Dan, spotting the cruisers, worked his way to the ground and rolled under an empty box car. Wayne crawled backward into an air vent on the roof and held his breath as two uniformed cops climbed onto the roof. Within moments both men were in custody. The bag of money was taken into evidence. Wayne and Dan had stolen $387.40.

At the police station Wayne sat, handcuffed, in a side room, when Lambeau walked in.

"So Wayne," Lambeau said. He held a bag in his hand. From it he pulled the nylon stocking and the chain that Wayne had left in the restaurant owner's car. "I guess you were just sitting in that guy's car with these that night, huh, waiting for him to leave for work. And what was it this time? You just happened to fall into an air vent, with a nylon stocking on your head just as an alarm went off?"

Wayne knew there was no stonewalling this time. He waived his Miranda rights and confessed to the attempted robbery of the restaurant owner, and he gave Lambeau the details of the break-in at the factory. He spent the night in the Des Plaines jail. The next day his mother bonded him out. For his crimes, he was given one year of supervision.

That July Wayne was a suspect in another burglary, this time at a metal company where he had once worked. Stolen from the company were five skids of scrap metal, over four thousand pounds of it valued at eight thousand dollars. There was no sign of a break-in, which meant to police that it was an inside job. Whoever did it had dragged the skids over the floor and opened the garage and loaded them onto a truck. Wayne, who was never charged with the crime, had been seen at the factory a week before the break, talking to some of the other workers.

Later that summer while other kids his age were crowding Axe Lake Park, Wayne Chaney purchased his own business and called it Affordable Landscaping. His crime spree, it seemed, had ended. He was maturing. Soon he discovered that he had a good sense of business and that he could make a good living without breaking the law.

August, 1980

Connie felt as if she were being pulled up from the bottom of a murky pond. As she rose higher and higher, the deep heavy darkness receded around her like waves passing over her. She felt herself getting closer to the surface. Of what? she wondered. Of sleep, she thought, of a deep sleep that felt like a coma. She opened her eyes.

A woman resembling her mother stood over her. Connie shook her head as she was coming to. Then she heard a familiar voice saying, "Connie, it's me, Chris, can you hear my voice?"

Now, as her eyes began to focus and her brain to clear, Connie could see, yes, it was her sister, Chris. She had never realized before how much Chris looked like her mother.

"Where am I?" Connie asked.

"In the hospital," Chris said. "Lutheran General."

"Lutheran General," Connie repeated. It was the same hospital where her mother had worked as a nurse. "What happened?"

"You passed out," Chris said. And then, "Connie. They say it was drugs."

"Oh," Connie said. Now the memory of the evening came back to her.

It had been a sweet summer night. Earlier, she remembered, she had been at Axe Lake Park and she had been drunk. The kids had been sitting around the campfire drinking beer and smoking dope. Wayne wasn't at the lake this night, so Connie partied with other friends. The cops had come. As the kids began to toss their drugs and scatter, Connie began to move, too, but in slow motion. She remembered the cops were shouting. She saw beams of light coming toward her. Then she had passed out.

"How did I get here?" she asked Chris now.

"One of the cops felt your pulse," Chris said. "He called for an ambulance."

Tears were streaming down Chris's face. She reached out and pressed a cold cloth against Connie's forehead, swabbing it gently from side to side. It felt cool and comforting and Connie realized that Chris had been doing it all along, even while she was sleeping.

"Connie, I'm here for you," Chris said. She took her baby sister by the shoulders. "I'm here, and I'm not going to let you die like mother. We won't let this happen."

"Die?" Connie said.

"The drugs," Chris said. "If you keep doing drugs, that's what can happen."

The door behind Chris opened and John Krauser walked in. Connie could see from the look in her father's eyes that he had been at the hospital for a while. He looked scared.

"Hey, Connie Rose," he said, forcing a smile. "Everything's going to be okay."

"When can I go home?"

"You're not going home," he said. "Not right away. You're going to Forest."

"Forest?" Connie said.

Forest Hospital was just down the street from Lutheran General. Connie knew it well. It was there that her mother had dried out, at least for a while.

"You're going into a drug and alcohol rehabilitation program, sweetheart," John Krauser said. "We're going to have our old Connie back."

Connie took a deep sigh and lay back against the white sheet. She felt powerless. Her life, she knew, had gotten out of control.

3

Acceptance

August, 1980

Placed in Forest, Connie met with other alcoholics every day in a room that was small and square and bare of furniture, except for a small desk and a dozen moveable brown metal chairs. She would sit in a therapy session circle with ten other patients. They were mostly older teens, some even twenty and twenty-one. She liked Forest most of the time; it seemed more like a wooded campus than a chemical dependency treatment center. But it sometimes felt like a prison. There were no bars on the windows, no alarms on the doors. But Connie was not allowed to go anywhere without telling someone when and where. And whenever her family brought her a gift, it was checked for drugs. Deodorant, panties, paperback books—if it came into Forest, it was suspect.

Still, despite all that, and though her moods swung almost daily from despair to optimism, she was relieved to be there. After three weeks, she was beginning to see the sense in the program. She came regularly to the therapy sessions and Alcoholics Anonymous meetings. She drew strength from the sessions most of the time, and if she faltered there was always a counselor nearby to talk to her and give her hope and sometimes just hold her while she cried. What Connie liked most of all were the weekly visits from her father, brother, and sisters. They brought her not only presents and hugs, but something deeper—their commitment to her recovery. For the first time since the death of her mother, Connie felt as if she had a family. And a friend. One afternoon, Wayne arrived with a bouquet of white daisies wrapped in green waxed paper from the local supermarket. The nurse took the flowers and began to unwrap them, looking for drugs.

"Hey, what are you doing?" Wayne said. "Those are for Connie."

"I'm sorry sir," she told him. "Our policy is that everything must be checked."

Now, as he walked into the day room with the separated flowers in his hand, Wayne felt stupid. Connie was reading literature from AA (Alcoholics Anonymous) when he came in. She looked up and smiled. She was delighted to see him.

Wayne smiled. He handed her the flowers. He sat down and listened while Connie told him how much she hated being there. She told him they wanted to send her to a halfway house in Springfield.

"Can I write to you?" Wayne asked.

Connie smiled. She took his hand and squeezed it. "Yes," she said, "I would love it." She was finally feeling connected to the world again. And Wayne would keep his promise.

But one day as she neared to the end of her stay at Forest, Connie worried that it would all be taken away. Her family had come to meet with her counselor, looking for guidance on the next step. Would she have to stay here? Could she come home? Would she be sent far away, as some of the kids had been?

Connie wanted to go home. She felt she was doing better. During her stay at Forest, they had been trying to get her to talk about what her mother's drinking and death meant to her. And for the first time Connie had let the reality of her pain come all the way inside her. It was like having her bones scraped. She had cried with the counselors and screamed at them. She had thanked them, and she had called them terrible names. And sometimes when they talked to her, she did nothing; she would get totally frustrated and not even know what to say or how to feel.

What Connie did know was that she began drinking shortly after her mother died. Losing her mother, her home, and her family at age twelve had been devastating. It had made her feel sometimes as if she didn't exist, or had become invisible.

She had wanted attention desperately. She had wanted to feel needed, and she got that feeling from her friends at Axe Head Lake. She had wanted not to feel awful inside, and the alcohol and drugs had freed her from those feelings, at least for a while. Now she was realizing she'd long sought comfort where none could ever truly be given.

Late that afternoon Connie was brought into the counselor's office with her family. Her father was there, along with Jane, Chris, and Tom. John Krauser, numbed by all that had happened, was the parent. But it was Connie's siblings who asked the questions. Jeff, the young red-headed counselor, sat behind a small desk and spoke frankly to the family.

"I am going to suggest a long-term care unit that has a special program for teens," he said. "Connie must be some place away from the life that led her into drugs and alcohol. She has to make new friends now, and she has to realize that she has a new family outside of Des Plaines."

Connie looked around. These people whom she loved were listening to every word and nodding. They agree, she thought. They would send her away. God, no, she thought, don't send me away from my family.

Jeff continued. "I don't want to seem like I'm preaching," he said. "But too often we see that when people return to the world of their drinking and drug-taking they relapse. We have to give her a chance."

The program that Jeff recommended was a part of the Gateway Foundation, a program for adolescents that was housed in an old three-story Victorian mansion in Springfield, Illinois, a four-hour drive from Des Plaines.

"It is an in-depth program," he explained. "It lasts for fourteen months. It's continuous treatment, not just a few hours a day. And she can continue her schooling there."

"No," Connie cried.

Everybody looked at her.

"Well, can't I just go to meetings here and be an outpatient? I'll be fine."

Jeff turned to her. "Change, Connie. Change. That's what's going to help you. We have to help you to learn new ways of coping with your feelings. We have to help you learn that you are no longer the victim, and you must believe in Connie."

"But I don't want to go away," Connie said.

Tom, who was leaving for school in Atlanta in the morning, leaned over, put a strong arm around her. He pushed her hair from her forehead.

"And we don't want you to be far away, Connie," he said. "But this is what we have to do because we care about you."

"Look, Connie, one of us will be there every month on visiting day, I promise you," Chris said. "This is a chance for you to grow and meet new people."

"God," Connie said, "if I hear that one more time I'm going to scream."

"Connie Rose," Chris said, "you are going to go there. I will not allow you to end up like Mom."

Connie began to cry softly. Through all the years of hiding behind drugs and alcohol, one thing had never changed. The mention of her mother could bring her to tears.

It was a few weeks later that Jane and Chris piled Connie's suitcases into Chris's car, and the three sisters drove off to Springfield to deliver Connie to her new home.

As she watched the outline of Des Plaines shrink in the distance behind her, Connie knew that she was leaving the city of her childhood behind forever. It was a quiet, middle-class neighborhood twenty miles from downtown Chicago. The main streets of Des Plaines criss-crossed the commuter tracks of the Chicago Northwestern railroad, but the town's only claim to fame is that Ray Kroc built his first McDonald's restaurant there. She would be back, she knew, but she would be different. Her sisters were chattering and listening to the radio. When there was a moment of quiet, Connie put her head down and said, "I'm sorry."

"There's nothing to be sorry for," Chris said. "We should have done this a long time ago."

"I want to make you proud of me," Connie said. And she would, she thought, and then everything would be all right.

November 11, 1980

It was just after dark on a cool November evening. Wayne Chaney had just pulled away from the curb at his parents' house when he saw the red glare of a flashing mars light in his rearview mirror. He pounded on the steering wheel of his new Camaro, exasperated. He believed that the cops were ganging up on him. Wayne had a number of court dates coming up—for burglary, possession of marijuana, open alcohol in a car, and battery—dates which he intended to keep. But in the meantime it seemed to him that everywhere he went there was a Des Plaines cop there to harass him.

"What in the fuck did I do now?" Wayne said. He stared up at the police officer who had just pulled him over at a busy Des Plaines intersection. "You are driving with no headlights or taillights on," Patrolman Frank Dziaduch said. Dziaduch was a veteran of the force, a much-experienced traffic officer. He had pulled Wayne over only for a warning.

Suddenly Wayne went into a rage. The door to the car flew open and Wayne leaped out. Dziaduch jumped back. He reached for his gun, but didn't draw it.

Wayne stormed around to the front of the car. "No fucking way," he shouted. "I had my lights on all the time. You cops are all jack-offs. All you do is hassle me."

Now people were stopping on the sidewalk to see what was going on.

Dziaduch remained calm. He knew that something wasn't right. This guy was reacting way out of proportion. He wanted to get him off the street, away from the citizens. He put his hands in front of him, away from his gun. "I think," he said, "that we should go into the station and talk about this."

Wayne got back into his car, slamming the door. He drove toward the police station with Dziaduch following. No sense running, Wayne thought, they will just come and get me.

On the way to the station Dziaduch called in. "Got a guy here who is really putting up a stink about being stopped for not having his headlights on. Let's run his license through, see if we find anything. I'm bringing him in."

The man who ran the check on Wayne Chaney's license was James Prandini, a four-year veteran on the force. Prandini, a man in his thirties, with a slender build, had just come on duty.

A few minutes later Dziaduch showed up with Chaney. Wayne moved defiantly into the police station, taking hard, quick steps. Prandini met them in a hallway near the entrance.

"Okay, I'm here now," Wayne said to the two cops. "What the hell are you going to charge me with?"

"How about disorderly conduct," Dziaduch said.

"Didn't you say that the license was on a 1972 Camaro?" Prandini asked Dziaduch. "Funny, but those plates check out to a 1972 Buick. How can that happen?"

Again Wayne exploded. "What are you saying? That I stole the car? Is that what you're saying, you crazy fucking cops?"

Instantly both officers had their cuffs out. Prandini, fifty pounds lighter than Wayne, grabbed him around the right shoulder and yanked his arm behind his back. He pressed Wayne's face against the concrete wall, cutting Wayne's lip. Dziaduch grabbed Wayne's other arm and pinned it against his back as Prandini pushed the cuffs around each wrist. Wayne cried out as the cuffs cut into his skin. Though Wayne soon stopped struggling, Prandini could still feel the violence in him. He swung Wayne around. Their faces were inches apart. Wayne pressed his lips together, ran his tongue over the blood from the cut on his lip. Then in a low and cold voice he said to Prandini, "I'm going to get a gun and blow you away."

They searched Wayne, read him his rights, and took him into a side room where he was fingerprinted and booked.

It took two hours to check out Wayne's plates and straighten out the paperwork. Wayne had just bought the car a few weeks earlier and switched his old plates to the new car. But the new registration, the license plate and the new title information, had not shown up in the computer. After they pulled up his arrest record they searched his car for drugs and burglary tools, but found nothing. In the end they had nothing on Wayne except driving without taillights and improper use of registration. He was told he would have to pay a thirty-five-dollar fine, and one more court date was added to his agenda.

As Wayne stood in the booking room, gathering the keys and wallet that had been taken from him, he glared at Prandini. He hated cops and Prandini had become the latest symbol of them. He massaged his wrists where the cuffs had bitten into him. He stared at Dziaduch, then back at Prandini. "Just remember what Manson did," he said.

"You son of a bitch," Prandini said. He had been threatened by prisoners before, but there was something particularly cold and ominous about this threat.

Dziaduch quickly stepped between the two men and motioned for Wayne to leave the room. When Wayne was gone Prandini turned to Dziaduch. "I want that statement in the report just as he said it," Prandini said. He had a feeling that this wouldn't be the last time he would confront Wayne Chaney.

4

The Change Within

September, 1981

After a year at Gateway Connie Krauser was a new person. She observed the changes in herself and noted them in her letters to friends. She felt good. She was happier.

"I've got a new sense of freedom," she wrote Tammy, "and I can accept disappointments and establish goals in my life."

The letters were part of her twelve-step program; the requirement of step nine is to make amends to the people she had hurt. In her letter to Tammy she wrote, as she did to others, "Most importantly, I'm asking you to forgive me for the way I acted when my mother was drinking. I felt angry and frustrated with my mother and I took it out on you."

Though Connie was happy now, as she wrote to her old friend, it had not been all pleasant. At Christmastime, she told Tammy she had been miserable and wanted to leave. Chris and Jane were even going to drive through a blizzard to come and get her on Christmas day. But the counselors said that was a bad idea. Between her desperate calls to her sisters, the counselors made her sit in a chair and think about whether her sobriety was more important than rushing back to Des Plaines after being at Gateway for only four months. It had been a moment of realization, she told Tammy. The fear of relapse was too real and she had given up her fantasy of Christmas at home. Her biggest thrill at Gateway, she said,

31

was when she celebrated her one-year anniversary and got a medallion with the number one engraved on it, along with the words "To Thine Own Self Be True."

In her letters she also talked about Wayne Chaney. He had come back into her life in recent months by writing to her.

Wayne, she said, had also gone through changes. He had moved in with a young married couple. He'd left his bad-boy days behind him and had bought a landscaping business that he named Affordable Landscaping. He was tired of always getting into trouble with the police and he didn't want to go to jail. Wayne, she noted, had proved himself a hard worker and a good businessman. He owned two pickup trucks that he filled each day with lawn mowers, brooms, garbage cans, and sod for new grass. He ran his business wisely and he made money. If he was not an angel, neither did he seem to be a devil.

Wayne's most attractive quality, of course, was the fact that he liked Connie. She was a girl who needed to be liked, and she was willing to overlook a lot in return.

After Connie left Gateway she moved in with her father and her father's girlfriend, Wanda, in a quiet bungalow of Des Plaines. One day Wayne was mowing a lawn when he looked up and saw Connie standing on the sidewalk. Quickly, he reached over and turned off the lawnmower. He was wet with sweat from the work. His hands were covered with dirt.

"Connie Rose, you're home," he said, smiling. He rushed to greet her. "Hey, when did you come home?"

"Came home Monday," Connie told him. "I'm on my way to McDonald's. I got a job there from Gateway."

"Well, welcome home," he said. He hugged her. Connie, pleased, kissed him on the forehead.

Wayne, suddenly shy and self-conscious, looked down. "Sorry, I'm so dirty," he said. "Hope I didn't mess up your outfit."

"I'm fine," she said. "Got your letters."

Wayne had written to Connie four times while she was away. "Would have written more," he said, "but I got so busy with the landscaping and all. Can I walk with you?"

"Yes," Connie said.

They looked into each other's eyes. She could see that he had missed her and that pleased her. "I think I like Wayne

Chaney,'' she said to a co-worker later. ''And he seems to like me.''

She worked evenings at McDonald's, and Wayne came by often. Sometimes he would arrive as she neared the end of her shift, just to drive her home. And he was always welcome, because otherwise Connie would have to take the bus. Other times Wayne would come strutting in with some of the guys who worked for him and he would flirt shamelessly with Connie and show off like a twelve-year-old.

Although she enjoyed the attention, Connie's first reaction had been to reject Wayne Chaney's romantic advances. But she had come to see his sweet and tender side, and as the weeks passed she began to feel more than friendship for him. He seemed in some ways to be as injured and lonely and she was, and her heart went out to him.

There was, however, during this time one major warning that Wayne was unstable. He came over one afternoon to help Connie work in her garden, and he became impatient with her.

''You're digging too deep . . . watch out for the roots . . .'' he had shouted. Then his face had gotten red and his muscles had tensed, as if he were being set upon by some attacker. Wayne had eventually calmed down, but not before his outburst was seen by Wanda. Later she told Connie that she didn't want Wayne coming around anymore. He was a troubled young man.

June, 1982

Connie went back to high school, the second of the Maine schools, Maine East, to continue where she left off. One day before her graduation, Connie asked Tammy to take her to the cemetery. She hadn't seen her mother's grave since the funeral. In fact, the thought of it had filled her with grief, and there had been times when she thought she would never visit the spot in the earth where her mother lay. But now she knew she had to. It was part of her healing and letting go of the pain and anger. With graduation a day away, the symbolic moment had arrived. Connie had somehow made it through adolescence safely, if not undamaged, and in the fall she

would be off to nursing school. She was, she now felt, a
woman. She had to let her mother know that she was okay.

It was a warm Saturday morning in June, and as Tammy
and Connie drove to the Holy Family Cemetery they talked,
as girls of that age do, about boys, especially Wayne Chaney.
At the cemetery, though, when they stopped in the office to
look up the location of Cynthia Krauser's final resting place,
their moods turned serious. Connie was somewhat embarrassed that she didn't know the location of her own mother's
grave. But it had been a long time and many drug-addled
nights since she'd last seen it.

They drove along the small winding tar roads between the
acres of gravesites until they found the spot. Tammy pulled
the car over to the side of the road, and they got out. Connie
stood stiffly and stared out across the rows of headstones,
which seemed to fall away in the distance.

"Krauser," she said. "Krauser."

"It's over there Connie, by that tree," Tammy said.

Connie reached out and softly grabbed Tammy's hand.
"Thank you," she said. "Thanks for coming." And then she
paused. This was a day for memories. "And thank you for
forgiving me ..."

"Nothing to forgive," Tammy said.

Connie walked alone to the grave. Tammy, sensing the
privacy of the moment, stayed behind.

When Connie reached the headstone, she pressed a finger
against the cool granite and slowly traced her mother's name.

"Well Mom, I made it," she said. "I did it."

And she had.

Since her release from Gateway, Connie had been a model
citizen. She'd gotten the job at McDonald's. She'd gone to
her AA meetings at Forest Hospital. She'd diligently done
her homework every night. She had been more active than
she had ever been, but she'd been in control of her life. And
now, as she sat down in the grass by her mother's grave,
with her legs curled beneath her, she felt proud of herself
and wished that her mother could be there to see her graduate.

For Connie there had never been another mother, though
her sister Chris had come close. Chris would call Connie
every other day. She offered advice, she helped Connie plan
for graduation. She would even go to open AA meetings with

Connie whenever she could. Connie looked up to Chris but she never felt that she could tell her sister everything about her life. She told her she was seeing Wayne Chaney, but said little else about him.

John Krauser's latest girlfriend also tried to mother Connie. Wanda was a kindly, middle-aged woman who gave Connie and her sister Jane their own rooms and made them feel as welcome as her own daughter, Kim. Wanda and Connie had gotten close. The older woman had been one of thirteen children, she had grown up in foster homes without a mother of her own, and she could understand Connie's feelings. She would listen to Connie, comfort her, but when she tried to offer motherly advice, it felt to Connie as if she had crossed a line, and Connie would clam up and turn away. She didn't want another mother. It felt disloyal.

Perhaps in time Wanda would have become a second mother, Connie thought now. Unfortunately, this new family of Connie, Jane, Kim, Wanda, and John had not endured for long.

John Krauser, like his late wife, had taken to too much drink himself. And, as he had with Cynthia, he'd gone out with other women. A few months after Connie moved in, John came home drunk one night and managed to set Wanda's house on fire while cooking.

Connie was awakened by shouting and the smoke, and when she rushed into the kitchen she found John and Wanda running about frantically, trying to rip down the flaming curtains. John finally threw them to the floor and slapped at them with a dish towel, while Wanda poured water over the cabinets, which were also burning. Then, after the grease fire was finally doused, all the frustration Wanda had been feeling came pouring out.

"That's it," she screamed. "I've had enough of your drunkenness. And I know you're seeing women. Don't deny it. I want you out of here. Out, do you hear me? All of you. I'm kicking you and everyone else out."

It had been a terrible moment for Connie, a ghostly reminder of her mother on the burning couch, and all the pain that had followed. She ran back into her room, and locked the door. She cried all night.

But Wanda did not back away from her threat and the Krausers had to leave.

If Connie was sure of one thing, it was that she did not want to live with her father. She and Jane found an apartment, which they shared with Jane's friend Mary Jo.

Certainly, if there was a moment when Connie could have slipped into relapse, could have turned to alcohol and drugs again, it was that moment when Wanda had thrown her and her family out. The breakup of yet another family. But she had not slid back. She would not allow anything to ruin her plans of graduating from high school. She would get her diploma. She would go on to nursing school in the fall. Nothing would stop her.

And as she sat in the grass by her mother's grave, her fingers still gently pressed against the stone as if she could once more connect with her dead mother, she wanted Cynthia Krauser to know.

"I'm okay, Mom," she said out loud. "I'm going to be a nurse. Like you."

She swept away the twigs that had gathered by the grave. She kissed her fingers and touched them once more to her mother's name, carved in the granite. And then she rose and brushed off her skirt, and walked slowly back to her friend.

5

Living Together

July, 1984

Wayne slowly slipped the end of the stiff nylon fishing line into the eye of the barbed hook. At the base he wrapped it around three times until it formed a small hangman's noose, where he could insert the line to make the knot taut.

From an old coffee can he pulled out a worm and laid it into his wet palm. The worm wiggled from side to side as Wayne pinched it between his fingers to hold it still. With the sharp point of the hook in the fingers of his other hand, he dug firmly through the hard midsection of the worm. Wayne knew how to set a hook so that the worm would be alive long enough for its frantic movements to attract a fish.

A few inches above the hook he squeezed together a small buckshot, for weight on the line. Then he flicked the line into the still, dark water. He unlocked his line and pulled enough slack so that he would feel the slightest movement of his prey.

Wayne sat quietly in the small rowboat as the large moon, white as a beach ball, cast its reflected light down on the lake. The August sky was bright with shimmering stars. He liked being out of the city, away from bright lights and harsh noises. Here, in the deep woods of Michigan, he felt most at home. He looked down at his twelve-year-old brother, Steve, who lay curled up, fast asleep on the bottom of the wooden boat. There was a slight chill in the night air, so Wayne took off his jacket and gently placed it over his brother to keep him warm.

With just Steve's quiet breathing and the squawking of a distant bird for company, Wayne waited, deep in concentration.

To Wayne Chaney, fishing was more than a sport. It was a battle between his shrinking patience and ever-growing excitement. A hunter at heart, he was thrilled to wait quietly for his prey to make a mistake. He loved to watch the ripple in the waters and feel the fish playing at his bait. He knew when to let the fish think it was safe, and when to jerk the line to set the hook. But it wasn't the fish that he wanted; he wouldn't even keep most of them. It was the thrill of catching them. There was a great sense of power in luring the animal to near death, and then taking it off the hook and setting it free. Sometimes he would reel in the same fish again and again as if it was as obsessed with being caught as he was with catching it.

It had been a long night of traveling with Steve. They had gotten lost along the way, and Steve had wanted to turn back. But no, Wayne had insisted they keep looking. He wanted to take his brother fishing at the very place where Wayne, his mother and father, and his brother Ken used to go when Wayne was five years old, long before Steve was born, and when Wayne had a goal, he would not be denied. Often he had talked to Steve about how beautiful and peaceful that place was and said that when he was five his dad taught him how to fish and they caught over twenty fish at a time.

"Yeah, right, twenty fish at a time," Steve had said, and Wayne had good-naturedly pulled out the photos of him and the folks proudly holding up trout of varying sizes.

He was pleased now that he had shared this with his little brother. He hoped that maybe he could create in Steve the same love of nature that he felt. Moments like this brought Wayne back to a time when his life was peaceful. For in nature, Wayne had a haven where no one judged him and he could rely on himself and no one else.

Thoughts of Connie often drifted into his mind. They had been dating now for about three months. As he fished he remembered sudden moments with her, like stills from a movie. Her eyes looking at him tenderly. Her face in the afternoon light. Her sun-tanned body naked on their bed's white sheets. These moments after making love—they lingered most in his mind. The closeness. The intimacy. That was what he was missing more than anything. Wayne loved to hold Connie and make gentle love with her, but there never seemed to be enough time together or privacy. He had suggested that they move in together and share an apartment. The vacation now gave them each time to think about it.

It was a decision that both frightened and thrilled him. Perhaps in the future he would find it less easy just to go off and fish whenever he wanted to. Perhaps he would have to explain himself. But he didn't want to fight for his time. He just wanted to be free to be able to go into the woods alone whenever he felt like it. That was his dream. But he had another dream, Wayne thought, looking down at his little brother sleeping peacefully, and he needed Connie for that. Wayne wanted someday to marry, and to have a boy of his own whom he could take fishing.

Wayne would not give up on her. She hated the idea of being able to make love at only certain times of the day when Mary Jo or Jane was not in the apartment, and Wayne would use that to convince her to leave. When he wanted something he stayed on it, just as he had during the trip up to the lake. Although Steve thought they had gotten lost in the woods and things seemed hopeless, Wayne had convinced him to continue on until they found their way.

Soon after that fishing trip Wayne convinced Connie, too, even though she, like Wayne, had never lived with a lover before, and found the experience a little scary at first. They moved into a small apartment in Des Plaines, and if Wayne took great comfort from the woods, Connie took just as much from suddenly living with a person who would love and protect her.

"God, you're beautiful," Connie heard Wayne say. "What did I do to deserve a woman so beautiful?"

It was shortly after they had moved in together, and she was getting ready for her first day of work at her new job in the deli department of Dominick's, a local supermarket chain. It was a busy and exciting time for her. She still dreamed of becoming a nurse and she took classes during the day. Now she stood in front of the bedroom mirror, brushing her hair and wondering if she liked the way she looked in the peach uniform she'd been required to wear. Connie never used much makeup or believed in beauty shop hairdos—she liked things simple. And so the uniform worked for her perfectly.

Through the mirror she watched him in the bed behind her. He lay naked on the white cotton sheets. He stretched his arms above his head and the firm muscles in his chest flexed, then he pushed the pillow under his head to stare at her adoringly. Connie turned quickly towards him. In his eyes she could see that he felt the same love and happiness that she felt. They shared the newness of the intimacy and it was a feeling that she hoped would last forever.

He rose up to his knees and slowly reached out for her with his long muscular arms. His fingers laced behind her waist, and he gently drew her in.

"Wayne, I have to go to work at the deli ... it's a new job," she said unconvincingly as his lips softly closed upon hers.

They fell to the bed and he rolled her beneath him, poising his large frame over her chest. Their eyes met and they seemed to melt into each other. Connie took her finger and softly ran it across the blond hairs on his pecs. Wayne bent low and kissed her throat. "I love you Connie Rose," he said. "You are the best thing in my life. I will always take care of you and love you."

They made love then and from the feel of the strong man inside her and surrounding her, Connie believed that sense of security would last forever.

From the apartment that she had shared with Jane, Connie had not brought much. Just her clothes and an antique cedar chest that had been her mother's. The one-bedroom apartment in Des Plaines seemed perfect for the young couple living together. Wayne had his prized custom-made oak office desk, which his friend Dan had made for him. Wayne showed it off to anyone who visited. "See," he'd say, "it's got these compartments for letters, and I can put my office supplies here ..." He wouldn't allow anybody to put a cup down on the desk without a coaster, and each week after sitting at the desk to write out his customer bills, he would polish it, filling the whole apartment with the smell of lemon furniture polish.

On a bookshelf nearby Connie kept her medical books from nursing school at the University of Illinois, where she was taking courses during the day. Connie would study in the afternoons, and then drive to the deli where she worked mostly evening shifts. With Wayne for a partner, Connie no longer had to take the bus. Wayne was a whiz with used cars, and he bought Connie an old clunker and had it tuned up like new in no time.

Because he had lived on his own for a while, Wayne had also learned his way around the kitchen, and often when Connie came home from her deli job after midnight, Wayne would meet her at the door, smiling proudly.

"Madam," he would say, bowing graciously, "dinner is served," and he would wait on her like the finest of waiters, presenting her the dinner he had cooked.

They were happy together. But if one of them was uncertain about the future, it was Connie, not Wayne. After her months at Gateway, Connie still experienced life as if it were something new, a game in which all the rules had not yet been explained. She felt herself growing, but wasn't always sure of the direction. She no longer went to AA meetings. Drinking and drugs seemed to be a distant piece of her past. Nursing school represented the new start in her life, and she was determined to give it all she had. Connie thought she wanted to marry Wayne, to have his children, to buy a house. But she wasn't positive. Wayne, on the other hand, knew that was exactly what he wanted: to be a family. Most of all, Wayne wanted to be a father.

Wayne's instinct for fatherhood had already found a sometimes unwilling subject in younger brother Steve. One afternoon, in between jobs, when Wayne dropped into his parents' home on Fifth Avenue, he was surprised to find Steve at home watching TV.

"Why aren't you in school?" he asked his brother.

Steve laughed. "Because I am here," he said.

Wayne was not amused. "Get up. I'm taking you back to school."

"What are you talking about?" Steve said.

"You ain't going to make the same mistakes in your life that I did," Wayne told him. "You are going to graduate,

get an education, go to college, and make something of
yourself.''

"Hey you made something of yourself," Steve said. "Shit,
you've got your own business.''

"I could have had a lot more if I stayed in school," Wayne
said. "But no, I had to have it my way." He walked over
to his little brother and grabbed him by the shirt. "Now get
up, let's go."

Though Wayne had never hit Steve, Steve understood that
it would be a good idea to do what his brother told him.

Connie, perhaps, understood this, too, that it was a good
idea to do what Wayne wanted, though the message was
often more subtle. The idea of being a couple was new to
Connie. She had never lived with a man before. There seemed
to be certain social rules that went along with it. And she
followed them without questioning. One was that if you live
with Wayne, you also socialize with his friends and other
couples at Boomer's Tavern in Des Plaines.

Boomer's was a storefront bar on a side street in a residential area of Des Plaines. The buildings around it were low-
rent apartments, and the people who frequented Boomer's
were mostly factory and warehouse workers. Often a string
of motorcycles would be parked up on the sidewalks in front.
They reminded Connie of western movies, with all the horses
hitched out in front of the saloon. The atmosphere inside was
western, too, with polished cattle horns mounted over the
bar and the latest country and western tunes blaring from
the jukebox.

No matter when Wayne and Connie went to Boomer's, it
was always crowded with men and women in their late twenties, drinking and laughing and shooting pool. It was a happy
and raucous place that seemed to find an excuse for a party
every night. If it wasn't Valentine's Day, or Halloween, or
Saint Patrick's Day, then it was "Western Night," or "Ladies Night," or "Funny Hat Night" or something.

So like many young couples, Wayne and Connie placed a
bar at the center of their social life. This normally is a disas-
trous idea for a recovering alcoholic. But Boomer's seemed
at first to be no problem for Connie. She had never hung out
in bars, and so the atmosphere did not bring up memories
associated with drinking. She only went there to socialize,

and she even tried to minimize that. With school and work, she didn't have much time for hanging out with friends, anyhow. Connie felt secure that she wouldn't backslide.

April, 1986

"I want to drop out of nursing school," Connie said. There. She had said it. And she had said it to her sister Chris, the person who cared most about her nursing career.

"I see," Chris said. She sat on a couch at her place, gazing sympathetically at her younger sister. Connie didn't know what she had expected—a bawling-out, a sermon, criticism—but she had built this moment up in her mind so much that it was one of the hardest things she had ever set her mind to do. She hoped it would be over soon, whatever her sister said.

"Why?" Chris asked.

By this time Connie had reached the point in her nursing school training where she was required to put in many hours working in a hospital with patients. That had brought her closer to Chris, who was working full time at a northside Chicago hospital. But it had also brought Connie closer to the reality of life as a nurse. And gradually, she had come to realize that it wasn't for her.

"It's hard to explain, but working with people who are helpless depresses me," she told her sister. "It brings up memories," she added, remembering how she had taken care of her mother when she was twelve.

For reasons Connie didn't fully understand, each new patient reminded her of her mother, and soon after she began her hospital work, she now told Chris, she began dreading the hospital and the prospect of becoming a nurse.

"I'm sorry," she said to Chris, after she had explained it as best she could. "I know I'm letting you down."

"You're not letting me down," Chris said. "You're just . . ."

"What?" Connie said.

"You're rushing your life," Chris said.

Chris, as always, was cool. She never yelled or demanded that Connie change. Instead, Chris would just lay out the facts. This is what's happening, she would say, always logical, always right.

"You're going too fast," she said now. "Moving in with Wayne when you're only nineteen. Working part time, going to school, and trying to build a career—it's all too much too soon. Take some time, Connie. Give yourself some space, and work on Connie. Don't focus on anybody else."

Telling Wayne her decision to give up nursing came a lot easier to Connie. He didn't mind if she dropped out, he said. He loved the idea of taking care of her.

Perhaps Connie should have been pleased that Wayne had made it so easy for her to change course. But she wasn't. Chris had planted a seed. More and more, Connie felt that she was losing her bearings. Just as she had turned her back on nursing school, she had also begun to doubt other decisions in life. Like Wayne. Was he the right person for her? Was this the right time to be with him? She was beginning to feel as confused and powerless as she had at sixteen.

Connie voiced these concerns to her friend Loretta Delavale. Loretta, a pretty, dark-haired women just two years older than Connie, also worked behind the deli counter at Dominick's. She and Connie had bonded quickly. Now, with Connie dropping out of school, Loretta often came to Connie's apartment, arriving early in the afternoon, and staying through all the hours that Connie used to spend in nursing school. They would spend the day talking, or shopping, and then they would drive off to work together for the four-to-midnight shift at the deli.

"Ever since I left nursing school I've noticed that something is happening with my relationship with Wayne," Connie told Loretta one afternoon. "Maybe I was just too busy to see it before."

As Loretta pressed her to articulate just what she was feeling, Connie felt as if she were back in therapy at Gateway. It was that sense of being protected by Wayne, she realized . . . it was gone. She was no longer like a bride on honeymoon. She was disenchanted.

As spring stretched into summer, Connie became more and more bored. Wayne was out all day, and even Loretta was often lost to her because Wayne got Loretta some jobs cleaning windows for some of his clients. Connie tried to work with Wayne, but somehow they always ended up arguing.

"You're just getting in my way," he would say. "Why don't you go home."

If the days were lonely, the nights became lonelier. Often as not, Wayne didn't come home after work. He would go on fishing trips and be gone for hours. More and more Connie and Wayne lived separate lives. On hot summer days, if Loretta was free, she and Connie would drive over to Axe Head Lake. They would toss a Frisbee, the way Connie did during her drug and alcohol years, then lay in the sun and tan and share their problems.

At Gateway Connie had been taught to say what was on her mind, to not hold back her feelings, and in these comforting afternoons she was more and more coming to terms with her confused feelings about Wayne.

"I need some space away from him," she told Loretta. "I need time to sort out what I am going to do with my life. I love him, but I can't work behind a deli counter forever."

Loretta understood. She, too, worried about spending her life behind a deli counter.

One afternoon when she was at the lake with Loretta, Connie found someone there she didn't expect. Wayne. He had gone off to work that morning, she thought, and here he was fishing on the lake and partying with his Boomer's friends. Connie couldn't believe what she was seeing. If he was free to take the day off and play, why couldn't he have taken her with him?

It might have been wise to discuss this at home, but Connie confronted Wayne right there at the lake in front of his friends. Not surprisingly, Wayne lashed out. He was a man with men, and she was a woman trying to read him the riot act.

"I finished work early, all right?" he said. "So shut your trap."

"Why didn't you come home?"

"I'll come home when I'm ready to come home," he told her.

It was an ugly scene, one which crushed Connie and convinced her more than ever that life with Wayne was some kind of trap.

When she came home from work that night, she was still upset from that afternoon's incident. It was after midnight, and as she sadly entered the apartment that had once been such a love nest, she was confronted with piles of empty beer cans. Wayne was asleep on the sofa with the TV still on. She needed to talk, to get it all out. She grabbed his shoulder and began to shake him.

Wayne woke up with a start. He bolted off the couch as if it were burning. "Jesus," he shouted. "What? What is it?"

"Wayne," she said, "I want ..." The words wouldn't come.

"What?" Wayne said impatiently. "What do you want?"

"I want to move out," she said.

"Move out? But we like it here," he said.

Connie stepped back from Wayne. She folded her arms in front of her chest, as if for protection. "I don't mean us," she said. "Me. I want to move out."

Wayne reacted as if she had punched him in the face. His head snapped back, his face became red suddenly, just as it had that day in the garden, and she could see that his fists were clenched.

"Why?" he said, half-pleading, half-shouting. "Why? What did I do wrong now?"

"It isn't you," she said.

"What the hell is this, you want to leave me just because I took an afternoon off with my friends?"

"No, no Wayne, it's not that. I've been thinking."

"Oh, great. You've been thinking."

"I need space in my life," Connie said. "Everything is happening so fast."

"Oh," he said. Now he stood dangerously close to her, fists tight, anger etched like scars on his face. "I see what's going on. You've been talking to your sister Chris again, haven't you?"

"This has nothing to do with her," Connie said.

"It's got everything to do with her," Wayne shouted. "She hates my guts, she always has, and you know it."

He began to pace, seeming suddenly as large and danger-ous as a bear in the small apartment.

"It's not Chris," Connie shouted. "It's you."

"Oh, now it is me, huh? A minute ago it wasn't me, it was just you needed some space, whatever the hell that means. Make up your mind, Connie."

"Well you're never here for me," she shouted. "You're too busy fishing and drinking beer. I don't need to live with someone like that."

He stared at her, his eyes widened in rage. His face and neck became redder than before. For a moment Connie thought he was going to pass out. Then he stopped pacing.

"You are not leaving me," he said, coldly. "You cannot leave me."

She thought he would hit her. But, instead, he turned from her and rushed to the wall of the living room. He pressed himself against the wall as if he could push it down. She could hear his breath becoming rushed.

"Wayne? Wayne, are you okay?" she said.

"I don't want to look at you," he said. "I don't want to see a betrayer."

"I'm leaving tomorrow," she said. Get it done, Connie, she told herself, don't back down. "I will find a place somewhere."

She moved toward the bedroom, thinking, how will we get through the night. Can we possibly sleep together on such a night? She hoped Wayne would have enough sense to spend the night on the living room couch.

Suddenly Wayne was upon her. "No," he said. Still not touching her, he hovered closely, smothering her with his presence. All of his muscles were tensed. He looked like an animal ready to pounce.

"I say no," he said. "You will not leave me."

"I can leave you," Connie said. Try to keep cool, she told herself, don't show him how scared you are. "You can't stop me."

"No," Wayne screamed, then his hands were on her shoulders, shaking her. It was the first time he had ever touched her in violence. Connie threw her hands up against his arms and broke his hold, pushing him off balance. He began to fall backward, and for a moment seemed to lose his footing, before he pulling himself forward and lunged at her. The force of his shove knocked the breath out of her, and Connie tumbled to the floor. Fearing he would pin her down, she rolled quickly to her side and struggled to stand. But when she was halfway up, Wayne leaned over her, waiting, like a boxer who would deck his opponent as soon as he got to his feet. He looked huge and monstrous. His eyes were merciless, and his hands were still clenched into fists.

Though others had seen this side of Wayne Chaney, Connie had not. Certainly, she had seen him lose his temper—in the garden, at work—but she had never seen him act violent before. For the first time Connie was terrified that Wayne might hurt her. But she fought the fear. She'd been taught that at Gateway. She couldn't let it stop her from leaving. She knew that if she did she would be lost to it forever.

Connie rose slowly. Wayne didn't move. She walked across the living room, expecting an explosion, but it didn't come. She grabbed her purse and looked at Wayne. What she saw was almost as shocking as the violence. The rage had drained from Wayne's body as quickly as it had appeared. His muscles were relaxed, his face almost white. It was as if he were an actor; the curtain had fallen and he had emerged from the role he was playing. The Wayne who faced her now was meek and tired and apologetic. When he reached for her there was no fist, and his hand settled gently on her shoulder.

"Connie I'm sorry," he said. "Honey, please don't leave me."

Connie was silent as she stood for a moment and looked him in the eye. She felt her throat tighten. The tears she had held back now flowed freely. She shook her head, and walked quickly to the door.

Wayne ran down the stairs after her.

"Connie, let's talk," he pleaded.

She turned around just once. He stood above her on the stairway. No longer threatening, he looked pathetic, like a small boy being abandoned by his mother. Connie felt sorry for him, but she knew what she had to do. The pain of the first time he had struck her still throbbed in her shoulders.

"Leave me alone, Wayne," she said. "Just leave me alone."

Connie could not have made a more foolish choice for her next stop. She went to Boomer's. It was a homing instinct, perhaps, that brought her to the place where there would be understanding friends. She needed someone to talk to and as she stood in the doorway to Boomer's and stared through the dim, smoke-shrouded bar mirrors reflecting the shelves of liquor, she spotted her friend Cathy.

"My God, what happened?" Cathy asked. She led Connie to the bar. There she reached for a napkin and began dabbing at Connie's tears.

"I'm leaving Wayne," Connie said. "I can't take this anymore. We had a fight and he ... he ... well I guess it was my fault, I shook him awake and told him I was leaving and we had a fight and he pushed me down."

They sat at the bar, women talking about men. Cathy softly rubbed Connie's shoulders.

"You'll be all right, don't worry," Cathy said. "Things will work out."

Connie shook her head from side to side and lit a menthol cigarette.

"Why does he have to be like that?" she asked. "Why? I don't even know why I'm with him."

Then without giving it a lot of thought, she turned to the bartender.

"I want a beer, a light beer, please," she said.

6

Back Together

September, 1986

The most significant change to emerge from Connie's leaving was the fact that she started drinking again. It was only beer, she told herself. And it was only at Boomer's. No big deal. She was sure that she had her drinking under control. It was not a problem.

In a way Connie was right. She did not develop a serious alcohol problem again, or even become a heavy drinker. But still it was a problem because she had allowed herself to return to something harmful. She had taken a small step down the path of self-destruction, and that was a path that led, inevitably, back to Wayne Chaney.

It didn't take Wayne long to show up at the deli with roses and a card. "I love you Connie Rose and I want you back. I will change, honey, believe me." And just as easily as he had changed his attitude, he won Connie over with his child-like ways of asking for forgiveness.

"Honey," he begged, "it was our first fight. Please give me another chance."

Connie could not refuse. Within days of her departure she returned to Wayne. Soon the moment of violence began to shrink in memory until it seemed to Connie so much smaller than it had really been.

Still, her rebellion had shaken Wayne. He was terrified of losing Connie, and in the days following her return, he was every inch the charming lover, making heroic efforts to provide Connie with the attention that she craved. Some days Wayne would go to work just long enough to give his crew their work orders. Connie would pack a lunch, and off the two would go to the placid fishing waters of some hidden lake that Wayne knew about. Connie was delighted that Wayne wanted to share his passion with her, and she tried to love fishing, but in the end she realized that sticking squirming worms onto razor-sharp hooks and gutting dead fish were not her idea of fun. Fishing would just have to be Wayne's thing.

But they did have fun at other times. In the weeks that followed their first physical fight, Wayne took great pride in showing off his girl. He often brought Connie to Chaney family activities. On Sunday afternoons, for example, they would join Wayne's family for dinner. These were carefree family days that nurtured both Wayne and Connie's instincts for nesting and building a family of their own.

Steve Chaney, who was sixteen then, loved to play football in the backyard with Wayne and Connie. Connie still had some tomboy in her, and Steve liked the fact that his brother's girl could give a pigskin a pretty good ride. From the days when she had played with her brother, Tom, Connie had developed an impressive spiral and a powerful toss. Steve would often laugh at the sight of his brother, Wayne, running furiously to get under the football when Connie fired it in the air.

For Steve Chaney, Connie was the sister he had never had. He loved tackling Connie in the backyard and tumbling in the grass with her. And he loved her sense of humor. Connie cracked jokes easily, and whenever she got off a good one she would lower her head so she could look up at him. She would smile from the side of her mouth. In each eye she had a freckle, and this devilish look of hers seemed to highlight them.

But most of all, Steve loved the fact that he could talk to Connie about the things that mattered to him at that age. Steve had become quite a good carpenter and he would brag to Connie at length about how he had refinished a chair or built a bookcase. Connie would listen patiently even to the most mundane details of carpentry. She really took an interest in what was important to him. With Connie, Steve could also discuss his problems at school, most notably the fact that teachers seemed to expect trouble from Steve just because his last name was Chaney.

"They're always comparing me to Wayne or Ken," he told Connie. "They think I'm going to deal drugs or cause problems just because I'm a Chaney."

Steve was not the only member of the Chaney family to grow smitten with Connie Krauser. Wayne's mother, Donna, was very fond of the girl, and had been since Connie was a kid, back when Donna Chaney used to sell Avon products to Cynthia Krauser. By the time Wayne started bringing Connie around for Sunday afternoon dinners, Donna was convinced that Wayne had found the perfect girl. She bragged about Connie to her friends at the Methodist church, and dreamed of the day when the two of them would give her grandchildren.

Though Connie was adored by Wayne's family, the same could not be said about Wayne and Connie's family. Connie often brought Wayne on visits to her sister, Chris, but the get-togethers were always awkward. Chris disliked Wayne. Sometimes she told herself that what she was feeling was just her motherly instincts toward Connie, that no man would be good enough for her little sister. But there were other times when Chris knew. It wasn't just any man. It was Wayne. She didn't trust him. And Wayne could feel it.

Chris was now Christine Musetti. She had recently gotten married and she and her husband, Al, lived on the northwest side of Chicago in a two-story frame house. Al, an architect, had redesigned the house interior to make it look more spacious, and Connie often dreamed that she and Wayne would have such a house. But it was a house in which Wayne always felt like an outsider. While Connie would sit with her sister and brother-in-law and talk for hours, Wayne would stretch out on Chris's couch, clutching the TV remote control in his hand, and just click his way from channel to channel until it was time to go.

The place where Connie and Wayne still felt most comfortable together was Boomer's. Wayne especially liked the freedom he felt there. With Connie's family, and sometimes with his own, Wayne felt that he was being judged. But at the bar he could drink beer, hang out with his friends, and act pretty much any way he wanted. He felt accepted.

Often Connie would meet Wayne at Boomer's after work. She would sit, smoke cigarettes and talk with her female friends while Wayne and the guys shot pool. Other times they would slam a couple of tables together, all their friends would gather around, load the jukebox with quarters, and listen to country music while they drank pitcher after pitcher of beer.

Connie, who loved country and western, often affected a cowgirl style of dress. She almost always wore boots and a sweater and skirt. She felt that she belonged at Boomer's, and she fit in a lot better socially now that she would drink with the rest of the crowd and wasn't going to nursing school. Wayne, who loved to dance when he was drunk, and would literally kick his shins, was gradually becoming more affectionate in public. He was especially frisky in the bar where, after a couple of beers, he would come up behind Connie and wrap his long arms around her and kiss her neck. At first Connie would redden and shrug demurely. Her shyness made her friends laugh. But as time went by she became less inhibited.

Wayne's business continued to thrive. With two pickup trucks and six employees, he seemed to be well on his way to becoming a big success. Behind him were the days of robbing factories. In fact, many of the police officers who had arrested Wayne during those reckless years were happy to see how well he was doing, and they often stopped by to say hello. James Prandini, however, was not convinced that there was a new Wayne Chaney. Prandini's run-in with Chaney had stayed fresh in his memory, and while he didn't go out of his way to find Wayne, when he did come upon him he would ask probing questions. What are you doing these days? Who are you working for? Prandini believed that Wayne was still a bad apple. He would carefully check the registrations of Wayne's trucks and sometimes he would ask Wayne or his workers if he could take a look into their toolbox or truck just to be sure nobody had slipped any drugs or burglary tools in there.

Connie's dream of a career in nursing was replaced by the dream of a career in business. Still working at the deli, she began to attend trade school, where she was learning secretarial and management skills. She was hopeful that if she could get into a good company, even as a receptionist, she could work her way into a career. And then, it seemed, all the other good things would fall into place.

June, 1987

It was on a sunny afternoon in June that Connie learned once more that good times don't always last. She came into the apartment around lunchtime, her arms loaded down with groceries. Summer had come in full force, so she was wearing only shorts, a skimpy halter, and sandals. As she placed her bags of groceries on the table a male voice said, "Hi." Connie jerked up, startled.

It was Wayne. He stood in the doorway to the living room, and with his arms stretched up to the lintel, he looked especially big. Still sweaty from the morning's work, he wore a t-shirt and held a can of beer in one hand.

"God, you scared me," Connie said. She laughed nervously. "Hey, why aren't you at work on a day like this?"

"I'm the boss, remember?" Wayne said.

"Great day for mowing and planting sod," she said.

"I thought I'd take a few hours off," Wayne said. He smiled, and took another sip from his beer can. His face was unshaven.

"Going to do the bills?" she asked. She pulled groceries from one of the bags and moved about the kitchen, placing them in their proper places.

"No," he said. He watched her intently, as she opened the refrigerator and put away Diet Coke, milk, and fresh vegetables. "I came home for another reason."

Connie stood and smiled. "You're out of luck, Wayne. I have too much to do this afternoon."

Connie was no prude. She had a healthy appetite for sex and a deep appreciation of its pleasures. But a quickie at lunchtime was not her idea of lovemaking. Though she liked spontaneity, she also required real intimacy and the lingering afterglow of being held and cuddled and told that she was loveable. She didn't like sex when it seemed that she was

simply being asked to extinguish a fire that burned in
Wayne's loins.

Wayne guzzled the rest of his beer. He crushed the can
and tossed it into the kitchen garbage can.

"You have cute knees," he said. "Do you know that?
Real cute knees."

"Well, thank you," Connie said nervously. She put on a
southern accent, which she often did for fun.

"And a nice ass."

"You're so sweet," she said.

She could feel his eyes looking her up and down. She
turned to face him. He was closer than she'd thought, and
now he grabbed her and pulled her to him. "And you smell
good, too," he said. He pressed his lips against her neck,
kissing her softly. She tried not to respond. He kissed her
harder and harder, working his lips up to her mouth. Then
he gripped her arms tightly with his powerful hands and
forced his tongue into her mouth. Connie pulled away.

"Wayne, please stop it," she said. "I said no."

"Oh, come on, Connie," he said playfully. "Don't be a
party poop."

"Maybe tonight," she said.

"Tonight?" he said. "Maybe? What if I get run over by
a truck this afternoon?"

"Wayne, you won't get run over by a truck," Connie said.

Suddenly he pulled her close again. He ran his tongue
along her neck again, this time moving down instead of up.
He pressed his tongue under the strap of her halter, then
pulled it down with his hand. He kept kissing her, licking
her, his tongue working its way down to her breast.
"Wayne," she cried. He sucked her urgently, his hands pressing hard against the small of her back.

"Wayne!" she pushed as hard as she could against his
sweaty chest, trying to wriggle free.

"No, Wayne. Now stop it, please."

"Hey, calm down," Wayne said. "This is me. I live with
you, remember. I pay your bills. I take you out. Now I want
a little. What is that, a crime?" His voice was still soft and
playful, but his hands were like iron, adamant. "Hey, you
are my girl, right?"

"Yes, I'm your girl, Wayne. But I don't want to have sex right now. So just leave me alone, okay."

Now his fingers dug into her painfully. "No," he said. "I won't leave you alone, okay?"

Connie could feel her face grow hotter. "I don't want to have sex with you," she said, but his grip only tightened. "Damn it," she said. She shoved her knee up between his legs and rammed him just hard enough to get him away from her.

"Jesus Christ," Wayne screamed. He bolted back, his hands rushing to his crotch. She could see from the pained look in his face that she had kneed him harder than she had intended. Wayne's legs buckled and he fell to the tile floor.

Now Connie was afraid that she had really hurt him. "Wayne, are you okay? I'm sorry."

For a moment he could not talk. He just rolled back and forth on his side, clutching himself, his face curdled with pain.

Connie started crying. "I'm sorry," she said. "I didn't mean to hit you so hard." She reached down to him, but he pulled himself up without her help.

"Why the fuck did you do that?" he said, still wincing. Wayne reached out and grabbed her arm, holding it firmly so she couldn't back away from his question.

"Because I said no," Connie said. She was surprised to hear herself shouting. Only now did she realize how angry she was at the way Wayne had tried to dominate her. "You wouldn't leave me alone, so I hit you. You deserved it, Wayne."

Wayne just stared at her. Was he hurt? Was he angry? Had she done the wrong thing? Suddenly Connie felt dirty, guilty, confused. All sorts of emotions swirled within her. She yanked her arm free and swung around. Connie rushed into the living room, leaving Wayne behind, and fell in tears to the couch. Why does it have to be like this? she wondered. Why can't we just always get along? She tried to focus on the happy times, the football in the yard, the laughing at Boomer's, even the stupid fishing trips with Wayne. Why couldn't there be just the good times? Why did there have to be this ugliness? She remembered how much counseling had helped her at Forest, and wondered if Wayne would get counseling if she asked.

These thoughts were interrupted by glass suddenly crashing. Then another, more violent noise came from the kitchen. Wayne was screaming. "Goddamnit, this is my place," he said. "I pay the bills." Another crash. Connie rushed into the kitchen. Wayne, red with rage, was tossing the groceries from the other bag all over the room. "Damn pickles," he shouted; then slammed a jar of them to the floor. "Shit." He whipped cans of vegetables at the sink.

"Wayne, Wayne," Connie cried. "I'm sorry I hit you. I'm sorry, I shouldn't have done that." Please stop." She rushed to the sink and ripped off a handful of paper towels and began sopping up one of the messes he had made.

"Stop it?" he screamed. "I'll stop it." Now he put down the objects in his hand and went for Connie. He grabbed her violently and forced her back against the doorjamb.

God, he's going to hit me, she thought.

She wanted to strike him first, just smash him with her fists, but she knew that would only enrage him more. She felt her body crash against the hard wooden frame.

"Don't you ever do that to me again," Wayne shouted into her face. He raised his arm back behind his body.

"God, Wayne, don't," Connie screamed, feeling more helpless than she had ever felt. "I'm sorry, I'm sorry. I won't do it again."

"You bet your ass you won't do it again," Wayne said. He smashed his fist into her face full force. Connie felt a moment of blackness, then dizziness, and then just the burning of her face where he had hit her. He grabbed her by the shoulders and pushed her through the kitchen, toward the bathroom, where he slammed her against the doorway. Now Connie threw up her hands to protect herself. She swung wildly at Wayne, but he easily pushed her hands back. Now, more irate because she had tried to hit him, he smacked her face even harder. Connie felt herself going faint. The stinging in her cheeks was almost unbearable.

"You bitch," he shouted, punching her in the right eye. The dizziness rushed over Connie again, and she felt her balance slipping away. As one hand went to her eye to protect it from another blow, she fell back and reached out with her other hand. She landed on the edge of the tub. She was crying hysterically, screaming, "I hate you, I hate you," waiting for the next blow to land. But it didn't come.

"Bitch," Wayne said again. He stared down at her, the anger still screwing up in his face. This time there would be no apologies, no outstretched hands, no begging for forgiveness. He stormed out of the bathroom and went into his office, slamming the door violently behind him.

Later, when she told her friends about it, Connie had no idea of how much time had passed while she sat there on the edge of the bathtub crying so hard she actually heaved to catch her breath. When she finally pulled herself up she looked in the bathroom mirror, and through her blurred vision saw that the skin around her eye had become purple and swollen. Blood oozed from a cut over her eye, where his ring had dug into the skin. There was a moment of panic when she thought the eye might be permanently damaged. But she closed it and told herself it would be okay. She took deep breaths. She splattered cold water on her face. Then she walked slowly into the kitchen, picked up her purse, which Wayne had flung to the floor in his rage, and went quickly out the door.

Barely able to drive with her vision so distorted, Connie made her way to Loretta's house. Loretta's father, Frank, let her in, and called to his daughter. The two of them tried to calm Connie down. Still hysterical, she spilled out the details of the fight. Her shoulders shook and she sobbed continually. "It's my fault," Connie said. "It's all my fault."

Frank filled a towel with ice cubes and placed it on her cuts. "Your fault?" he said. "That this guy hit you? Hell, I've been on this earth for fifty-two years and I've never hit a woman." He began to wipe away the crusted blood on her forehead.

"Dad's right," Loretta said. "I don't care what you did. No man has the right to hit a woman. You are not going back to that man. He has no right, no right at all. You don't have to be ashamed of anything. You said no, and he didn't respect that. So he hit you. Connie, honey, that is not love, that is not someone who treats you like a human being. Who does he think you are, some tramp he picked up that he can do with as he wants? Forget him. This time you are not moving back in, you are staying here."

Loretta put her arms around Connie. Connie, comforted, burrowed her head into Loretta's shoulder and sobbed.

Later that afternoon Connie called Tammy. She came to the house and the three women discussed ways to keep Connie hidden from Wayne.

"You have to stop seeing him," Loretta said. "That means no talking to him. No sitting down for a beer or anything."

"When they start to beat you, that's too much," Tammy told her.

"I don't know why I stay with him," Connie said. "There's that something."

"The only something is that he's a man," Loretta said, "and you haven't known enough other men. Look, you knew this guy since you were sixteen. You're almost twenty-one. You haven't dated many other guys. You've got to know more men than Wayne."

They spent the afternoon talking in that vein. Men were great. Men were horrible. They hated them. They loved them. When the phone rang Connie tensed. She knew who it would be.

"Let me speak to Connie," Wayne said. "I know she's there."

"She's not here," Loretta said. "And please don't call here for her." She put the phone down without saying goodbye. She turned to Connie and Tammy. "See how easy it is," she said.

Thirty seconds later the phone rang again. This time Loretta just picked it up and put it down without speaking.

"He'll get tired of calling after a while," she explained.

Maybe it would be easy to just walk away, Connie thought, maybe it would.

Certainly freedom from Wayne Chaney seemed possible during the days that followed. Connie missed Wayne. It hurt not to see him. But she forced herself to stay away from him, just as she had stayed away from drugs and alcohol all those years. Loretta and Tammy did what they could to keep Connie distracted. They took her shopping. They took her to parties where they knew Wayne wouldn't be.

The father of one of the boys who worked at the deli had a room to rent in his house on Graceland Street. Connie agreed to take it. Three days after the beating, when they were sure Wayne would not be home, Loretta drove Connie to the apartment. They dashed around like burglars, gathering as many of Connie's things as they could carry or stuff into big plastic garbage bags. Connie took her clothes and makeup and her cedar footlocker, all the time listening for the sound of Wayne coming home early. After they got safely away, Connie moved into her new home. It was a small room, but the family was nice and the house was peaceful. The room was her private place where no one could hurt her.

Connie was anxious to date other men. She thought that would help her purge the poison of Wayne out of her system. It was not so easy, however. She was still shy, and she had no idea of how to strike up a conversation with a stranger. So she gravitated toward men she already knew and when she finally settled on one, she chose unwisely.

It was at a pool party later that summer. The party was at a friend's house. Loretta and Tammy were there, and Connie thought maybe there was a chance that she would meet a new guy. As it happened, Dan Roberts, Wayne's friend and former partner in crime, was there. When she saw him, Connie was surprised by her own emotions. She was happy to see Dan, even excited about it. Connie had always liked him, and she had always felt that Dan was attracted to her. Now, free of Wayne, he looked better than ever to her.

In the pool Dan splashed Connie with water like a twelve-year-old boy trying to get a girl's attention. She splashed him back. It was a mild flirtation and they both knew it. Dan even joked nervously about it. "Imagine what Wayne would do if he caught me flirting with his girl," he said. "His ex-girl," Connie replied.

Throughout the afternoon the flirting continued, somewhat at a distance. They were both feeling awkward about the situation. But in the evening, after they both had been drinking, such inhibitions faded. Connie stood in the pool beside Dan. She pressed herself against him, lightly fingering his bare chest. He did not pull back from her. Instead, he slipped his arms around her. It was an exciting feeling to have someone new touching her, wanting her. Now she put her hands around him. There was a moment of concern. Ex-girl or not, they knew Wayne would not exactly be happy for them. And then they threw caution to the wind and kissed. Later, they would look back and consider this pool party to be their first date.

When the news got back to Wayne, he did not take it well. The news came from Steve Chaney, who had run into Dan at a bar. Dan had told Steve what was going on and wanted to know if it was okay with Wayne; were he and Connie really finished with their relationship? Steve, knowing the answer was no, had held onto his secret for a while and when he finally told his brother, Wayne flipped.

"That's it," Wayne shouted. "The bastard has stabbed me in the back. I will never talk to that son of a bitch again."

Wayne, as usual, acted out his rage physically as well as verbally. He banged his fist into a wall until it bled.

"Dan is history," he shouted. "He betrayed me, betrayed me."

July 22, 1987

Connie drove her red Oldsmobile Cutlass into a parking spot behind the Des Plaines theater adjacent to the mall on Miner Street where Connie worked at the delicatessen. But she wasn't working this morning. She was with Loretta, and they were going shopping in some of the mall's department stores. It was a fine day for an outing, sunny and warm. Connie carefully locked her car and, as she and Loretta walked across the parking lot toward the stores, Connie talked about what she would buy. During a break from work at the deli one night, she had done some window shopping, she told Loretta, and she had her eye on a few blouses and a new pair of jeans. This was a significant moment in Connie Krauser's life, though she didn't know it. It was on this morning that she would begin her day as a stalked woman.

Soon after the women left the car, Wayne Chaney, slowly cruising in his yellow Chevy pickup truck, drove onto the parking lot. He had been watching the lot, knowing that sooner or later Connie would show up. This was his chance. He had seen her turn off the road and into the parking lot.

Now he drove up and down along the lines of cars, looking for Connie's Cutlass. For Wayne, this was like tracking a deer in the forest, the Oldsmobile his quarry. When he found it he could feel the excitement growing within him. He had bought the car for Connie shortly after they had started living together, and in Wayne's mind, this entitled him to take it away, too. What was about to happen was Connie's own fault, he reasoned. If only she had responded to his phone calls. He had tried to get messages to her through Tammy and Loretta, but they had refused to help. He had even gotten Connie's new phone number and called her at all hours. But she had not answered. Now she would have to be punished.

Still in his truck, he slowly circled the Cutlass, studying it from every angle, as if it might suddenly bolt and get away. This was the moment before the kill and he would milk it for all that it was worth. He could feel his heart pounding, the adrenaline rushing through him. Finally, he found the angle he wanted, and he swung his pickup truck around so that the rear of the truck was aimed at the passenger side of Connie's car.

He glanced around the parking lot. He spotted a Des Plaines detective in an unmarked car, one of the many local officers Wayne knew from various encounters. He waved to the detective and smiled. The detective waved back and drove by.

Now Wayne jammed the gear shift into reverse, pulled his foot off the brake, and stomped on the accelerator. The pickup lunged backwards, and Wayne braced himself as it smashed into the Oldsmobile. There was a wrenching of metal as the doors caved inward, and a splattering of glass as the side windows exploded. The Oldsmobile reared up to one side and landed a few feet from where it had been. Wayne was thrilled. He let out a shriek of victory. It had been as exciting as the kill. He glanced back once at his handiwork, then shoved the truck into forward gear and sped out of the parking lot.

Connie and Loretta returned to the parking lot a few minutes after noon. The sight of her wrecked car hit Connie like a fist to her heart. For a moment she was silent. She felt like crying. She had no insurance.

"It was Wayne," she said. "He did it. I know it."

Connie, distraught, frightened, and angry, had her car towed. She was told that the car was totaled and not worth trying to repair. She walked home dejectedly, counting her dollars in her mind to see if there was some way she could afford another car.

Wayne, in the meantime, had called Dan Roberts. "Dan," he said coldly, "I just smashed up Connie's car." Then he hung up.

Connie was in her kitchen, putting away the clothes she had shopped for, when the phone rang.

"Hi, Connie," he said, almost cheerfully. "I just smashed into your car." And he hung up, just as he had with Dan.

Connie, who had been frightened by the knowledge that Wayne would do such a thing to her car, was now more frightened by the fact that he didn't even try to hide it. She immediately called the police and told them about the phone call.

The officer who went to see Wayne this time was Ron Sharin, a fifteen-year veteran who had arrested Wayne when Wayne was eighteen. Then, there had been a report that somebody was breaking into an Elk's Lodge. Sharin had gone into the lodge and found Wayne Chaney hiding under a desk in a darkened office.

Now Sharin checked out Wayne's truck before going in to speak with him. There was glass and red paint imbedded in the rubber on the truck's rear bumper, and on the trailer hitch.

At first Wayne denied hitting Connie's car. But when he saw that Sharin wasn't buying it, he changed his story, saying he had hit the car, but that he had a right to.

"How's that?" Sharin asked him.

"It was mine," Wayne said. "Connie used to be my girlfriend. I gave it to her."

Wayne was charged with criminal damage to property and set free on one hundred dollars bond to await a hearing.

The possibility of another arrest apparently placed no fear in the heart of Wayne Chaney. A few weeks after the incident in the parking lot he struck again.

Connie had gone with Dan to a movie at the Des Plaines theater. They left shortly before midnight, and as they turned the corner around the building and entered a narrow alley they came upon Wayne, leaning against a wall. He just stood there. His body language was unthreatening. His hands were pushed deep into his pockets and he just shrugged when he saw them. "Hi Connie, hi Dan," he said, seemingly without emotion. Connie was afraid. She stepped back quickly. Dan moved forward to protect her. For a moment the two men glared at each other.

"Let's go," Dan finally said. He took Connie's hand and led her away. As they moved away from the alley Connie glanced over her shoulder, thinking Wayne might follow them. But all she saw was Wayne, standing in the same place, staring at them with eyes that seemed to Connie, very sad.

Dan took her for a nightcap at a nearby lounge. By this time, having a drink was as normal for Connie as having a Diet Coke. It was one o'clock when they came out of the lounge and headed back to Dan's car, a red Pontiac Grand Prix. Connie was still feeling edgy about Wayne. They were getting close to the court date for the incident with her car, and she was afraid he might try something. Suddenly Dan started shouting.

"Goddamn it," he cried. "Goddamn it, goddamn Wayne, I'm going to kill him."

"What is it?" she asked. Then she looked ahead at the car and she saw.

"He slashed all my tires," Dan said. "He slashed them all. Shit, shit, shit."

In court a few days later for the first attack, Wayne told the judge that all he had done was smash up a car that he owned. He showed the judge the car's registration, in his name. The judge agreed that the car belonged to Wayne. There was no law against destroying your own property. The judge asked Connie if she wanted to pursue any other charges. She said no. Wayne was released and his bond was returned.

A few days after that Wayne had his own surprise. When he went out in the morning to begin work he discovered that all the tires on his car and all the tires on his trucks had been slashed. He called the police and filed a report. Later that day a woman who worked at a local lounge said that at three o'clock in the morning she had seen a man running away from the trucks. Her description sounded like Dan Roberts, the very man that Wayne Chaney suspected. When the police

presented her with a photo lineup of five subjects she picked
Dan out. Wayne signed a complaint against his old pal and
Dan turned himself in.

The feud between Wayne Chaney and Dan Roberts was in
full fury now, and Connie blamed herself for it. She called
Wayne and pleaded with him to drop the charges.

"I might," he said. "On one condition."

"What's that?"

"Have dinner with me," he said.

"Okay," she said.

They met at a local restaurant. Wayne, the auto wrecker
and tire slasher, could not have been more of a gentleman.
He was scrubbed to a polish, dressed in a jacket, and smelling
sweet of cologne. He was charming, apologetic, remorseful.
Over dinner he told Connie that if he acted crazy sometimes
it was because he loved her so much. He told her that he
would change. He begged her for forgiveness. And Connie,
as emotionally troubled in her own way as he, looked into
his deep sorrowful eyes and melted. Of course he loved her.
Nothing could be more obvious. He loved her, and that was
the most important thing in the world to her. She held his
hand all through dinner. Connie Krauser was being pulled
back into Wayne Chaney's web. Or perhaps she was rushing
enthusiastically into it.

Within days Connie and Wayne were an item again. It was
as if all of Wayne's violence had occurred in a bad dream
that now had ended. Connie was as certain of Wayne's sincer-
ity as she was that the sun would come up in the morning.
She told friends that the time apart had been good for their
relationship. When she was reminded that this was a man
who had beaten her up, smashed her car, stalked her, and
slashed her date's tires, Connie replied that these dramatic
actions only showed how much Wayne loved her.

Wisely, Connie did not move back in with Wayne. Instead,
they dated. They went to movies and concerts. It was a full-
fledged courtship and he wooed her with flowers and charm.
On Christmas, Wayne's favorite holiday, he decorated his
apartment with every note and card and letter she had ever
given him, and every photo of her that he could find. The
happy couple bought a small spruce Christmas tree and decorated it together. They hugged and laughed and sang as they

strung the lights. They kissed under the mistletoe. It was the happiest Christmas moment Connie could remember since those yuletides of her childhood, when her mother and father were still together.

After the tree was decorated, Connie and Wayne toasted it with spiked eggnog, and they slipped gradually into a sweet and tender lovemaking under the tree. Later, she would remember the moment well and say that it was then that she felt their love coming alive, that she felt it growing inside of her, like the beginning of a new life.

7

A New Life

March 16, 1988

"I think I became pregnant in December," Connie said. She sat on a cold examining table in the office of Dr. Bernard Greenwald.

Greenwald, a gynecologist-obstetrician who had been doctoring to area women for more than forty years, smiled at her. He was a kindly man, robust and good humored. Now seventy years old, he had delivered more than ten thousand babies. Connie had come to him because her friend Cathy Sullivan worked for Greenwald. And because Connie's home pregnancy test had indicated she was pregnant.

Greenwald put on his gloves and began the examination.

"And there's something else," Connie went on, nervously. She realized she'd been talking nonstop since she got into the office.

"Oh?" the doctor said.

"I'm not married," she said.

Greenwald smiled again. With ten thousand childbirths behind him, he'd met a few unwed mothers-to-be.

"The most important thing is that we determine if you are pregnant and how long you have been pregnant," Greenwald said, "and that we do the best to make sure that you and your baby are healthy."

Connie had hoped that Dr. Greenwald would not be the type to judge her harshly and now she was reassured.

The exam took only a few minutes but it felt endless to Connie because it embarrassed her and because she was so anxious to know for sure if she was pregnant. When it was over, Greenwald did not keep her in suspense.

"Congratulations," he said. Connie felt her heart soar. "It looks as if you are three months pregnant."

"Three months?" Connie said, quickly subtracting the months in her mind. It was important to her that it be December and that it be Wayne. "Yes," she said. "December, I knew it." I did know it, she thought, that night under the Christmas tree with Wayne.

Connie got dressed, and she sat patiently on a low and cold metal chair. Greenwald stood before her, a clipboard in his hand. He asked her a series of questions, and each time she answered he scribbled a note. Connie wanted to jump up and scream for joy, call all her friends, write letters. Her mind raced. Pregnant. Will it be a boy or a girl? Which of her girlfriends should she tell first? How would she tell Wayne? Where would they be, what would he say?

"What about your mother?" Dr. Greenwald was saying.

"My mother?" Connie said. As always the mention of her mother could shatter her mood, at least for a moment.

"Did she have any difficult pregnancies?" Greenwald asked. "Any problems or complications?"

"Oh," Connie said. "I don't know. She died when I was ten."

Greenwald patted her shoulder. "Well you look very healthy to me," he said. "Next, I want to set you up for an ultrasound."

"Ultrasound? Is there something wrong?"

"No, no," Dr. Greenwald said. "This will show you that your baby is alive within you. It is our way of making sure that everything is okay with you and your baby."

By the time Greenwald had set her appointment Connie was weeping with joy. She wanted to share her news as quickly as possible with a friend, so she asked if Cathy could come in. Cathy started smiling when she reached the door, sensing Connie's big news before being told. The two women hugged. "I am going to have a baby, Tinker, a baby," Connie cried. "Just think, Connie Rose Krauser is going to have a baby."

Cathy was the first of four women that Connie told that day. She also told Loretta, Chris, and Tammy.

By the time Connie met Loretta later at the McDonald's where Connie had once worked, her joy had been tempered by a number of practical considerations. For a while she sat silently across from Loretta, delaying her announcement not because it would be such a thrilling surprise, but because Loretta did not approve of Wayne. Loretta knew something was troubling Connie. Connie kept grabbing french fries and then tossing them back in the package.

When Loretta pressed her, Connie finally announced, "I saw the doctor today."

"Are you okay?" Loretta asked.

"I'm three months pregnant," Connie said.

Loretta was taken back. "God, Connie," she said. "Wayne's the father?"

"Of course he is," Connie said.

For a moment she was silent. She stared off at the small children playing on the slide in front of the restaurant, perhaps imagining her own kid in a few years.

Gradually, though, her fears rose to the surface and Connie then spilled out all her apprehensions about motherhood. For one thing, she told Loretta, she had no health insurance. For another, she was haunted by her own memories of growing up without a father, and she was fearful that the same thing could happen to her baby.

"Wayne and I have always been on and off," she said. "I want this baby to have a real family."

It seemed to Loretta that Connie wasn't sure of how to break the news to other people. It was the great moment in her life, and she didn't know how to share it with the people she loved.

Connie's problem, though she didn't quite say it, was that the people she loved didn't love Wayne, and while they might have been joyous about her pregnancy, many of them would be saddened to know that Connie's link to Wayne Chaney had been tightened.

Still, by the time she said good-bye to Loretta that day, Connie knew she had no choice. She had to tell her sister, Chris. She drove to Chris's house and dropped in unexpectedly. This was rare for Connie, so Chris knew that something was up.

Chris, who had been relieved when Connie had left Wayne, had been annoyed, exasperated, and frustrated when Connie went back to the man. It had not been easy, but Chris had held her tongue about it. Chris had come to believe, probably correctly, that whatever she said would make no difference, and there was no point in fighting. Still, she worried. It was difficult to understand why her sister would gravitate toward such a jerk, and it was difficult not to grab Connie by the shoulders and say, "Smarten up, get a man who will treat you the way you deserve to be treated."

All these thoughts passed through Chris's mind as she sat in her living room with her little sister. But she sensed that fate had intervened, that something had made a break with Wayne even less likely, and she had a pretty good idea of what it was. Chris, whose daughter was now two, was three months pregnant with her second child. She had a sixth sense about such things.

"Connie," she asked, "are you pregnant?"

Connie, stunned by her sister's intuition, began to cry. "Three months," she said.

"Oh Connie," Chris said. She held her sister. "We are going to have our babies around the same time." Then she stopped and looked at Connie. "Who is the father?" she asked, not looking forward to the answer.

"Wayne," Connie said. "I'm thinking of marrying him."

"Are you sure that's the best thing?" Chris asked.

"He's asked me many times," Connie said. "I've always put him off. But I think we should now. I can get Wayne's insurance benefits and a child needs a father ... and ..."

Chris felt then that she could see Connie's future with Wayne, and what she saw was not a pretty sight. "Look," she said, "let's not jump into things. There are other alternatives. Do you really want to raise this baby?"

"Well, of course," Connie said. "Why wouldn't I?"

"I've got a two-year-old daughter, remember?" Chris said. "Connie, we are talking about a lot of work and a responsibility that lasts a lifetime."

"I know."

"You could put the baby up for adoption."

"Chris," Connie said, "I know you're worried about me. But ... well, the baby needs a father and a home and a family. Wayne isn't that bad. He's changed, he really has, and maybe this will be good for all of us."

Chris shook her head. She was unconvinced. "Connie, I love you," she said, "and I want what's best for you. But, frankly, I don't think you should marry Wayne. There is something I don't like. A feeling. A premonition. Call it what you want. Wayne Chaney is bad news. I think you should just get away from the guy. You can be a single mother—we will all help you."

Connie, not wanting to fight with her sister, or disappoint her, said that yes, Wayne had been a problem in the past, but that now things were better and that, in any case, she hadn't decided definitely to marry Wayne.

By the time she left Chris's house, Connie was a zephyr of whirling emotions. Joy over the pregnancy. Worry over the health insurance and the time she would lose from work. Uncertainty about what she should say to Wayne.

She stopped next at Tammy's house, put on her happiest face, and revealed the news straight out. Tammy's first question was "Did you tell Wayne?"

Connie told Tammy no. Their relationship, she explained, was still somewhat iffy, and she was still seeing Dan from time to time. She said, "I didn't think this would happen, but this is Wayne's baby. Should I get married?"

"Times have changed," Tammy told her. "You don't have to." Like Connie's other friends, Tammy tried to make it easier for Connie to get by without Wayne. She told Connie that her mother would help, that she would teach Connie about changing diapers and washing bottles—she *could* raise a child by herself. She didn't have to marry someone.

By the time Connie left Tammy's that night it must have been clear that there was a theme to the day's conversations: Don't marry Wayne. But it wasn't necessarily what Connie wanted to hear.

She put off telling Wayne. Instead, she called Dan Roberts and asked to see him. If nothing else was clear, it was clear to Connie that carrying Wayne Chaney's baby was sufficient reason to end her relationship with Dan.

She met Dan at a local restaurant and told him she was

pregnant by Wayne then she asked for his advice. Perhaps
Connie imagined Dan being happy for her and a tender good-
bye, let's stay friends, no hard feelings, and all that. But the
meeting did not go that well. Dan was angry, jealous. He
lashed out at Connie verbally. It was Connie's fault that his
friendship with Wayne got screwed up, he said. "We never
should have got together," he told her. "It was a mistake."
Then he yelled at her. "This is Wayne's baby. I'm not going
to marry you, that's for sure. I got enough problems with
Wayne. He's the father, you go to him. I'm done with you."

Dan, apparently needing to tie up loose ends, then drove
to Wayne's. He stood at the bottom of the three steps leading
up to Wayne's house and asked to see his old buddy. When
Wayne came to the door, the two hot-tempered young men
stared at each other, as if each was waiting for the other to
draw a pistol.

"What do you want?" Wayne asked.

"Connie's pregnant," Dan said. "And I want you to know
that it's your baby and I am having nothing more to do with
her." Then he left.

After this encounter, though Wayne still regarded Dan as
a traitorous enemy, Wayne told a number of people that he
admired Dan for coming to him that way. Perhaps Wayne
was just in a generous frame of mind. He was ecstatic about
the pregnancy—this was Wayne's dream come true. A child
of his own. Within minutes of Dan's departure Wayne was
on his way to a department store, where he bought a life-
sized black and white panda bear for a child that wouldn't
even be born for another six months. Then he drove to Connie's place. When she came to the door, he wiggled the panda
in her face and said, "Look, honey, our baby's first teddy
bear."

Connie was not pleased that Wayne had found out from
somebody else, especially Dan. But at least he knew now,
and the smile on his face made her think that everything was
going to be all right.

In the days that followed, Wayne glowed as if the child
had just been born. He told everybody he knew, and some
he didn't know, that he was going to be a father. Many of
the people he told remember Wayne being as happy and
excited as they had ever seen him. He was simply overjoyed

at the prospect of fatherhood. And there was, he told Connie, no reason not to get married now. Business was good, the baby was coming, he was straightening out. Everything was coming together, he said, and he began to make plans. Donna, his mother, insisted that Wayne and Connie have a church wedding. "We have to do this right," she insisted. "We will hold the reception right here in our own backyard."

When Wayne's brother Steve heard the news it crossed his mind that the baby could be Dan Roberts's, but Steve was wise enough not to give voice to such an idea. Wayne's brother Ken was less wise. Ken had not forgiven Connie for turning to Dan Roberts, and when Ken heard that he was going to be an uncle, his first comment to Wayne was, "How do you know that it's your baby? I sure as hell don't want to be around if that baby is born with red hair."

March 30, 1988

In March Connie went to Dr. Greenwald's office for the ultrasound examination. The purpose of the test was to give Dr. Greenwald a look at the fetus, so that he could be sure the child was developing normally, and also to determine more precisely how long Connie had been pregnant.

Wayne, who wanted to be included in every aspect of the pregnancy, went along, and acted the nervous daddy through every moment. Connie later told Tammy that she found the process fascinating. Her belly was coated with jelly and a probe was attached. The probe was then hooked up to a TV monitor and Dr. Greenwald turned it so that Connie and Wayne could watch the emerging sound picture. First they saw what looked like a dark swirl of clouds. Then Dr. Greenwald began to trace his finger along the dark image. He pointed out the black imprint of her baby's nose and mouth, the white of the baby's skeleton. Connie watched intently. Yes, yes, she could see it. The image seemed to float from side to side, the small head with the hand up towards the face, and the outline of the bones in his fingers. The baby, Greenwald said, was sucking his thumb, though it was hard for Connie to make it out that clearly. Her heart beat wildly. I'm looking at my child, she thought, a baby that Wayne and I made. It was an exciting moment for both of them. Wayne, extremely touched by it all, kissed Connie softly. She was thrilled to see him so gentle.

"This is the head," Dr. Greenwald said, "and here, you can see the heart beating."

Wayne watched anxiously. His great concern was that the baby be a boy. He reassured Connie that a girl would be fine, but they both knew he had his heart set on a son. And if the baby were a boy, Wayne had announced, he wanted to name him William Max Jackson, after his grandfather.

Dr. Greenwald joked with him. "If the child cooperates and shows us his genitals, we'll know," Greenwald said. "Otherwise, you'll have to wait until he is born."

Dr. Greenwald told the couple that the fetus looked healthy and he estimated its age at three months and nine days. "But," he added, "I am sorry, this baby is not helping us in determining his sex."

Dr. Greenwald could see how excited Wayne was about the wedding. "It will be a real wedding, in a church," Wayne said. "Connie will wear a gown and we will have flowers, music, everything. Nothing is too good for my Connie and my baby. You are invited."

"Fine," the doctor said. "And you, young lady," he said, pointing at Connie, "you have to take good care of yourself, Connie. Don't do too much. Remember, no alcohol, no cigarettes, and no drugs. You want a healthy baby."

"I will take care of myself," Connie promised. "And my baby. I'm going to be a good mother."

June 18, 1988

The wedding of Wayne Chaney and Connie Krauser took place at the First Methodist Church in Des Plaines, a small flagstone structure that had been erected on the corner of Graceland and Prairie in 1950. The church was not air conditioned and so on this very hot day, with the temperatures climbing into the nineties, fans had been hauled out of closets and brought by guests, and placed strategically around the sanctuary to keep everyone from wilting.

Before the wedding, Connie stood in the ladies room at

the back of the church, surrounded by female friends and family, all of them fussing with her clothes and makeup. Though she was six months pregnant, Connie was radiant in a white lace wedding dress, the handiwork of her sister Jane. In her arms she held a bouquet of pink roses, white carnations, and baby's breath from her sister, Chris, who had tried to put away her apprehensions long enough to enjoy Connie's big day. In her hair Connie wore more flowers from Chris.

Loretta was the maid of honor and she wore a sleeveless satin gown.

"The lipstick is too bright," Connie said to Jane, who was carefully applying the makeup to Connie's lips. Connie had never been much for makeup and now this pink color seemed strange on her face.

"Connie, relax," Chris said, though Chris was on edge herself. She fumbled with the flowers in Connie's hair.

"I'm so scared," Connie whispered.

"I know, I know," Chris said. She stepped away now and studied Connie at arm's length. "You look great," Chris said. "And I have something for you."

From her purse she pulled a small black velvet jewelry box.

"Earrings," she announced as she snapped open the box and revealed a pair of small looped earrings. A small diamond glistened in each loop.

"They were mother's," Chris said.

"They're so beautiful," Connie said. "I could cry."

"I wore them when I got married," Chris said.

"Thank you, Chris," Connie said. And then she turned to the others. "Thank you all for being here," she said, holding back the tears. "Jane, for the dress. Chris, for the earrings; Cathy, Loretta, and Tammy, thank you. I love you all."

Then there was a distinctly unladylike knock on the door and it was time for Connie to be escorted out by her brother Tommy. She stepped out carefully. Loretta lifted the trail of the gown. Tom took her arm in his and led her to their father. "My baby sister has grown up," Tommy whispered along the way. "You have turned into a beautiful woman."

Meanwhile, Wayne was going through his own prenuptial jitters. In the photo taken with his father and grandfather in front of the house before the wedding, Wayne looks particu-

larly uncomfortable. He was not used to suits and his arms
hang awkwardly by his side.

If Wayne was not totally at ease about this wedding, he
was not alone. Steve, who was an usher, remained uneasy.
He still worried that the baby might not be Wayne's and he
knew that nothing in this world could crush his brother now
more than that. But Steve showed up at the church early, and
hoped for the best.

Ken Chaney was also a long way from being at peace with
Wayne's marriage to Connie. Though he had agreed that his
two daughters would be flower girls in their uncle's wedding,
Ken was still on unsteady terms with Wayne. In front of the
church on the wedding day, the brothers exchanged sharp
looks. Ken, perhaps nervous and not knowing what to say,
said the wrong thing. "Hey, you can still back out," he said.

Wayne gave him a look that could kill. He pointed a finger
at his brother. "Look," he said. "This is my wedding day,
okay. I am marrying Connie. I love her."

Ken, hurt and frustrated, stayed outside of the church for
awhile, but finally walked in.

Neither of Wayne's brothers had gotten the call to be best
man. That honor had gone to Jerry Wessel, a fellow who
worked with Wayne in the landscaping business. Jerry had
been a drifter before hooking up with Wayne, but he was
quiet and the two young men worked well together. Jerry,
not troubled by issues of paternity, was strictly happy for his
friend, because if one thing was clear it was that Wayne
was in love with Connie, was thrilled with the prospect of
fatherhood, and more than anything wanted to get married
and raise this child.

The other person who had no reservations about this wedding was Gramps, Wayne's grandfather. He was happy about
Wayne finally getting married, and he was excited about having a great-grandchild.

As the moment approached, Wayne took his mother's arm.
Donna Chaney, who adored Connie, might have preferred not
to have a pregnant bride, but at least the wedding was being
held in church, not in front of some justice of the peace, and
she was pleased. She wore a large white carnation and a pink
rose that matched the pink of her flower print dress. She

smiled at everyone, and held on tightly to her son's strong arm.

The organ music began. The bride, on her father's arm, marched in, and Wayne stood, transfixed. Connie looked so lovely he almost cried. He had behaved poorly at times, he knew, and he often suspected that he did not deserve such happiness. But here it was, his dreams were being fulfilled. Things would change.

Connie, too, felt that the past had drifted away, and as she walked down the aisle to be with the man she would marry, she was sure that better days lay ahead. Bouquets of roses and carnations had been placed around the pulpit. A red drape hung over the altar table beneath a seven-foot cross. The June heat pressed upon her as she moved forward. She could feel the baby moving inside of her. It seemed that the warmth of the air around her, the presence of the people she loved, the soft, vulnerable child moving within her, somehow all merged into a single secure nest that embraced her, and as she took the hand of Wayne Chaney and his strong fingers entwined with hers, Connie felt, perhaps for the first time since the death of her mother, that she was whole again.

"I love you Connie Rose," Wayne whispered.

"I love you too, Wayne Chaney," Connie replied.

Before the Reverend Merlin Mather spoke the words that would make Wayne and Connie a married couple, there was a single moment when Wayne allowed his hand to brush Connie's stomach gently. It was a gesture noticed by only a few of the guests. But it was, clearly, Wayne's way of sharing the moment with his unborn child.

October 6, 1988

Connie screamed in pain and grabbed at Wayne's hand. Wayne, dressed in his lime-green hospital scrubs, stood silently by her in the delivery room, not wanting to do anything to disturb the doctor. He just wanted to take care of his wife and see his baby born.

They were in the birthing room at Lutheran General Hospital and Connie had good reason to scream. She had been in labor for twenty hours. After she'd become four days overdue, Dr. Greenwald had decided to induce birth.

As Wayne looked around, the room didn't look as cold and sterile as he had expected. The walls were cream colored, the bed framed in wood—nice, homey touches. But the machines of medicine were also there. A fetal monitor strip had been placed on Connie's stomach to detect any distress of the baby, and one of Connie's arms was hooked up to a blood pressure machine.

Dr. Greenwald called out for pain killer for Connie. "This is a wonderful moment and it should not be painful for you," he said to his patient. "Having a child should be a happy experience. You will get enough pain when you raise the child."

He held up a black Polaroid camera. "A photo finish," he promised. "I promise you a picture of your baby in the first twenty minutes or the pizza is free."

Things, not surprisingly, had been getting tense and Greenwald was doing his best to cut the tension with humor. Wayne smiled. He liked Greenwald. This is the guy who is going to deliver my baby, he thought. My son, he hoped. Wayne crossed his fingers.

Dr. Greenwald pulled up a chair and pushed aside the sheet that covered Connie. Wayne sensed that this was really it. This was the moment.

"Okay," the doctor said calmly. "Connie, are we ready to push?"

Connie nodded. Wayne moved closer. He had not slept for more than twenty-four hours, and he had stayed with Connie all that time. But adrenaline washed away his exhaustion. This, he thought, is magical. A child is being born. My child. Our child. Two nurses and a resident stood by as Connie, enervated but anxious to go on, began to push.

"Come on, push," Greenwald said. "Come on, do it. Push again. Push. Push. Come on push. Good girl. Now you're doing it. I see the head. Keep pushing."

"I'm trying," Connie said. "God, I'm trying." Her face was wet with tears.

Wayne knew she was in awful pain, but still she smiled, or tried to. He was proud of her.

"I can't," she said. "I can't."

Wayne, frantic just to somehow be needed here, held Connie's hand with both of his. He stared down at her silently. He didn't know what to say, what to do.

"Come on, just a little more," Greenwald said. "Come on, Connie, we need that photo finish."

He put his hands close to her. Oh God, Wayne thought, he's going to do it, he's going to get the baby. "Come on, that's a girl, come on. Now we've got you."

Suddenly Greenwald stopped talking and Wayne knew that there would be no more need to urge Connie to push. Slowly, Greenwald worked his hands around the soft body emerging from Connie. The head of the baby was face down and Greenwald gently tilted the head to the side and cleared the nose and throat of the fluid from the placenta.

"You got your wish," he said to Wayne. "It's a boy."

Minutes later Wayne's brother Steve was allowed into the birthing room. He came in shyly, uncomfortable at seeing Connie bare-breasted.

"Get in here," Wayne said. "Have a look at my son."

Steve placed flowers next to Connie. He kissed her cheek. Then he looked at his nephew. "Gee, Wayne," he said. "He's got your chin."

Connie smiled. She knew what he meant.

8

The Promise

May, 1989

Long before he became a father, Wayne Chaney had decided
that his grandfather, William Martin Jackson, "Gramps," was
the man who was most like a father to him. Wayne had
many powerful memories of times he had shared with his
grandfather, and it was with him that Wayne felt most accepted. In the birth of Max, Wayne saw his chance to give
something back to the old man, who by then was seventy-
five, though still strong and stalwart. He would give the baby
William as his middle name. Gramps was touched and
thrilled by the gesture. This, he knew, was Wayne's way of
saying that a family name would continue, that the child was
a part of him.

William Martin Jackson, after all, had been the most significant person in Wayne's life. After Wayne's falling out
with his father, at age twelve, he gravitated toward Gramps,
who had moved in with Donna and the family after his wife,
Evelyn, had died. The sweetest moments of Wayne's childhood were long, fun-filled days with Gramps. Gramps would
take the boy hunting and fishing, and fill Wayne's imagina-
tion with vivid stories of his own childhood in Kentucky.
Gramps was born in Warren County to a farming family, he
said. Later the family had owned a general store. When
Gramps told Wayne tales of the townfolk and the store, and
the colorful characters who came in to shop, his language

was rich with the texture of the land, and Wayne sometimes felt as though he could smell the sweet air and touch the merchandise in the old store. Though Gramps and his two sisters had moved out of Kentucky long before Gramps had a grandson to tell about it, one brother remained there, and Gramps had held onto the farmland he owned in Kentucky. "Never been able to part with it," he told Wayne. Instead he rented it out to tobacco and cotton farmers.

"I bought it in 1943 for six thousand dollars," Gramps told Wayne at least a dozen times. "Can't buy much of anything for that price now."

Wayne often went with Gramps to the farm. Located on Route 1 in Smith Grove, near Bowling Green, it was 155 acres of land on Drake Creek. For Wayne, who would gladly have spent his life as Huck Finn, the farm was as perfect as a cool breeze off the Mississippi. And it was there that Gramps helped Wayne develop his deep attachment to the land.

In addition, Gramps was hardworking, enterprising, and frugal, a man who believed in giving a day's work for a day's pay. He had gone into the construction business as a young man, supplying rocks and gravel to contractors, and did well enough over the years to eventually expand into Illinois. Though Gramps was rumored to be rich, he was a man who drove the same car year after year, and if he did have money, Wayne and his brother Ken had never been able to pry any of it out of him.

From this example Wayne also developed a strong work ethic and the drive to own his own business, though the old man would have been horrified to think Wayne had pulled robberies to finance that business. As Wayne Chaney grew up he was certainly inclined to skip out of work from time to time and go fishing, but when Wayne did work, he worked hard, like his grandfather.

May was Gramps's favorite time of year. The pink and white flowered dogwoods would bloom and the earth would just seem to come alive with the scent of freshly plowed soil and honeysuckle blossoms. In May he was always drawn homeward to Kentucky, where he would stay for a few weeks or a few months. In years past he had often been able to take one of his grandsons, but now their lives were getting crowded. Steve was busy with work. Ken was in jail on a narcotics charge. And Wayne, of course, had a wife and a new baby and a business that boomed in May. But Gramps came by, anyway, to invite Wayne, and like any grandparent, mostly to see the baby that was named after him.

Max was eight and a half months old when William Martin came to the apartment that Wayne and Connie had rented shortly after their wedding.

Wayne and his grandfather talked about much of their history that day. The birth of a new generation had put them both in mind of the family's past. Gramps, sitting at the kitchen table, balanced his great-grandson on his knee, as he had Wayne. Wayne sat next to him, sipping a cold beer, and listening again to tales told a dozen times.

"He's a Jackson, all right," Gramps said, talking again about the baby. "Looks like you when you were this big. Those eyes and that Jackson chin. He's got your grip, too. I wish you could bring him down to see the farm. To walk in the fields, to fish."

Wayne told his grandfather that he looked forward to the time when he could take little Max to the farm, and teach him to hunt and fish and to love the land. Then the two men talked for a while about the values that William Martin had passed down to his grandson.

"Take good care of this boy," the old man said. "Promise me that you will raise him right. A part of me is in him." He held Max above his head and watched happily as the infant kicked his feet from side to side. He laughed and pulled Max towards him and kissed the child on the forehead for the last time. He stood. Wayne took Max from his grandfather, and, with his free arm, embraced the man he loved most in the world.

As his grandfather headed for the door he turned one last time and said, "Remember your promise to me. Raise the boy right."

"I will, Gramps, I promise," Wayne said.

Though the day was not significant at the time, Wayne recorded much of it in the diary he'd begun to keep. Perhaps he had a feeling about the day. As it turned out, this meeting of the two Williams would be the last time Wayne would ever see his grandfather. On May eleventh Wayne was at his mother's house when she got a call from a friend of Gramps. William Martin Jackson had died of a heart attack in Kentucky.

Wayne's first reaction was to deny it. It's a mistake, he said. There's a mixup. But when it sunk in that his Gramps was really gone, he collapsed into a front room chair and cried like a baby.

From Des Plaines along Highway 65 through the flat barren land and cornfields of Indiana to Kentucky, Wayne and Connie and the baby drove somberly to the funeral. Wayne's spirits rose—and then only slightly—when he saw the rolling hills of the Bluegrass State. It pleased him that Gramps would be laid to rest where he had spent some of his happiest hours. At times Wayne pointed out landmarks of these times to Connie. Spotting one gas station, he remembered clearly standing out in the sun with Gramps, drinking Cokes out of bottles. At another spot on the highway Wayne recalled a conversation they had. The subject they discussed was lost now, but the feeling of being with Gramps remained, like a wind that lifts a sagging tree and holds it, for a moment, tall and proud.

Connie said little throughout. She held the sleeping baby Max in her arms much of the time, and stared out at the highway. She had gone through the death of her mother, a memory that was as real as yesterday to her, and she knew the pain that Wayne was feeling. It was not a pain that needed to be talked about, at least not yet.

When Wayne spoke, he voiced his concerns about Gramps's farm. What was going to happen to it? Who would own it? Would baby Max ever get to run and fish on those acres as he had? He was troubled to think that his son might grow up without ever knowing the peace, contentment, and sense of freedom that he had, walking endlessly across the open fields and pastures of that Kentucky farm.

They stopped first to see relatives in Smith Grove. There, with the long ride behind them, Wayne, Connie, and Max cleaned up and changed clothes. Still Wayne was very quiet as they drove into Bowling Green and finally the circular driveway of the Hardy & Son funeral home. The building, a mansion once owned by restaurant tycoon Duncan Hines, was a white colonial, elegantly southern, fronted by large white columns.

Wayne took his sleeping son out of the car seat in the pickup, and cradled him in his arms as he moved toward the building. Connie walked next to him.

"Wayne, I'll take care of Max when you go up there," she said.

Wayne shook his head, "No, I want him to be with me when I see Gramps."

As he stepped into the funeral home, Wayne froze in place for several seconds. It looked to Connie as if he might not go through with it. He stared around, lost. Then Wayne spotted a small sign noting that William Martin Jackson was in the main room. Reassured, as if offered a hand, he moved on.

Connie followed him into the room where Gramps lay. The air smelled sweet, and soft music flowed from a speaker in the walls, but still Wayne's steps were slow and heavy. Huge arrangements of flowers in large urns fanned out from the coffin. The rest of the family was already present. His mother, Donna, and his father, Tom, looked up at him and Connie, but they did not move. His brother Steve approached him, offering small words. But Wayne, still stunned and grief stricken, heard nothing.

As he moved toward the open coffin at the front, Wayne held baby Max up by his shoulders. Wayne's own body grew rigid as he came close enough to view the body of his grandfather, stretched peacefully out in white satin. Tears flowed freely down Wayne's face and he made no attempt to hide them or wipe them away. Still holding Max, he kneeled to pray.

He kissed the boy softly and said, "Max, I want you to say good-bye to your Gramps. I don't want you ever to forget him. There is part of him in you and you carry his name." Then Wayne began to shake uncontrollably.

Connie, seeing that Wayne was overcome with grief, quickly reached out and took Max from him. Wayne began to weep. His body heaved, and deep pathetic wails of sorrow rose from him. "Oh Gramps," he cried. He stretched his arms out over his grandfather and leaned into the coffin. For a moment it looked as if he might actually climb on top of his grandfather like a child. He pressed his face down onto

Gramps's chest and wrapped his hands around the old man's embalmed shoulders as if he would never loosen his grip.

In his mind he saw Gramps again—in the kitchen, handing Max back to him before leaving. And he heard clearly Gramps's final request of him: "Raise Max right." Then Wayne heard his promise voiced. "I will." And his voice cracked and he could not speak any more. Then he felt the gentle hands of Donna and Steve on his shoulder.

That promise, now renewed, became for Wayne a sacred vow. The grief he felt at losing Gramps never left him and the only antidote for his pain, in Wayne's mind, was his determination to keep the promise, to give to his son as much love and guidance as the older Gramps had given to him. To Wayne it was very real that he could keep the spirit of his grandfather alive in young Max, that his son was his last remaining link to his grandfather.

9

Nothing Changes

October, 1989

The birth of Max seemed to shift the course of the Connie and Wayne's marriage. Connie no longer showed up at the homes of friends with bruises on her face. There were no more late-night tearful phone calls, no wringing of hands, no plans of escape. Connie and Wayne were happy. A magic spell had been cast over the once-troubled couple, and his name was Max.

The baby was a force that drew Wayne and Connie closer, and he made a difference in both of their lives. Every activity centered around Max. Every conversation led to Max. Every decision came down to what was best for Max. And they both wanted it that way. Connie and Wayne had their arguments; the constant crying and attention-seeking of the baby made them both short-tempered at times. But the arguments came only in words. Fatherhood, it appeared, had drained from Wayne all the aggression, all the meanness of his earlier self. He was happy with his new family and he would do anything for Connie, his queen, and Max, his prince.

At a Halloween party at Boomer's Wayne dressed up as an old cleaning woman—Connie and Max were hobos—and won first prize. At the local Octoberfest he pushed Max in a baby buggy, and showed off his son like a new sports car to Des Plaines police officers Mike Lambeau and Bob Schultz, who had arrested Wayne back in the days when Wayne was breaking into vending machines. The two officers were delighted to see the transformation. It seemed there was one less potential felon for them to worry about on the streets of Des Plaines. No longer surly and reckless, Wayne seemed to have matured, to have been tamed by marriage and fatherhood.

Wayne loved to bring Max into Boomer's, where the infant's eyes would shift constantly from the colorful bottles, to the shiny mirrors, to the green felt pool tables with its musical clacking of billiard balls. At Boomer's, Wayne would hold Max's tiny arms and try to get the baby to walk along the top of the bar. The child would giggle, and his feet would wobble forward in something like steps while Wayne held him up. Then Wayne would roar triumphantly and hug his little boy as if the kid had just walked a mile without help.

He would tell Max, "Hey, you have a daddy who loves you and I'm going to take you hunting and fishing and we are going to have a house and a dog."

Wayne could hardly wait for Max to grow older. Even before Max's first birthday Wayne set his mind on taking the family to Disney World. Connie and Steve tried to convince Wayne that Max was too young to enjoy the Magic Kingdom. But Wayne was adamant. "What are you talking about?" Wayne said to his brother. "Kids love Disney World." Wayne, so anxious to do things for Max, was projecting his own childhood dreams upon the child. As it turned out, Max seemed to enjoy the plane ride to Orlando, and a few of the kiddie rides at Disney World, but in the family snapshots taken during that Florida vacation it is clear that Connie and Wayne were having a lot more fun than Max.

Though Wayne's landscaping business brought in enough money to support the family, it did not provide any extra to be put away for their dream home. So if they were to have a house of their own, Connie had to work at the deli. Soon after the baby was born, Connie went back to Dominick's, where she again labored behind the processed meats and prepared platters in an eight-hour swing shift every day. At four in the afternoon she would turn Max over to a babysitter, who would watch the baby until Wayne got home. Connie would go to the deli and work until midnight. Wayne, fortunately, was a responsible father. He adored his child and he nurtured Max as much as he played with him. Though she trusted Wayne to take good care of Max, Connie was still a nervous mom when she was away from the boy, and whenever she took her break at the deli she would call home to make sure Max had eaten supper and had been asleep by nine.

On the other hand, when Connie was with Max, she took him on small adventures. She loved to ride her bike and would strap Max into the children's bike seat carrier she'd put on the back. Wearing his white crash helmet, he would giggle as they rode down the side streets to the store or took rides at dusk to Frankie's hot dog stand.

Connie's female friends were still a big part of her life. They doted on the new child. When Max was around, Connie called them "Aunt Tammy" and "Aunt Cathy." But, until they met Jim and Kathy Hoshell on a fishing trip, Connie and Wayne had no friends with kids Max's age. The Hoshells had a son, Travis. He and Max became fast friends, and so did Connie and Kathy. Now everything seemed to be in place. The Chaneys loved their kid, business was good, and they were putting away money for the house. Connie did not have the kind of job she wanted, but she had good friends, a stable marriage, and a happy baby. For now, that seemed to be plenty.

Winter, however, is a slow time in the landscaping business, and it is also a time when light is scarce and people are forced indoors. The bulk of Wayne's winter work was snow plowing and if there was no snow, there was no work. This was not a great financial hardship. Anybody in landscaping expects to do most of his work and make most of his money in the spring and summer. But it did leave Wayne with lots of time to sit around the house drinking beer and watching television. Perhaps too much time. Certainly it was difficult for Connie to force herself to go to work at the deli every afternoon while Wayne was sacked out on the couch, sipping on a cold one and watching Stallone and Schwarzenegger movies. Connie's job was already a curse to her. She lived with the dread that she would never rise above the level of delicatessen clerk. She wanted more than anything to go back to school. Her goals were not even lofty, she just wanted to learn how to use a computer. The gap between her work reality and her work dreams fostered tension, and having

Wayne on the couch while she went to work didn't help. The tension cord was pulled even tighter as Max grew bigger and began to walk and call for even more attention. And tighter still by the fact that Wayne was still deeply troubled by the death of his grandfather.

As the anniversary of his grandfather's death grew closer, Wayne became more irritable. He missed his Gramps terribly and it rankled Wayne that his mother was being forced to sell Gramps's farm and farm machinery. Even before Gramps had died, Wayne had idealized Kentucky into God's country, a perfect place where a man could breathe clean air and walk on quiet pastures and not be hassled by anything or anyone. He would talk often about how beautiful the Bluegrass State was, and how he had wanted to bring up his boy on a farm and how maybe he would pull up stakes and take his family to Kentucky or Tennessee.

When the deadline for the sale of the farm was only a few weeks off Wayne decided that he must take young Max south to see his grandfather's grave and the farm before it was taken from the family. He announced his plan to Connie one afternoon while she was in the bathroom getting ready to go to work.

"I'm taking Max down to Kentucky to see the farm," Wayne said. He leaned against the doorway to the bathroom. Connie stood in front of a mirror, fixing her hair with the little can of mousse she always kept in her purse. Little Max sat on the floor in front of the bathroom, playing with toy trucks that Wayne had bought him.

"Wayne," Connie said, "I don't think that's a good idea." It made her nervous to think of Max being so far from her. Still a new mother, she had never had a day of not taking care of Max, and she wasn't ready to be separated from her son.

"Well, he has to remember my grandfather," Wayne said.

"No," Connie said firmly. "Not by going there."

"No?"

"No. You can't just go galloping off to Kentucky with Max, while I have to stay here and work."

"It's just for a day or so," Wayne said.

"No," Connie said again. "I am his mother and he is not going."

Wayne stiffened. This, she recognized, was the way he got when he felt attacked.

"He will be with me all the time," Wayne said.

"I said no," Connie said. It was time to go to work. She pushed her makeup into a cosmetic bag and zipped it up. "No means no." As she walked through the doorway she pushed Wayne aside. "Now please move," she said. "I have to get to work."

Suddenly Wayne grabbed her. "Don't you push me," he said. Then he shoved her back into the room.

Though Wayne did not shove her hard, Connie lost her balance. "Wayne," she shouted, but he couldn't catch her. She fell back and landed in the bathtub. Oh God, she thought, it's starting again, he's going to hit me. She stared up at him. His face was red, his temples throbbing. His hands were twitching as if he were trying to decide whether or not to hit her. Suddenly they both became aware of the hysterical shrieking of Max, who had been frightened by the sight of his mother falling.

At that moment Wayne reached out, not to help Connie out of the tub, but to pick up his little boy. "It's okay, Max," he said, "it's okay. Mommy just fell, that's all."

Connie lifted herself from the bathtub. She was shaking, but tried not to let her son see that she was hurt and scared.

"Please give me my son," she said coldly. Wayne handed her the child. "Connie, I'm sorry," he said, putting Max into her arms.

Connie turned away. She held Max to her. "Everything is okay, honey," she said. "Mommy is okay. Daddy didn't hurt Mommy. She is okay." She looked at Wayne. "Now Mommy will give you to Daddy. You see. Everything is okay." She passed Max back to his father. Then, without speaking again, she left for work.

Wayne's need to use Max to relive his own experiences with Gramps made Connie uneasy. This incident haunted her. A voice inside told her that it would happen again and again.

If incidents like this made Connie fantasize about not being married to Wayne, she didn't have to look any further than her new friend, Kathy Hoshell, for a role model. Soon after Connie and Kathy began sharing confidences, Kathy revealed that she and Jim were getting divorced. In the weeks that followed, the Hoshell's divorce sometimes became quite bitter and Kathy, a husky young woman with long blond hair, would come to Connie for comfort. Though Kathy had never been beaten, her stories of dissatisfaction in marriage struck Connie's heart and helped to crystallize Connie's own unhappiness. Though she felt that divorce was not even an option, the idea of it fascinated her.

When Kathy began driving into Chicago to make court appearances for her divorce procedure, Connie went with her. They were usually early in the day, and Connie didn't have to be at work until four, so she would feed and dress Max, and they would ride into the city with Kathy and Travis. Connie was awed and sometimes horrified by the workings of the Daley Center in Chicago's loop, a massive building with thirty-one floors of courtrooms and offices. She was amazed at how the people who worked there could keep track of all the court business. She thought it was all very sophisticated and her days in the courthouse fueled her dreams of someday working at something with a little more status than slapping together ham, mayo, and rye.

Connie watched the Hoshells' divorce proceedings with a keen eye. They were much less complicated than she had imagined. It seemed as if the attorneys did all the talking and Kathy and Jim, though they had to show up, didn't seem to actually do anything.

Some days Connie would stand out in the marble hallways and study the divorcing couples. So this is what it is like, she thought. Men and women who had been incredibly happy together, who had made love to each other, now averted their eyes to avoid seeing each other. Occasionally someone would start shouting and a lawyer had to rush in to calm him or her down. It was all so incredibly emotional that Connie could hardly imagine herself going through it. In the courtroom the pain, she thought, was pushed deeper inside. Wounded-looking men and women would stand quietly and dull-eyed while lawyers argued over child custody and property settlements and visitation rights.

Wayne was not overjoyed to learn that his wife was attending divorce proceedings in Chicago. He felt threatened. He didn't like his wife getting so involved with someone else's breakup and he said so often and vociferously. Not wanting to know what was going on with Kathy and Jim, he drifted away from them as friends. "Kathy is a bad influence on you," he once told Connie.

Throughout the period of her divorce, Kathy did not know about Connie's being pushed into the tub. She didn't find out that Connie was a battered wife until after an incident that occurred in June, 1990.

June, 1990

On June twenty-sixth, Max began crying at five o'clock in the morning. Because Connie had gone to sleep at 2 a.m. after her night shift at the deli, she shook Wayne and told him to get up and make Max a bottle of warm milk. Wayne, still in a stupor, crawled out of bed. Unable to find any milk, he poured orange Kool-Aid from a plastic pitcher into the baby bottle and brought it into the room. He tried to feed the baby with the Kool-Aid, but Max just pushed the bottle away and cried even louder. Connie sat up in bed. Through bleary eyes she stared at her husband and child, trying to understand why Max had not stopped crying. Then she realized that the bottle Wayne was holding did not contain milk.

"Hey, that's not milk," she said. "He needs warm milk. What is that?"

"Kool-Aid," Wayne said. "We ran out of milk last night."

"If you knew we were out of milk why didn't you go and get him some more? You were home all night, while I was working."

Wayne went rigid. He said nothing.

"Get him some milk," Connie said.

Suddenly Wayne flung the baby's bottle at the wall. "Get it yourself," he yelled. The nipple popped off the bottle and the orange Kool-Aid splattered on the wall. Max began to wail even louder.

Connie bolted from her bed. "Stop it, stop it," she screamed at Wayne. "You're upsetting the baby." She rushed to the child. "Get him some milk, Wayne. Babies do not drink Kool-Aid."

It was attacks like these, real or imagined, that would set

Wayne Chaney off. Now he heard Max screaming. Connie
was holding the empty bottle and shouting about the Kool-
Aid and the mess he had made on the wall. And so Wayne
threw it all back at Connie in a blow to the side of her face.
Her body arched back and she fell against the bedroom wall.
Connie flung her hands up in front of her face to protect
herself from another blow, but Wayne grabbed his jeans from
a chair instead. He shoved his bare feet into a pair of shoes,
grabbed a shirt and jacket, and went out the door. "I'm going
to work," he shouted, slamming the door behind him.

Connie, stunned, slowly rose, then stood motionless for
several seconds as if she had been welded to the bedroom
wall. An understanding had been gaining on her, an aware-
ness that she had denied, but could deny no longer: Whatever
strange and dangerous demons resided in her husband's mind
might have rested for a while, but they had never gone away.
Her mouth ached. She tried to ease the pain by wiggling her
jaw, but that only intensified it. Kathy, she thought, I've got
to call Kathy. But Kathy did not have a phone. And Max,
Connie suddenly realized as she emerged from her daze, was
crying hysterically. She picked him up to calm him and decided to go to Kathy.

The sun was just coming up when Connie reached Kathy's
door. She had been sleeping, but when she peered through
the peephole and saw that it was Connie with Max in her
arms, Kathy let her right in. Kathy could see that something
had happened. Connie had a yellowish purple mark on her
face and Max's face was red. He had obviously been crying
for a long time. "Wayne hit you, didn't he?" Kathy asked.
Connie said yes, and told Kathy it wasn't the first time. That
night Wayne hit her because there wasn't any milk for Max.
Kathy went into the kitchen and grabbed an empty baby
bottle and poured milk into it. She told Connie to sit down,
everything would be okay. Then Kathy asked Connie if she
had ever filed a police report against Wayne.

"No," Connie said.

"Well that's what you've got to do, right now. You are
going to report this to the police, and you are going to get
help," Kathy told her. "Otherwise, your son will learn that
it's okay to hit people and be violent. You don't want to

teach Max that, do you? If you do that, then everything else you taught him will mean nothing.

"Max must learn to respect people and learn that a wife is to be respected," Kathy told Connie. She placed the milk in the microwave. When it was ready, she handed Connie the warm bottle and Connie gave Max the nipple. Soon he was quiet and content, and she stared lovingly into his face, thinking about his future. Kathy had said something very powerful to her, and now the idea that Max could grow up to be a wife beater if Connie didn't stand up to Wayne began to take hold in Connie's mind.

Kathy made coffee and the two women talked. Kathy told Connie about Life Span, a support group for battered women in Des Plaines.

"I think you should talk to them," Kathy said. "You need proof of what he is doing to you, you need support. If you ever divorce Wayne . . ."

"Divorce him?"

"Well, yes, if you ever divorce him, then there will be a report for every time he beat you up. You don't have to file charges, just file a report, that's proof enough. They will not come after him if you don't press charges, but that report is always there if you need it. Connie, do yourself a favor, don't go back to him without doing at least that. Support groups are good. You can't live with a guy who beats you. I say divorce him."

Connie was stunned and confused. She knew all about support groups. After all, she had been in AA for years. But still, the idea of getting involved with one made her uncomfortable. And divorce? After what she had seen in the Chicago courthouse, it seemed unthinkable. Connie didn't know what to do. She wanted to call the police, and she wanted to call Life Span, but she knew that both of those things would only bring more grief down upon her and Max.

Later that afternoon she turned, as she often had in the past, to Chris. Chris told her to go to the hospital and to file a report. That set Connie straight.

Connie went to Holy Family Hospital, and Kathy went along to watch Max while the emergency ward doctor looked at Connie. They took X rays of her face. The doctor recog-

nized the signs of wife abuse, and he brought a Des Plaines
police officer in to talk with Connie.

"Do you want to sign a complaint?" the officer asked.

"No," she said. She was scared, but she added, "But you
can write it up as a report, can't you? Then there's something
on file."

"Yes, I can write it up as an incident report. But you are
sure you don't want to press charges?"

"Yes," she said.

"Because, you know, there's nothing I can do to help you
if you don't file a complaint."

"Really, I'm sure," she said.

"Okay," the cop said. He gave her a handout from Life
Span.

Connie, still afraid to go home, went back to Kathy's to
stay while she tried to figure out what to do next with her
life. Later, Wayne began calling her at the deli. He was contrite. As in the past, he begged forgiveness, promised he
would never hit her again. He told Connie that he wanted
her home. He didn't like the idea of her being with Kathy.
She wasn't likely to see things clearly, he said, since she was
in the middle of a divorce. Kathy was not a good person for
Connie to turn to.

Abused wives often move around from house to house like
slaves in the underground railroad. And this was the case
with Connie Chaney. She moved from friend to friend, and
each time the pressure of imposing on a friend increased,
Wayne's promises seemed more and more inviting.

"I think we should leave Des Plaines and get away from
here and start a new life," Wayne told her on one of his
many phone calls. "We can get a house."

Connie was frightened and unhappy and she knew that
Wayne might not change, but her language was the language
of a woman who was coming back. "Listen, Wayne," she
said, "I need to be away from you for a while."

"What about Max?"

"You can see Max. But I need to live someplace else."

"Well, I'll be away for a few days. I've got to go to
Kentucky because my mom's selling the farm and all."

Connie then went to see Chris. They sat at the kitchen

table drinking while Max and his cousin Alexandria played and Connie told her sister what happened.

"How many times has this happened before?" Chris asked.

Connie felt uncomfortable. "Never," she replied.

Chris knew what that reaction meant. She set her cup down hard on the table. "You're lying," she said in a slow stern voice. Now was not the time to coddle her.

Connie then pressed her lips together like a child and gave in. "You're right. Three times, but it's been my fault."

Chris was so shocked that she wanted to shake her sister. "Oh Connie. How can you say that? Haven't you watched enough 'Oprah,' 'Geraldo,' 'Maury Povich,' to know that it's not your fault?" Chris was being honest, but she wondered how good her advice would be to Connie—since Connie always had to do things her way.

Connie's next stop was Loretta's. Loretta was now living with her boyfriend in an apartment, and the addition of a woman and child, as one would expect, caused turbulence. Loretta told her landlady that Connie was a cousin who would be gone in a month, but the landlady, who lived upstairs, complained constantly about the sound of the child crying and running around. Connie knew that there was a limit to how long she could stay there.

Wayne called several times a day. He was desperate. More and more he was afraid that Connie would divorce him and take away his son. Like a salesman trying to sell a product, Wayne would run his spiel by Connie: Give me another chance, we'll move, we'll get a house, I'll change ... and then he would talk to Max. With each call, Connie became more confused and guilt-ridden. It's not right to take Max away from his father, she thought. Sometimes Wayne would come over and he would sit on the floor with Max and they would play with Max's toy trucks. When Wayne left, Max would cry, and it broke Connie's heart.

At the end of July Wayne asked Connie to move with him to Knoxville, Tennessee. Knoxville, once called the gateway to the West, was a good-sized city and Wayne was sure that he could drum up business for his landscaping. Also the cost of living was lower than it had been in Illinois and he felt that in Tennessee they could afford to buy their dream house. And there, he said, they would get a fresh start. There would be no more hitting. "There's a university in Knoxville," he told her. "You can go there. My mother will pay part of your tuition if you'll just make us a family again."

Connie didn't like the idea of moving away from her friends and family, but she wanted whatever was best for Max. To her, that meant a complete family, a mother and a father who loved him. And she never doubted that Wayne did love his boy. The memories of her own broken family and the death of her mother had been painfully carved in her memory. She didn't want Max to grow up fatherless. So her main concern couldn't be whether Wayne hit her.

Tammy convinced Connie to see a marriage counselor. Connie went with Wayne three times and the counselor told her to give the marriage one more try. Wayne promised also to go to counseling in Tennessee. Connie had always trusted counselors since she was fourteen, but still she spent many days agonizing over her decision.

After work she would sit up late with Loretta and discuss her options, none of which were very attractive. Trying to raise her son on what she made at the delicatessen would mean always living in close quarters, sharing apartments with friends, and counting pennies. She would never have a house. But going with Wayne meant putting miles between her and her emotional support. Her friends and her family were everything to her. But so was Max.

Loretta knew that Connie didn't want to leave Des Plaines, but she also knew that Connie felt she was becoming a burden on her friends and would have nowhere else to live if she didn't go with Wayne. Loretta told her, "You have to make your own decision, you have to feel comfortable with yourself and you have to think about Max."

Connie's sister Chris was dead set against Connie's leaving for Tennessee.

"What will you do, where will you go, if he starts to beat on you down there?" Chris asked. She had sensed all along that Connie was bound for tragedy, but it was like standing in the distance and watching her sister drive toward the edge of a cliff. Nothing she could say could make a difference.

Wayne, meanwhile, was determined to show Connie how much she meant to him. He sold his equipment and accounts to a landscaping firm in Arlington Heights. At the beginning of August he headed for Knoxville to look for a house for Connie and Max. He placed advertising for his new landscaping business. He rented a large white two-story frame house on Delden Street, in an older section of town. After a few weeks in Knoxville, Wayne took a job with a landscaping firm, but he was still determined to have his own shop again. He started buying landscaping equipment. Still the outdoors man, he spent his weekends fishing in the motorboat he had bought before leaving Illinois.

Connie, meanwhile, was not ready yet to go that far. She moved again, this time into Wayne's parents' house. Donna Chaney spoiled her grandson with homemade cookies and gifts from her variety store. Tom Chaney watched Max when Donna and Connie were both at work. Wayne called often to give Connie reports about the house and jobs. He told her Labor Day was the perfect time for her to move out.

Connie still did not make up her mind, despite the fact that Wayne had already settled into a life in Tennessee. On a weekend visit in August they argued about her hesitation.

"Wayne, I don't know if it is the right idea to just move."

Wayne was stunned. He glared at her. "You got to be kidding, Connie. I sold my business. I rented a house. I'm starting out from zero just so we can begin a new life."

Connie shook her head. "Wayne, I didn't ask you to do that. You just did it on your own."

Wayne moved close to her. "I can't believe what I am hearing. Connie, we are going as a family."

"I don't know," she said.

Wayne grabbed her arm, shook her. "Damn it, Connie. It is too late to change your mind. We are going down there."

Connie pulled away. "Leave me alone," she said. "I don't want to go."

Wayne's face got red. "How could you do this to me," he yelled. Suddenly he raised his hand and slapped her across the face. Connie jumped back. Wayne, realizing what he had done, grabbed her and hugged her. "Connie, Connie, I'm so sorry . . . but I gave up everything so we could be a family and then you say no."

For the rest of the weekend Wayne sweet-talked, he pleaded, he promised, and in time he convinced her. Connie forgave him for the slapping. She felt it was her indecision that enraged him, and she worked it around in her mind so that the three of them could be a happy family. She wanted to give them one more chance.

On Labor Day weekend Wayne drove up to Des Plaines and he and Connie and all of their friends got together for the last time at a festive backyard party at the home of Donna and Tom Chaney. Connie did comedy routines, putting on her famous southern accent. When someone put on a rock and roll record she stood and made gestures to Tammy and Cathy, as if she were playing the drums. The two women joined her, and they jerked their heads back and forth in time with the music, just as they had as kids.

Connie had many fine memories of times spent in the Chaneys' yard, of her and Wayne and Steve tossing the football, of sitting in the grass with Steve while he told her about his carpentry and the way the teacher eyed him funny when they found out his name was Chaney. She talked about this with Tammy and Cathy, and the women recounted their own stories of times spent together with Connie. She didn't tell anyone about the slapping incident. She was too embarrassed. There were lots of tears, lots of hugs, and lots of people writing down Connie's new phone number.

At one point Connie, touched by all the friendship, turned to Loretta and said, "Maybe I shouldn't go."

"Too late now," Loretta said. "But remember, you can always come back. We're always here for you."

As the party wound down there were more hugs and kisses and promises to stay in touch. By the time Connie had made the rounds, her ribs ached from hugging and her face was wet with tears. Then Donna Chaney, who had spent much of the afternoon holding onto her grandson, reluctantly turned the boy over to Connie and Wayne. "Be good to each other," she said.

The sun had set below the Illinois sky by the time Wayne and Connie and Max climbed into the pickup truck and headed out. The truck, loaded down with furniture and towing Connie's car behind, still seemed peppy as Wayne steered it through the neighborhood streets and finally onto a south-bound highway. Connie sat quietly, still wiping at the tears she had shed through all the goodbyes. Max snuggled in next to her and closed his eyes. He was asleep by the time they crossed the state line into Indiana and Connie turned to say good-bye to Illinois.

All in all, it had been a warm and loving afternoon. Connie had basked in the glow of her friendships, and perhaps the knowledge that so many people still cared about her filled her with hope, as she drove farther and farther away from the state of her childhood. Certainly, there was reason at least for the proverbial "cautious optimism." Connie was giving her family one more chance to be whole. She hoped that the move would somehow create the happy family that Max needed. For her, there was also the promise of school, the chance to be more than a deli clerk. And for Wayne there was plenty of landscaping work, it seemed, and one more chance to share with his son the things that Gramps had shared with him.

There had been only one unpleasant moment that day, and it was easy enough to push it from her mind. It had occurred when Wayne stood by the barbecue, cooking up a hamburger, and Kathy Hoshell had stood next to him. By this time things had gotten very cold between them. Wayne saw Kathy as a woman who promoted divorce to her other female friends, and he felt that she had been a bad influence on Connie. Standing next to her, he made some comment about her perspiration, that it made him sick. It was a strange thing for him to say, and he and Kathy had words about it. In time the argument cooled down and they went their separate ways and in the good feelings of the day it was lost. But Kathy never forgot the look in Wayne's eyes when he had talked to her. It was frightening, she thought, a look of absolute hatred.

10

Making a Move

Fall, 1990

The move to Knoxville did not go exactly as Connie had hoped.

Instead of getting their dream house, Connie and Wayne moved out of the house Wayne had rented, and into a used 1978 two-bedroom mobile home, which they bought for four thousand dollars.

In his diary, Wayne wrote, "Connie and I decided to look for a home of our own. We couldn't purchase a house due to just moving there, so we set forth to buy a mobile home trailer. We had plenty of money left, so we went out one day to look at one. The first and only trailer we looked at was a good thirty miles out, taking the beautiful country road."

The metal frame home, as Wayne described it in his diary, was twelve by seventy, had tan siding and a large brown awning at the entrance where three concrete steps led to the front door.

They installed their mobile home on lot number 441 at the Black Oaks Park in an area of Knoxville known as Halls Crossroads. It was a nice enough area, Connie thought, lots of cedar and maple trees, a good place for Max to be. Connie took a job at the nearby Kroger's supermarket, again as a deli clerk. Wayne continued to get landscaping jobs, but being new in town, he got fewer and smaller jobs. Still, he was bringing home about $180 a week and they were getting by.

Connie also did not go to college as planned. She visited the University of Tennessee, a sprawling four-hundred-acre campus, to pick up literature, but by the time she got to Knoxville it was too late for the fall semester. She was determined that she would enter school in the spring. The promised financial help from Donna Chaney, however, was not forthcoming. Wayne explained that the expenses involved in selling Gramps's farm had left his parents short of cash. Connie tried to be understanding, but when she drove by the campus and saw the students strolling about with their books, all of them career bound, it brought a lump to her throat.

As in the past, this reunion of Connie and Wayne brought its own honeymoon period. There were, for example, long idyllic days of fishing on the lake. Connie would pack lunch and Wayne would take the family out in his motor boat. Max loved to stand up in the boat and feel the wind blowing at him while Connie held him tightly. He seemed to love the noise of engines as much as his father did. Wayne, wearing his red baseball cap, would steer the boat across the lake, intensely happy as the mist from the lake washed his face. He loved the sense of freedom he got from being in control of a powerful engine. Sometimes he would pull the boat close to shore and turn down the engine. As they drifted quietly toward the tree-lined shore Wayne would point out small animals. "See, Max, it's a beaver," he would say, and Max would giggle with delight over the antics of the woodland creatures. It pleased Connie to see her son and her husband so happy. For Wayne, every day seemed like a vacation.

Connie had always been quick to find female friends, and at Black Oaks she hooked up with Therese Lynch.* Therese, in her early twenties, was divorced. She lived alone in the trailer park. She became not only a confidant for Connie, but also a baby-sitter who could watch Max when Connie and Wayne were both working. Therese's son, Mark, was only a year older than Max.

So again there was relative happiness in the Chaney family. But the warning signs were always there.

In November of 1990 Wayne's brother, Steve, flew to Knoxville to visit Wayne and Connie. They met him at the gate, along with Max, who was fascinated by the airport and loved to watch the big silvery planes rise from the runway. It was a warm reunion, with lots of hugs and kisses. Steve called Connie "Sis," and that's how he felt about her.

Steve's two-week vacation in Knoxville was not supposed to be all fun and games. He brought along a crate of tools with which to build a shed behind the trailer for his brother.

"I bragged about you to all my friends," Wayne told Steve as they worked their way out of the airport terminal that morning. "Told them my brother is coming here, he's a carpenter and he is going to build me a shed."

Steve smiled, "You bet," he said. "I am going to build the best damn shed in Knoxville."

They loaded the tools into Wayne's truck and headed for Black Oaks. It was fall, but the air was still warm as they drove along the country roads that took them from the airport to the mobile park. Connie was in a good mood. To Steve she seemed happy. She pointed out sights along the way, talking in her southern drawl. "Yonder there is McDonald's," she said, "where only eight folks can fit in at one time, mind you, yet we all happy here."

When they got to the trailer, Connie served beers all around. The two brothers, in no rush to get to work on the shed, kicked back and caught up on old friends. Wayne bragged about what a smart thing he had done in moving to Tennessee. "It is so laid back here," he told Steve, "that you can stand in line at the grocery store and people will talk to you just as if they have known you for years."

"Not like Chicago," Connie said, "where people are afraid you'll come at them with a knife."

When the brothers had talked on the phone before Steve's trip, Wayne had made it clear that the shed was important to him. And Steve had made it clear that he was pleased to be able to do this thing for his brother. So he was taken by surprise on this first day in Tennessee when Wayne said, "You want to go fishing?"

"Now?" Steve said.

"Sure, we can bring Connie back some dinner, what do you say."

Steve said yes, and Wayne and Steve went fishing, taking Max with them.

Wayne was happy to show off what Max could do. Even though Max was little, Wayne had given him a small green and white plastic fishing pole and shown him how to hold it and crank the reel to bring in the line. Max had learned fast by mimicking Wayne. Wayne would bait the hook and Max would watch the line and the little bobber. He also liked to look over the side of the boat at the small fish in the lake. "Look, baby fish, baby fish," he would say.

The next day the two brothers bought freshly sawed lumber and laid the planks in the back of the pickup truck. At the trailer park excitement was hard to come by, so people stopped and watched as Wayne and Steve unloaded the planks and stacked them as high as the tin roof of the mobile home. Steve plugged in his saw and Wayne helped him cut the boards into exactly measured pieces. Steve then used a power gun to drive nails into the boards. After they put up just a few boards they had something resembling a stage. But Wayne took a look at the bright blue sky and he smiled at Steve and Steve smiled back. And they knew it was much too nice a day to waste working. Instead, they went fishing again. "After all," Wayne explained to Connie, "we're catching fish."

A week later on a rainy and thunderous day, the shed still had not been built, though a lot of fish had been caught. Wayne stood at the door of the trailer early that morning and looked out disgustedly. Thunder echoed through the canyons outside of Knoxville, and lightning slashed at the sky. The sound of rain pelting the roof vibrated through the trailer. The area around the trailer was filled with murky brown puddles. It was clearly no day for outdoor work.

"We got to work on that shed today," Wayne said. He never looked away from the rain as he spoke. "I told everyone how my brother the carpenter would build me a shed. You'll be leaving soon and we hardly got the thing started."

Steve, still half asleep, sipped at his morning coffee. The last thing he needed to hear about was building a shed in the pouring rain.

"We'll finish it when the rain lets up," he said.

"We'll do it today," Wayne said.

"Come on Wayne," Connie said. "Leave it be for now." She stood behind him, softly pressing her hands against his shoulders. Sometimes when Wayne got fixated on something like this, she could charm him into submission. Now she teased him with her fingertips, kissed him softly on the cheek. "Come on honey, let it go for now, let it go."

Wayne succumbed, and soon he and Steve and Max were watching television in the small room at the back of the trailer.

Connie stood at the kitchen sink washing the breakfast dishes and staring out at the wild rain. She did not like what she heard coming from the television. It was the sound of police sirens and rapid gunfire. "Man," she heard Wayne shriek, "did you see how that guy blew him away!"

Now it was Connie's turn to get in a mood. How many times had she told Wayne that she didn't want Max watching violence on television? She threw down her dish cloth and stormed into the TV room.

"Damn it, Wayne," she said, "what have I said about Max watching these violent shows?"

Wayne gave her a look and then he angrily turned off the TV. He looked out the window, then at Steve.

"Okay, so it's raining," he said. "That tree will shelter us if we cut some boards and finish the platform."

Steve understood what was going on. If Connie was going to whine about the TV, then Wayne sure as hell was going to work in the rain. Steve had known his brother long enough to know that Wayne wouldn't back down a second time.

"You are just set on doing that damn shed today, aren't you," he said. He threw his hands in the air. "Okay, okay, I'll do it."

Now everybody was in a bad mood.

The men walked out of the trailer, slamming the door behind them.

Wayne plugged the cord of the power saw into the outdoor socket and began to cut into the wood. Steve couldn't believe that Wayne could do anything so stupid, but he held his tongue. He could see Connie watching them through the window. The rain soaked Wayne's shirt and streamed down the bill of his red baseball cap. Steve held the board. He could barely see through his safety glasses, they were so wet. Wayne began to cut. Finally, Steve couldn't hold back anymore. "Wayne, are you fucking nuts?" he said. "You'll get electrocuted."

Wayne gestured to the maple tree behind them. "The tree will get some of the water away."

Then a blue and white spark flew out of the saw and Steve jumped back. "Hey, no way man, put that saw down," he yelled at Wayne. He dropped the board. "You are nuts, man . . ."

Wayne, his face filled with anger, yanked the cord out of the socket and wrapped it around the saw as if he were strangling it.

"Okay," he said, "here's your saw, take it." His eyes were intense. Then he went to his long metal tool box and pulled out a hand saw. He pushed it at Steve.

"I told everyone you were going to build me a shed, so you and I are going to build this shed. You came here to do a shed, and you're going to do it."

"You'll get your damn shed, but not now," Steve yelled back.

"Well, you're leaving in four days and they say it's going to rain for four days, genius. When do you think you're going to do it?"

"Wayne," Steve shouted, "you can be such a fucking asshole sometimes." Steve stomped off and rushed into the trailer. He was seething.

"How do you live with that guy," he asked Connie as she handed him a towel to dry off. "He's possessed. Everything has to be his way, he just won't listen to anybody."

They stood by the window and watched Wayne maniacally go about the business of trying to build the shed he had been promised. He pushed the saw into the wet wood and struggled to cut through the boards. He would stop and raise the teeth of the saw back into the grooves of the cut. Every now and then he would swing his muscular arms out, to throw off the water that had gathered on him. The sky outside grew blacker, and the branches on the dogwood trees bent under the rain and wind. But still Wayne kept working, a man on a mission.

"He's nuts, Connie," Steve said. "He is a crazy man."

"Wayne's driven," Connie said. "He will stop at nothing to get what he wants."

Steve was fed up with his brother, as he had been many times in the past. He changed his clothes and came back into the front room of the trailer carrying his bags.

"I'm leaving," he said.

Connie asked him not to leave, told him he would have to pay hundreds of dollars in airline penalties, but Steve was as adamant about leaving as his brother was about getting the shed built.

Before Connie drove him to the airport, Steve stood by the open door to the trailer. The bags by his sides made it clear to Wayne that Steve was abandoning him. The rain beat down on Wayne, the thunder crashed around him and lightning flashed across the Tennessee sky. But he kept working his saw. Wayne looked up at his brother. To Steve his eyes looked small, his face reflecting both anger and hurt. Steve felt as if he were looking at someone else, someone insane. The look on his brother's face that day would always stay with him. But as time passed and tragedy ripped through the lives of the Krauser and Chaney families Steve would remember the hurt more than the anger, and he would forever feel guilty, blaming himself that he had let his brother down. Wayne finished the shed himself that day.

By the end of November Connie and Wayne had nearly used up the money Wayne had gotten from selling his land-scaping business. Connie made one hundred dollars a week at the store and Wayne was still bringing in the occasional paycheck, but winter was coming and landscaping work was dwindling. They were approaching dire straits. They drove into Knoxville to apply for food stamps.

Connie felt crushed by the need to use food stamps. This was not how things were supposed to go. On the way back to the trailer park she cried. Wayne reached out his hand to her and touched her softly. He could be extremely gentle and sensitive at times. "Honey," he said, "things will be okay. This is just temporary. I was making money when we first got here and I will again. We're still paying our bills."

Connie looked into Wayne's eyes and saw that he was disappointed and hurt. It was important to him to do well, make a living for his wife and kid. "I know," she said, "I know," but inside she was breaking.

Later Connie told Therese about the food stamps, and when

she found that Therese was also using them, she felt better. But the cash shortage was raising tensions in the household, as it inevitably does, and it was on the day that Connie got the food stamps, while she and Therese talked, that another issue came to a head.

Connie said she was feeling poor. She got a couple of beers from the refrigerator. Therese told her, "I use them all the time and no one ever says anything to me. Heck, if it feeds us, I'm happy we have them." Connie shook her head. She said she would give it a try. She figured things couldn't get worse. Then they heard the sound of gunfire coming from the television and people screaming, and Connie got upset. She shouted to Wayne, "How many times do I have to tell you I don't like Max watching violence on TV." Then she told Therese, "Wayne even buys him toy guns, not cowboy and Indian things, but commando guns. They both loved that movie *The Terminator* with Arnold Schwarzenegger, about a killer who can't be stopped." Then there was another gun blast and Connie slammed her can down hard on the table and walked to the living room.

On the TV screen there was a man in a black leather jacket and sunglasses. He was holding an automatic gun and in rapid action he was shooting at people in a crowded bar. He had a shotgun in the other hand and he shot a man in the stomach. Max and Mark, Therese's son, were watching intensely, sitting between Wayne's knees. Max was holding a toy gun and aiming it at the screen.

Connie had seen enough. "Max, give me that gun," she shouted. She took the gun from his hands. Max began to cry. Now she turned to her husband.

"Wayne Chaney, your son is two years old. I don't want him to see this stuff, people being shot and killed before his eyes. Look at what you're teaching him."

"Come on, Connie," Wayne said. "Kids watch this stuff every day. It's on TV." Then he turned to Max. "Mommy is grumpy," he explained.

Now Connie was more forceful. "Wayne, this is our son. I don't want him to watch this. It will scare him."

"It doesn't scare him," Wayne said. "It's okay."

Connie walked to the TV set and pushed the off button. There was a tense silence. Wayne lay back on his hands. His lips were pressed tightly, his eyes narrow. He looked at Connie. He said nothing. But Therese could see that inside he was burning.

Thanksgiving, 1990

For Thanksgiving Connie and Wayne drove four hours along mountainous roads to Atlanta to visit Connie's brother Tom, who had just gotten married. Connie's father, John, who had become a U.S. Customs agent, flew in to be with his kids.

Tom was not happy about Wayne's behavior. Wayne, it seemed, was in his grumpy mood, real unsociable. He just wanted to sit in front of the TV and not do anything.

The Thanksgiving dinner featured a number of tense moments. Connie's father asked how she was doing with school, and there was a long silence while Wayne gave his wife a meaningful look. Finally Connie said, "I'm going to try again in the spring. We just don't have the money for me to go back to school and pay our bills, too, right now."

"I thought you were going to get help with that?" John said.

"Don't worry, she will make it," Wayne snapped. It was clear to him that the Krauser family did not think he was providing a proper life for Connie.

When Tom and John Krauser asked Wayne about his work prospects he took it as criticism. "Everything will be fine," he said. "Everything will be fine."

Things did not improve on Friday. Tom had an old washer and dryer to give Connie. On Friday he told Wayne to rent a dolly, so they could haul the appliances out of the garage.

Wayne said, "No, we don't need a dolly."

Tom said, "Listen, you asshole, rent a damn dolly. Here is ten dollars." He threw the money at Wayne. Tom was annoyed that Wayne was too cheap to rent the dolly. Wayne just wanted to pick up the washer and dryer and carry them for forty yards. Tom, who wasn't feeling well because he had just run a marathon, told Wayne, "I don't need to carry this stuff." Connie was embarrassed about how obnoxious Wayne was, but they got the dolly. Tom and John Krauser had to go with Wayne.

Connie and Wayne were supposed to stay until Sunday. Tom's wife had planned a huge meal for Friday night. But Wayne said no, they had to get back. Tom thought Wayne was being ungracious. It wasn't as if Wayne had a job he had to get to. So Tom said "Fine, just get the hell out of here, Wayne."

Later Connie told Tom about a terrifying incident that happened that night on the way home.

They loaded the washer and dryer into Wayne's truck and began the drive back to Tennessee. It was a thickly overcast night, and dark along the narrow mountain roads. Max and Connie both fell asleep during the drive, but Connie woke up when she heard the popping sound of Wayne opening a beer can. She didn't think it was a good idea for him to be drinking alcohol while he tried to navigate the dark winding roads on such a dismal night, but she decided not to complain. Wayne had had enough criticism for one day.

Wayne had one hand on the wheel and one on his beer can when another car caught up with him, its high beams blinding him through the rearview mirror. Then the car, a black Camaro, swung into the center of the highway and began to pass Wayne, sideswiping him in the process. Wayne dropped his beer can and grabbed the wheel with two hands. He swung the truck quickly to the right to avoid being hit. The truck swerved wildly. Connie was knocked to one side, then the other, clutching protectively at Max to make sure he didn't bang his head against the side of the door.

Wayne was incensed. He steered the truck back to the center of the lane, as the passing car pulled away in front of him. "That asshole tried to run us off the road," he yelled.

"Calm down Wayne, we're okay," Connie said. Max had woken up and was crying.

"That asshole doesn't know who he is dealing with," Wayne said. He pressed down on the accelerator and the truck picked up speed. "I'll fix that son-of-a-bitch."

Connie's heart pounded wildly. Wayne was obsessed. He pressed harder and harder on the gas pedal until he was right behind the car that had passed him so rudely. When he got close he flicked on his high beams to blind the driver, then he swerved his truck so he could get alongside the passenger side of the car. He rolled down his window. He hurled his beer can out at the car, swearing, "Motherfucker."

The metal can smashed into the window of the speeding car, causing the driver to swerve out of control. Wayne floored the truck and pulled away, laughing.

Soon the bright headlights of the Camaro were on them again. Connie turned. The car was getting closer and it looked as if the driver was trying to ram them. Wayne began to swerve left and right across the road to prevent the Camaro from passing.

"Wayne, stop it," Connie cried. Now Max was wailing hysterically. Connie pulled him close to her body and wrapped herself around him to protect him if there was an accident. "Stop it, stop it," she cried.

But it was as if she wasn't even there. Wayne had a crazed, determined look in his eye.

"Wayne . . . please . . ." she pleaded.

Wayne's eyes were glancing from the road ahead to the side view mirror, so he could watch the car behind him and cut him off every time he tried to make a move. His foot was heavy on the accelerator as he moved the truck around the winding curves in the highway. On one straightaway Connie saw the speedometer move past ninety. Suddenly, as they moved around one curve, swerving into the wrong lane, Connie saw the lights of what appeared to be a truck coming at them. Wayne jerked the wheel to the right, rattling the washer and dryer around in the back. The seatbelt seemed to cut into her chest as she lost her grip on Max and was pounded to the side of the truck. There was a sound of screeching tires. The Camaro swerved off the road away from the approaching truck, and into the dark. The oncoming truck whizzed by. Connie sat back and took deep breaths. Wayne began to ease up on the accelerator. He smiled. He had been victorious.

"You could have killed us all," she said.

Wayne looked at her. "He didn't know he was dealing with Wayne Chaney," he said, his hands still tightly wrapped around the steering wheel.

Christmas, 1990

When Christmas came Connie didn't have much money for presents. But she liked the idea of making gifts for

friends. She ordered a rhinestone kit she had seen on TV.
Then she bought glitter and paint and made designs on t-shirts
as Christmas presents. She also made everyone an ornament.
Connie had become an expert in making do.

Wayne and Connie went back to Des Plaines for Christmas, where she caught up with all her friends. When Wayne
was with them, she raved about Tennessee and the great
weather, however, when Wayne was out of the room, she
confessed that she was unhappy. "But I'm giving it a
chance," she always said. "I'm giving it a chance."

Her friends were still with her and they all told her that if
she ever decided to come back, there was a place for her and
people who loved her.

Most of Connie's friends came to see her at Wayne's parents' home, where the couple stayed, but Wayne would not
allow Kathy Hoshell to enter that house. Instead he drove
Connie to Kathy's trailer for visits and he set a strict four-
hour time limit.

Kathy was shocked when she saw Connie and Max at her
door. They immediately hugged each other and then Connie
began to cry. She was confused. She looked at her friend.
"Max is my whole life," she said. "I love him so much and
I want everything for him. I want a home, a father who cares.
It's his laughter that makes me hang in there. Max and
Wayne get along so well."

They spent Christmas Eve at Chris's house and Christmas
Day with Wayne's parents. Wayne bought Max a black commando gun that made violent sound effects when he pulled
the trigger. Connie was disgusted, but she didn't want to
make a scene. It seemed as if nothing she said to Wayne
about violence and children made any difference.

Later, in his diary, Wayne wrote, "My little family and I
set out for Christmas in which we were all looking forward
to see our friends and families. We had a lovely Christmas.
Bragging to friends and family about the weather and Tennessee. Especially Connie. She was excited about our new lives
as much as I. We stayed until about Dec. 29th or so, had to
get back so Connie doesn't lose her job."

By the afternoon of New Year's Eve they were back at
the trailer park in Knoxville. It was a warm afternoon and
Connie got out of work early. When she pulled up in Black

Oaks, Wayne was out in front of the trailer with a couple of guys and Max. Max was riding a hobby horse. All the men were carrying handguns. Wayne had bought five bottles of Korbel champagne and he already had one of them opened. He told everybody 1991 was going to be their year, his and Connie's.

As Connie greeted Max with a kiss, she was startled by one of the men, who tossed a beer can in the air, then aimed his pistol at it and started shooting. The can twisted in the air and Connie could hear the sound of bullets whizzing through it. Max clapped his hands and giggled. He was delighted. Connie took the boy inside.

A few minutes later her friend Therese came in.

"Hey, don't get scared about the gunfire," Therese told her. "Everyone here has a gun. At midnight this place will be like a shooting gallery. Revolvers, shotguns, you name it, they'll all go off at midnight."

"You've got to be kidding," Connie said.

"No. They just stand outside, aim their guns in the air, and fire."

"We don't do that in the north," Connie said. "We just go to a party, blow horns, and kiss."

On New Year's Eve Connie and Wayne watched television and drank champagne. By eleven o'clock Wayne, even though he was drunk and slurring his words, was feeling horny. Connie put the sleeping Max to bed, and then Wayne kissed her softly and led her into the bathroom where he said he had a surprise waiting.

She followed him into the bathroom. Around the tub were a dozen little glowing votive candles, a bucket filled with ice, and a single red rose in a vase.

"Oh Wayne," she said.

Wayne, though he swayed slightly from his long day of drinking, did his best to stage a smooth and romantic seduction. He kissed her gently on the lips, on the neck, pressed his fingers softly against her hair. Connie, stirred by his gentleness, gradually disrobed. Soon they were both in the bathtub, touching intimately, making the kind of gentle love that always filled Connie with joy and hope. The candles glowed around them. It was the beginning of a new year, she thought, a new chance for things to go better. After they had made love, Wayne stayed with Connie, held her tight and whispered words of love in her ear. Then, feeling playful, he poured champagne on her naked body. He took a large swallow from the bottle and dropped it to the floor. Then he quickly put his hand to his mouth and began to vomit into the bathtub.

"I'm going to pass out," he said. "I'm going to pass out."

Just as she reached out to comfort Wayne, Connie heard the sounds of gunfire blasting through the air outside her trailer. This was followed immediately by the piercing sounds of Max crying. She pulled herself out of the tub and ran naked into the room where Max slept. She pulled the child into her arms. "It's okay, honey, Mommy's here, Mommy will never let anyone hurt you," she told him. The gunfire outside continued and she pulled Max close to block the sound from his ears. The year had begun in a strange way, and she wondered what the events of the evening meant.

In his diary Wayne wrote, "Made love to my wife in the bathtub and ended up getting sick soon after. We were both truly in love with each other."

11

The Escape

January, 1991

It was ten-thirty on the night of January twelfth. Connie paced nervously in the small back room of the trailer, while a local newscaster on television droned on about murders and auto accidents. She was a wreck. Where was Wayne? Exasperated, she jabbed the button on the television to shut it off. She didn't need reminders of all the dreadful things that could happen to a man driving home at night. Max, thumb in mouth, was sound asleep. She envied Max his ability to sleep in innocence of such things. "Where could your daddy be?" she whispered, careful not to wake the child, yet needing to communicate to somebody. She pulled back the delicate curtains that hung over the trailer window and stared out at the dark empty road. No sign of her husband. She picked up the phone for the umpteenth time to be sure it was working, but all she heard was the impersonal dial tone. Why didn't he at least call? It was at moments like these that Connie realized how much she worried about Wayne.

Wayne had gone fishing early that day, but darkness had come hours ago, and Wayne had not arrived or called. Connie was afraid. What if Wayne's boat had capsized? What if he was somehow stranded at the lake? She imagined him trapped on a dark shore, cold and alone. She imagined even worse things, but pushed them quickly from her mind. She didn't know what she and Max would do if they ever lost Wayne.

Finally, unable to take the uncertainty, she picked up the phone and began to dial the police. Her call was interrupted by Max, who awakened, yawning and stretching and crying.

She put down the phone, lifted Max into her arms and took him into the kitchen for warm milk. She tickled his stomach and talked softly to him. It distracted her from her worries.

By the time Max fell back to sleep in her arms, and she was ready again to call the police, she heard the humming of Wayne's pickup rolling into the trailer park. Soon the flash of headlights appeared against her window, and Connie knew that everything was okay. Thank God, she thought.

With Max in her arms, Connie stood rigid in the front room of the trailer, waiting for Wayne to make his entrance and his excuses. She wasn't sure whether to hug Wayne or yell at him. She heard him talking to himself even before he came through the door, muttering about fish and singing a song. She knew he was drunk. She heard him stumble on the small steps in front of the trailer. And then he came through the door with a fishing pole in one hand and a string of stinking dead fish in the other. From across the small room she could smell the fish.

"Hi honey," Wayne said. Proudly, he held up the string of fish. The shine had gone from them, and Connie could only wonder how long they had been out of water.

Connie, still holding Max, looked at her husband disgustedly. Now that she knew he was safe, her fears dissolved to anger. "Wayne Chaney it is almost eleven o'clock. I've been alone here with Max, worrying myself sick. Why didn't you call me? Look at you, you're drunk and you smell like dead fish."

"Oh honey," Wayne said, good-humoredly, "I just stopped and had a couple of beers with some of the local boys." He walked across the kitchen and tossed his catch into the sink.

"Judging from the smell of those fish, it had to be a couple of hours of drinking," Connie said. "We're trying to save money, remember, not spend it in bars."

Max was wide awake now and Connie strapped him into his booster chair. She was angry. How could one man be so inconsiderate, she wondered. Wayne didn't seem to care about her or even Max, just himself. Always himself. She remembered now that it had always been this way. Even when she and Wayne were first living together, he would often abandon her in the evenings and go off drinking with his friends.

Earlier Connie had slipped into her pink cotton night shirt, an oversized t-shirt which hung down over her thighs. Now as she bent down to strap Max in, her night shirt rode up to her hips and Wayne could see her white panties. Suddenly she felt his big hands on her waist.

"You turn me on," he said, playfully.

"Go to bed, Wayne," Connie snapped. She was in no mood for sex with a drunk who didn't even have the sense to call.

"Not until I get a little love," Wayne said. He held her again, now more aggressively. Connie pushed him away.

"I said no."

She expected him to get a wounded look and lumber off to bed. But Wayne reached for her again, his big body swaying in the small trailer. "No, Wayne," she said. She jumped away and dashed behind a small square table. Didn't he understand that she couldn't make love when she was mad at him? Max, sitting in his booster chair, began to giggle at what looked like a game.

Wayne came toward her. "Come on, Connie, we're going to have some fun."

"Wayne, stop it. Our son is right here."

As Wayne came at her, Connie dashed to the other side of the table.

"Oh, you want to play tag?" Wayne said, now a little sterner. "Okay." Suddenly he lunged forward. He got his arms around Connie and pulled her to the floor of the trailer. She began to struggle. He was hurting her.

"Jesus, Wayne, stop it," she cried. He grabbed her flailing arms and pinned her to the floor. Connie, gagging at the smell of beer, fish, and sweat, was suddenly frightened.

"Get off me now," she yelled, the understanding gone from her voice. She tried to roll free of him, but Wayne held her down with his body. Connie moved her hips up to push him off and struggled with her arms until she got one free. Then she reached under him to push his body up. When there was a space between them she kicked desperately, jamming a knee into his groin. Wayne shrieked. He went limp and she pushed him off.

No longer playful, Wayne was now enraged. Though still in excruciating pain, he reached out and grabbed Connie by the shirt and pulled her back to the tile floor. She struggled. She pulled away from Wayne and began to claw her way up from the floor by latching onto the handles of drawers that were built into the trailer walls. But before Connie could get erect, Wayne righted himself on one knee, shoved her against the wall, and whacked with his left hand. It was a fierce blow that snapped Connie's neck to the side and knocked her senseless for an instant. Wayne smacked her a second time, and Connie screamed in pain. She clutched her face as she slipped to the floor. Wayne, still in agony from her kick, fell backward.

Max began to scream at the sight of his two parents lying in pain on the ground, both of them moaning.

Connie, hearing Max, gasped for air. She turned and righted herself up on an elbow, her jaw pulsating. She crawled to Max. "Okay, honey . . . shhhhhh." She pulled herself up and unstrapped Max. Desperately, she pulled the child into her arms and ran into the back room and locked the door. She grabbed the phone, dialing frantically, fearing every second that Wayne would come crashing through the fragile door.

Wayne, in the other room, pulled himself up. He knew that Connie was calling somebody to tell what had happened. He wanted to know who. He picked up the phone in the front room and wrapped a towel around the mouthpiece so that it would muffle out the sound of his breathing.

Connie had called her brother Tom.

The sound of her voice indicated that she was hysterical. "He hit me," she kept saying. "He hit me."

"What happened, Connie?" Tom asked. "Are you okay?"

"Wayne was drunk. He wanted sex and I said no. I kicked him and he hit me."

Tom told her to take deep breaths, try to relax, and tell him exactly what was happening. He told her she could leave if she wanted to. He asked if she wanted him to come and get her right then. She said no, she'd be all right.

Tom asked if Wayne was still there and she told him that Wayne was in the other room. Tom was aware of the other beatings. He and Chris had talked with Connie about them and they had all agreed that if it started again she should file for a divorce. Now he reminded her of that conversation.

"Listen, Connie, you can come down here and spend a week," Tom told her. "Do you want to go back to Illinois? Do you want to file for divorce? Do it before he does? You don't want a divorce in Tennessee. Don't answer me now Connie. Just stay there and think about it—just relax, simmer down, get your thoughts together and just stay away from him. Don't say anything to provoke him, okay."

Tom stayed on the phone with Connie until she had calmed down. She ended the conversation saying, "Okay, I know what you're saying, it's all right, we'll see."

Wayne, of course, heard every word. Later he noted in his diary that the word "divorce" frightened him.

When Connie finally unlocked the door and walked out to the kitchen, she carried a pillow and blanket. She tossed them on the floor. This would be Wayne's bed for the night. Her face was swollen, her cheeks purple and yellow. On her arms were black and blue marks from where he had grabbed her.

"Honey," Wayne said. To Connie he sounded pitiful, like a small boy.

Connie took a swallow and stepped back. "It's all right, Wayne," she said. Don't provoke him, Tom had cautioned her.

"Your brother has a good head on his shoulders," Wayne said. "You ought to listen to him."

Connie stared at him, slowly realizing what Wayne had done.

"Ha," Wayne said, proud as a little boy who had performed a successful prank. "I'm not stupid, you know. I picked up the phone. I heard everything. I know everything you do, Connie."

This invasion of her privacy made Connie angrier. She felt more violated. She wanted to scream and shout and throw things at him and hurt him. But Tom's advice echoed in her ears.

Wayne was no longer on the edge, however. His violent moments often dissipated as quickly as they had erupted. And now he dutifully lowered himself to the floor, knowing that he had been a bad boy who would have to sleep on a hard bed. To Wayne this was just another spat. He would take his punishment and soon he and Connie would make up and everything would be normal again.

Max, still traumatized by the incident, cried himself to sleep, but for Connie it was a long and lonely night. She lay awake until dawn, recalling the past, and planning her future. She felt trapped. In just a few violent minutes she had gone from worrying about how she would ever survive without Wayne, to a near certainty that she could never survive *with* Wayne. She decided that she would ask him to go into counseling. And if he said no, she would leave.

While Connie made breakfast the next morning Wayne woke up slowly. Hung over, he sat up on the kitchen floor.

"Wayne, I think we should go to counseling," she said. After all, Wayne promised her that would be one thing he would do in Tennessee.

"No."

"Why?"

"I don't think we should go to some stranger," he said.

"Wayne, you have to change your ways."

"We don't have the money."

"Oh, but we have the money for beer with our pals, don't we? Listen to me," she said. "This is not working. You have to change, Wayne Chaney. Otherwise . . ."

"What?"

"I don't know," she said.

For a long time the tension hung in the air, each waiting for the other to speak. But neither did. Wayne left the room. Skipping breakfast, he dressed and left the house without saying another word to Connie.

If Connie still had second thoughts about leaving, an incident that morning alleviated them. As she was trying to feed Max, the boy resisted, a common occurrence. But this time it was different. Instead of turning his head from the food, Max struck out at Connie, hitting her hand and knocking the spoon to the floor. He had never done that before. Connie felt suddenly fearful for the future of her son, and later she would say that this moment was the one that made her finally leave. She remembered Kathy warning her, "You can teach Max everything, but if he sees that Daddy can beat Mommy then he learns that too."

Shortly after breakfast Connie called Tom at work. She told her brother that Wayne had been listening to their phone call.

"Doesn't surprise me," Tom said. "He is a cunning little shit."

Tom told her to start calling him and Dad at home from a pay phone, or he would call her at work. He told Connie he would get her out of there, but that they had to wait for just the right time.

Connie was distraught. "Tom, I want a divorce, I don't want to go through this. I never should have come down here. But I already have a Tennessee driver's license."

The significance of the driver's license was that if Connie was a resident of Tennessee she would have to divorce Wayne in Tennessee, which meant she would have to travel back from Illinois. Tom promised to look into it.

After he hung up Tom called Chris at the hospital where she worked as an administrator.

He told Chris that Connie had been beaten up again and wanted to run away and file for divorce in Illinois.

"I hope she kicked him in the nuts," Chris said. "I would have done that long ago."

Though Chris was haunted by mental pictures of her little sister being beaten, she was at least happy to know that Connie was finally leaving. She told Tom she would talk to a lawyer whom she had contacted a year before, when she'd been worried about Connie.

In Tennessee Connie began to plan her escape. She went through Max's clothing, looking for things she could put aside, without their absence being obvious. She called Therese and asked to store some of Max's things in her shed. But she didn't tell Therese, or anybody else, her plan. Wayne, it seemed, had ways of finding things out.

In the days following the attack Wayne was again Mr. Wonderful. He made French toast and bacon for breakfast. He slept on the couch in the back room and behaved himself. He tried constantly to make up with Connie. When she went to work early one afternoon because they were short-handed at the store, he kissed her softly on the cheek and promised, "I am going to clean up the house today, when you come home it will be clean ... you'll see."

While Wayne was dusting and straightening, Connie was making the phone calls that would facilitate her getaway. From the pay phone at the deli she called Tom collect at his office. He told her that an Illinois divorce was still possible, since she had not been out of the state for a year yet.

"Did you give up your Illinois driver's license?" he asked.

Connie, seeing hope, dropped the phone and let it dangle while she opened her purse and nervously reached into her wallet and pulled out all her identification. There, in her hand was a current Illinois driver's license.

"No," she said excitedly, "I still have it."

Tom was delighted. "Good girl," he said, "good girl. Now listen to me, Connie, you have to file first, because if he does it, then you can't leave."

Tom was even thinking of driving to Knoxville, and taking Connie to Chicago, or possibly meeting her halfway and taking her home.

The decision was made. The only question hanging over Connie was, when? When would she leave without getting caught? She had frightening visions of Wayne catching her in the act of running from him.

As it turned out, luck was on her side.

Connie cooked dinner for Wayne and made small talk, all the time wondering if there was something in her voice, in her demeanor, that would give away her secret. Wayne was becoming a larger-than-life figure for her, a man who could plumb the secrets of her soul. But if Wayne had an idea of what she was thinking, he didn't let on. In fact, he made an announcement that made her feel safer than ever.

"I am going to Florida on Thursday to meet Darrell." Darrell* was a friend who did landscaping with Wayne. "I'm going to help a friend of Darrell's move back up here. Darrell is already out there."

Darrell already sent him fifty dollars to make the trip in the pickup truck.

Connie couldn't believe what she was hearing. This was too good to be true. She almost dropped her frying pan. Act natural, she told herself, don't act happy about it. "I will be back in three or four days," Wayne was saying. Three or four days, she thought, three or four days. She and Max would be safely in Illinois before he even got back.

The next day she told Wayne that she had to go in to work early to cover for another worker. Wayne was happy. That meant she would be paid overtime. Connie left early while Wayne was still sleeping. What she really wanted was to firm up her escape plans. She went immediately to the pay phone. She looked up attorneys in the phone book and called a local divorce lawyer to ask him about taking Max to Illinois.

"All you have to do is leave a note telling him where you are at," he advised.

She then phoned Tom.

"Tom, you are not going to believe what happened!" she shouted to her brother in Atlanta. Connie told him about Wayne's plan to go to Florida.

Tom was thrilled. "Great," he said. "Pack the car the day he leaves and drive to Atlanta. I'll get you on a plane to Chicago."

After the call, Tom phoned Chris, who looked through the yellow pages until she found the ad placed by Chicago divorce lawyer John Collins. She asked him to represent Connie and made an appointment. Collins, who had been practicing divorce law since 1955, said he could format a divorce petition in less than two hours.

For the next few days Connie felt as if she were treading water. She could see the shore, but she could also feel the presence of Wayne in her life and it felt as if he could push her under at any moment. Perhaps he would sense her plan. Maybe he would beat her. Maybe he would cancel his trip. She worried, but she also planned. She secretly packed as many things as she dared. In her mind she composed the letters that she would send back to her Tennessee friends after she was safe. For now, she dared not tell anybody.

The night before Wayne was scheduled to leave, Connie asked him if she could go out with her friends from the store. She was nervous, because she knew that it was a farewell. After a moment of thought, he allowed her to.

January 19, 1991

"Daddy will be gone for a few days," Wayne said. He hugged Max, still wet from his evening bath. "Now you be a good boy. Daddy loves you. I could never live without you and Mommy." Softly, he brushed his son's hair.

Max giggled. He was beginning to talk. "Daddy," he said. "Daddy."

Connie, standing nearby, could see that Wayne was crying. God, she thought, he knows he is saying good-bye. But no, she told herself, that's crazy.

Later that night, after Max was sleeping, Wayne kissed Connie good-bye. He climbed into the pickup truck and drove off into the night. Connie was numb with anticipation. Was it really over? Was Wayne Chaney really gone from her life? She remembered the couples in the courthouse in Chicago. Would that be her soon? She felt the tension in her stomach. She felt the same nameless sensation that swept over her years earlier during her first days of recovery at Gateway. Is Wayne the drug I'm trying to kick now? she wondered. Like drugs, he had held her back. Now, she had to do whatever it took to make sure he was out of her life to stay. She had taken him back before she realized, as women like her often did with men like him, but now *Connie* vowed that this time would be different.

Connie slept poorly that night. She tossed and turned and listened to the night noises, half expecting to hear the truck return. "Honey, I changed my mind," Wayne would say, and her dreams of escape would be shattered. She looked at the clock constantly. But Wayne did not return. As the darkness turned to dawn she began to believe more and more that her dash for freedom would succeed.

In the morning she called Tom. "He's gone," she said.

Tom told her, "The lawyer said to leave a note for Wayne, so that you cannot be accused of kidnapping Max. Just write that you have gone to your sister's."

Connie hurriedly packed her Toyota with clothes and Max's toys. She just took one suitcase of her own things. She wanted to take a large chest that had belonged to her mother. It was the only thing she owned of her mother's, but no matter how hard she struggled with it, she could not squeeze it into the car. Sadly, she gave up and put the chest back in the trailer. She wrote her note to Wayne, set it on the table, and waited for him to call. She reasoned that if she

Wayne Chaney, age 19. *Family photo*

Connie Krauser, age 8. *Family photo*

Left to right: Steve, Wayne, and Ken Chaney at Wayne and Connie's wedding in 1988. *Family photo*

The Krauser siblings at the wedding. *Left to right:* Chris (eight months pregnant), Tom, Connie, and Jane.

Family photo

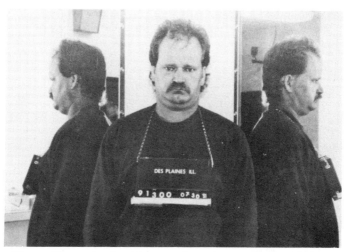

Wayne Chaney having his mug shot taken at the Des Plaines police station on July 30, 1991, hours after he pistol-whipped Connie, raped her, and kidnapped her and his son, Max.

Photo by the Des Plaines Police Department

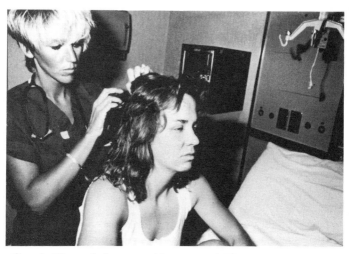

Connie Chaney being treated by a nurse in the emergency room at Holy Family Hospital after Wayne finally released her.

Des Plaines Police Department evidence photo

Cook County Assistant State's Attorney Toni Winninger at the Skokie courthouse.

Photo by Sharon White

Cook County Circuit Court Judge Sheila O'Brien on the bench in her courtroom.

Photo by Sharon White

Connie's friends meet in the kitchen of her childhood home. *Left to right:* Catherine Sullivan, Kathy Hoshell, Tammy Delaney, and Loretta Delavale Wagner. *Photo by Sharon White*

Left to right:
Des Plaines detectives
James Prandini and
Terry McAllister, and
Detective Division
Commander
Al Freitage at the
Des Plaines police
station.

Photo by Sharon White

Cook County Sheriff Police who were involved in the shootout with Wayne Chaney. *Left to right:* Dan Marshall, who was shot in the chest but saved by his bulletproof vest (on the desk), Paul Cagle, Mark Caridei, and Robert Arrigo, who was shot twice in the legs. *Photo by Sharon White*

The 9-millimeter pistol that Wayne Chaney used to murder his wife. *Photo by Sharon White*

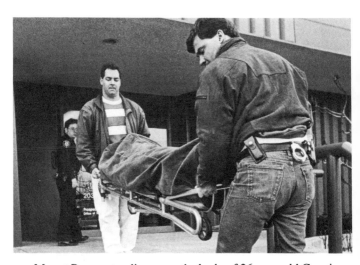

Mount Prospect police carry the body of 26-year-old Connie Krauser Chaney from her workplace, where Wayne killed her on March 17, 1992.

Photo by Bob Wessell, Journal & Topics *newspapers*

A Mother's Day drawing Max made for Connie in 1991 and a farewell letter Connie wrote two months later.

Photo by Sharon White

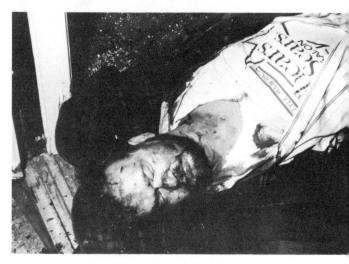

Wayne Chaney minutes after police fired over fifty rounds into the apartment doorway where he made his final stand.

Cook County Sheriff Police photo

Max William
Chaney, age 2.

Family photo

left immediately after talking to him, she would have the longest possible head start.

She sat by the phone, nervously twisting her fingers in her hand. Stay cool, she told herself, just act natural. Tell him you miss him. Don't be nervous. She took deep breaths. Finally, the phone rang.

"Honey, I'm here," Wayne said. "Does Max miss me, huh? Is every other word out of his mouth, 'Daddy'?"

Connie kept her composure. She gave Wayne the answers he wanted.

"Yes," she said, "He misses you and every other word is Daddy."

The conversation was brief. Wayne was worried about running up a phone bill.

"When will you be home?" she asked cautiously.

"About four days. We'll pick up a load of furniture, do a little fishing, and head back."

Fish for a month, she thought, fish forever, for all I care. "Have fun," she said. Then, "I love you." And as she hung up the phone she knew it was not true. But she loved herself, and he didn't leave room for her to love both of them.

She took a deep breath, lit a cigarette, and called Tom.

"I'm leaving now."

Three hours later she was in the embrace of her brother Tom and his wife, Marilyn. They all cried together and talked about a brighter future for Connie and Max.

"Everything will be okay now," Tom said, holding his sister longer than he had in years. Wrapped in Tom's arms, Connie felt like a little girl again. She had been so afraid— she was still afraid—but she had finally returned to the arms of her protector.

Tom and Marilyn drove Connie to the Birmingham, Alabama, airport and put her and Max and two suitcases on a plane to Chicago.

"Thank you for getting me out of there," she said.

"Chris will be waiting at O'Hare when you arrive," he told her. "You will be safe, Connie."

With her brother Tom and her sister Chris nearby, with the warmth and love of family surrounding her, Connie Chaney felt, at last, safe. Nothing, she thought, could hurt her now. The violence that had ripped her life was finally ended.

The strange power of Wayne Chaney over her had been destroyed. She felt the way she had years before when she had finally reached the bottom and been turned over to the constructive hands of Gateway House: at the beginning of a new life, one she would control, and she was taking the first step.

12

Court Battle

It was after midnight when Wayne and Darrell pulled into the driveway alongside the mobile home. The barren branches of the dogwood tree rustled in the wind against the dark half-moon sky. Wayne heard the sound of a neighbor's dog barking as it strained against the links of its iron chain. Wayne later reported in his diary that he had an eerie feeling as he climbed out of the truck. Something was wrong. And then he realized that Connie's yellow Toyota was not parked in the driveway.

He unlocked the door of the home and quickly stepped inside, rubbing himself to keep warm. Darrell came in behind him. Wayne flipped on a light and spotted the note on the kitchen table.

"I have gone to my sister's," the note said. Nothing else.

"Max," he cried. "Max." He ran to the back bedroom and turned on the light. The room was empty. He dashed to the crib and pulled back the sheet. The powder blue blanket that Max always carried with him was gone, along with his tattered yellow teddy bear. Wayne felt a chill sweep over him. He yanked open the drawers. Max's clothes were gone. All of them.

"She left me," he said to Darrell. "My wife left me and she took my son."

"Jesus," Darrell said. He could see that Wayne was enraged. "Calm down a minute. Maybe she is just visiting with her sister."

But Wayne was not listening. In seconds he was on the phone, dialing 911. He told the police that his wife had kidnapped his son.

A few minutes later a young officer arrived to hear Wayne's complaint. The officer tried to explain that there was nothing he could do. "This isn't a ransom note," he kept saying. "There are no threats, no demands. Mr. Chaney, there's been no crime committed here. You should get some sleep and call her in the morning."

But Wayne was inconsolable. "You don't understand," he said. "That is my son, Max William Chaney, that she kidnapped. She took him away and she has no intention of letting me see him again."

After the officer left, Wayne told Darrell to sleep in the bedroom. Wayne would sleep on the couch. But he knew he wouldn't be able to sleep. His mind was racing.

"She's got my son," he kept repeating to Darrell. "What do I do?" There were tears in his eyes.

Meanwhile, in Chicago, Connie felt safe. On her first morning at Chris's house she awoke to the sound of children's laughter. Chris had two girls, ages three and one, and they were delighted to have their cousin Max as a playmate.

Chris came in while Connie was still in bed. The two sisters talked and hugged, and promised each other that everything would be all right now.

"I'm taking the day off," Chris told her. "Any day that my sister leaves Wayne Chaney is a day worth celebrating. You go into town and see John Collins, the lawyer. I'll stay here and watch Max and the girls."

While they were talking, the phone rang, as Connie knew it would.

Chris answered. It was Wayne.

"Connie doesn't want to talk to you," she said, and hung up with all the finality Loretta had done five years earlier.

Wayne, on the other end, listened to the click. He couldn't believe how he was being treated.

"That sister of hers is a bitch," he said to Darrell. "I'm going to Chicago."

Darrell told him to get some sleep, to eat, to calm down.

"Chicago," Wayne said. "That's where my son is."

Connie wasted no time. She drove to LaSalle Street, where many of Chicago's largest law firms have offices, in the tall buildings across from city hall or a block from the main courthouse at the Daley Center. "The lower the address the more expensive the suites are," Chris had explained to her before Connie left. Connie didn't know how much her lawyer would cost and she was afraid to ask.

The office of John Collins was on the twentieth floor at 134 North LaSalle, across from city hall. Collins was tall and stocky. And efficient, Connie thought, because when she arrived, Collins handed her the petition for dissolution of marriage, ready for her signature.

The lawyer sat back in a red leather chair, with the Chicago skyline behind him. "The most important thing," he explained, "is to make sure the divorce is done here, not in Tennessee. Wayne is going to fight you on this, so be prepared. He is going to try to get this dismissed. He is going to fight against your sole care of your son."

Connie read the three-page document. When she got to the part that read "the respondent has been guilty of extreme and repeated mental cruelty towards the Petitioner without cause or provocation on her part," she smiled at him. "You got this right, for sure," she said in a southern drawl.

Collins told her to sign. It would all be notarized and filed in a day.

Connie was relieved. "Is that all?" she asked.

Collins leaned forward. "No," he said. "We are just beginning. You have a son. There will be a custody battle. Your husband will fight for visitation and he will fight against child support. If he threatens you in any way we will get an order of protection from a judge. That will keep him away from you and Max."

"Does that work?" Connie asked.

"If he violates it we can send him to jail," Collins said. "The courts will protect you and your son."

Before Connie left, Collins added one point. He didn't

want to spook her, but he felt he had an obligation to look out for her interests.

"I always tell clients to look into life insurance policies," he said, "to make sure that their children will be looked after."

In Tennessee Wayne brooded. He drank beer. He watched television. He dialed Chris's phone number all day. Late in the afternoon, he got lucky. Connie and Chris had just gotten home from their visit with Collins, and Connie picked up the phone.

"Connie, what is going on?" he said. "I want you to come home. How is Max, honey?"

"Max is fine," she said, cold. She realized she had been lulled into a false sense of well-being. Wayne was not exactly gone from her life. "Connie, what is going on?" he said. "It can't be that fight. That was days ago."

"Wayne, I'm going to hang up now," Connie said.

"Wait, Connie," he pleaded. "When can I see Max?"

"I'll talk to you later. Bye," she said. But still she didn't hang up the phone.

"Why are you doing this to me?" Wayne said. Now he sounded angry. "You took my son away from me."

Connie couldn't answer. Suddenly she was afraid. She had visions of Wayne coming to Chicago, stealing Max.

"Connie, I'm talking to you," Wayne said. "You think that was a beating. Well, that was nothing. I warned you about what can happen. I want to see my son. I have the right to see my son, and you can't stop me."

Now she hung up.

When Connie told Chris about the conversation, Chris said they would call Collins in the morning and get the order of protection. Order of protection, Connie thought. It sounded good, but could it really protect her or Max? The phone rang again. They let it ring.

At 9:00 a.m. on January twentieth Donna Chaney answered her door and was greeted by a process server.

"Does Mr. Wayne Chaney live here?"

By this time Donna knew what was going on. She had talked to her son and taken his side.

"Wayne doesn't live here," she told the process server. "He and his wife moved to Tennessee six months ago."

As soon as Wayne heard from his mother, he started looking for a lawyer. He flipped through the yellow pages frantically. He had it in his mind that he needed a top lawyer and would find one in the richest areas of Memphis. When he found Douglas Toppenberg, he was impressed by the fact that the man's office was on the nineteenth floor of a building on Gay Street, and picked him.

Wayne got dressed up and drove into Memphis for his first meeting with Toppenberg.

The law office was in a modern high-rise that overlooked the city. Toppenberg was a middle-aged man, who wore a tailored three-piece suit. Wayne was impressed by the leather-bound law books that filled several shelves, and the large oak desk in the center of the office. To Wayne this meant that Toppenberg had money to spend, and that meant that he must do a lot of business.

The lawyer asked Wayne for a small retainer and told him there was a chance that the divorce could be contested in the state of Tennessee. He told Wayne that they would ask for custody of Max. Within an hour the complaint for divorce was ready and Wayne signed it.

Driving back to his empty home that day, Wayne was filled with emotions. He was devastated that Connie had left him. He wanted her back, but he had filed for divorce to protect himself. He also wanted to see Max and decided that now, with his complaint filed in Tennessee he could go to Chicago, although his mother tried to talk him out of it. Through a lawyer who had defended Wayne on burglary charges many years earlier, Wayne got in touch with a Chicago lawyer who would work for him up there.

Connie began connecting with her old girlfriends. Loretta, Tammy, Cathy, and Kathy all listened sympathetically to her stories about Wayne, and when she told them she was divorcing him they agreed that she was doing the best thing. Donna Rubenstein, who had worked at the deli with Connie during Connie's pregnancy, urged Connie to reapply for her old job. She did and was hired. It amazed Connie how quickly she slipped back in the swing of things in Illinois. The months in Tennessee had shattered her self-esteem and she had not taken good care of herself. But now she took more care with her makeup, and studied her appearance a little longer in the mirror before leaving the house. The divorce would be rough on everyone, she knew, but she could feel herself once more becoming a person she could like.

When Wayne got to Des Plaines he moved into his mother's house and started calling Chris's. Chris was short with him. "Don't call here anymore," she told him. "We are trying to help Max adjust to the new situation." Once more she hung up.

Later, in the section of his diary which he called "Heart Attacked," Wayne wrote, "You don't go off and tell someone that, after his family left. She's a real bitch. Chrissy always ran Connie's life, always directing her where to go and what to do."

The next day Wayne called again, getting Connie this time. He told his wife that he was in Chicago, that he wanted to see his son. Connie, fearful of a kidnapping, told Wayne she would meet him only in public. They agreed to meet at a McDonald's restaurant at the corner near Western and Armitage under the el tracks. Then Connie called her lawyer and told him Wayne was in town. She wanted to know about the protective order. Collins told her it was no good unless Wayne knew about it and had been served with it.

"Then what good is it?" Connie said. She was exasperated and afraid. It sounded as if Wayne could just grab Max and there was nothing she could do about it. Collins told her to meet Wayne in an open area, but not for more than fifteen minutes.

The next day Connie stood nervously inside the front door of the McDonald's. Max kept asking if he could play on the restaurant's outdoor gym equipment, but she had to say no, she wanted him close. Her heart was pounding. What would she do without Max? Wayne pulled up in his pickup truck. As he climbed out he glanced around, nervous himself, as if he were expecting the police to grab him.

For a few minutes there were no words between husband and wife. Wayne embraced his son tenderly, as if the two of them were alone. "Max, Max," he said, "your daddy missed you."

When he finally spoke to Connie he asked her, "Why did you leave me?"

"We've been over it and over it," Connie said. "I don't want to go over it again."

"I filed for divorce," Wayne said.

Connie was stunned. "When?" she asked.

Wayne smiled. He acted as if he had tricked her. "You don't want to know why? Just when. I guess that's because you filed, too. Connie, where's the Toyota?"

"Why?"

"I want it, for a second car," he said.

"I'm leaving," Connie said. "Come on, Max." She reached out a hand to the boy. Don't let him see how scared you are, she told herself.

"It's only been ten minutes," Wayne said. "Not enough time for a man to see his son." He looked at her coldly. "Why did you leave me?" he said.

Connie took a deep breath. She picked up Max and walked away. She knew Wayne was capable of violence. She prayed that he wouldn't make a scene here.

Wayne let them go. Then he got into his pickup truck and began searching for the Toyota. He drove by Chris's house, then to Des Plaines where he looked in Tammy's driveway, then Loretta's. He drove past the houses of as many of Connie's friends as he could think of. Then he returned to Chris's house in Chicago and parked the truck so he could watch the house. He would know when Connie and his son went out and when they came in. If they stepped past a window, turned on a light, even sat in a chair, he would know. The stalking of Connie Chaney had begun again.

The first court appearance for Wayne and Connie came on February fifteenth. Wayne, wearing a white shirt and sport coat, drove for eight hours from Tennessee to Chicago. He arrived in court with his Chicago lawyer, Wayne Shapiro, a slightly-built man in his late thirties. Wayne smiled when he saw Connie. She did not smile back.

That day John Collins asked Judge Aaron Jaffee to issue an order of protection for Connie. Both Wayne and Connie were sworn in as witnesses. Connie, in trying to explain why she needed an order of protection, had difficulty in remembering exactly on which dates Wayne had hit her. Wayne, when he took the stand, was calm as he told the court that he had never hit or kicked his wife.

Judge Jaffee, noting that the husband and wife had two different senses of reality, said he was more concerned about the child than either Wayne or Connie. He ordered family counseling, and told them to arrange for a place where Wayne could meet with Max and Connie would feel safe.

On the following weekend Wayne saw his son, but after his visit, he was more depressed than ever. He drove back to Tennessee, obsessing about his wife and son every mile of the way. Back in the trailer he called Chris's house constantly, but got no answer. They had unplugged the phone.

An order of protection had been issued against Wayne. He was not to talk to his wife. In the days that followed his visit with Max, however, Wayne did find a way to speak to Connie. He spoke into a tape recorder. He talked about his feelings. He said that sometimes his pain was so great that he would smash his fist onto a table just so the pain in his hand would distract him from the pain in his heart. He was having panic attacks. He thought of his wife and son constantly. He could not work, he could not fish. He picked up the minnow bucket one day, and he could hear Connie saying, "Look, Max, baby fish, baby fish." He said that sleep was the only escape he had from his terrible depression. He said that he saw his life with Connie and Max like a film running through his mind. He saw Max bundled up in his life preserver when they went fishing. He saw Connie laughing. He said that everything reminded him of his family. When he picked up a box of Corn Chex he was filled with images of Max splashing milk into a bowl.

For hours at a time he would sit in the back room of the trailer, hunched over the tape recorder, drinking beer, crying. "I love you and I love Max so much," he said. "This is the hardest thing that has ever happened to me. We had our problems. A lot of marriages have problems. My mom said if she got a divorce every time she got into a fight I wouldn't have been born. Connie, I miss you so much. You are my wife, I love you."

Throughout the recording, Wayne broke down crying. He

whispered, "I love you, I always loved you, honey, and I always will." He would turn the tape recorder off, then on again as new thoughts came to him. He talked about the landscaping business he had given up, and how he was making progress in Tennessee. "I know you can't live off scenery," he said, "but I am making it, honey, I am making money. For fourteen weeks I have averaged $179.00."

Wayne sent the tape to Connie. She did not want to listen to it at first, so Chris listened to it to see if Wayne made threats. Then Connie played it and responded by putting it in the file folder she kept for her lawyer.

When Wayne finally started getting through to Chris's phone, he got an answering machine. He would call with the intention of being sweet and contrite. "Please come home, honey," is what he wanted to say, but often the frustration would erupt in him and he would scream, "Bitch, fucking bitch," into the phone. His love was turning to hate.

March 7, 1991

Wayne needed to communicate with Connie personally. If only he could get through to her, he thought, he could make her see how much he loved her and everything would be okay. But she would not take his phone calls. It was Chris, he thought, the bitch sister, she was the problem.

Wayne drove back to Des Plaines, for his court dates. On March seventh Wayne's problems deepened. He got a notice ordering him to appear in front of a judge and produce all records of income. If that wasn't enough to get him crazy, Connie was asking for a motion of temporary custody, and expecting Wayne to pay all court costs.

"I've got to talk to her," he kept saying in phone conversations with his brother Steve. "I've got to talk to her."

Finally, Wayne calmed himself enough to sit at the kitchen table at his mother's house and write a long letter to his wife. Despite his violence, he was capable of great sentiment, and as he expressed his tender feelings for Connie and his son, Wayne found himself moved to tears. When he finished he folded the letter neatly. He had decided he would place it on the windshield of Connie's car at work. He drove to the shopping center where Connie worked.

The long trip, however, soon depleted his measure of equanimity, and Wayne, often reckless behind the wheel of his truck, became particularly dangerous this day. He sloshed anxiously through the Des Plaines traffic, cursing the dozens of drivers he cut off. When he got to the parking lot of the deli, he swerved in quickly. Suddenly there was a young woman in front of him, pushing a cart of groceries with her son. "Jesus," he screamed and jerked the wheel sharply. The woman pushed her son out of the way. Wayne swerved again, barely missing both mother and son and whacking the grocery cart to one side. The woman screamed at him, but Wayne kept going. He was a man on a mission.

When he spotted Connie's Toyota, he pulled up and got out of his truck. Clutching his plaintive letter, he moved around the Toyota, trying the doors. He now wanted to leave the letter in the car, if he could. While he was yanking on the doors, trying to find one that wasn't locked, he was approached by Tara Baggot, a young recruit officer with the Des Plaines police. Baggot had witnessed the incident with the woman and her son.

"I want to talk to you," she said sternly.

Wayne sneered. She was practically a kid, and she was going to give him a hard time? Not likely.

"What are you doing?" she demanded.

"Fuck off, bitch," Wayne said. He jammed the letter under Connie's windshield wiper and climbed back into his truck. As he sped off, Baggot wrote down his plate number. Then she called it in, and called in the plate number on Connie's car.

Within minutes Connie heard her plate number being announced at the grocery store.

God, she thought, what has he done now? Her heart was pounding. All she could think of was the incident a few years earlier when Wayne had deliberately smashed into her car.

When Connie got outside, Baggot asked her to step into the squad car, and handed her the letter.

"Who is he?" Baggot asked, while Connie read.

"Wayne Chaney," she said. "I'm divorcing him." She showed Baggot a copy of the order of protection. "He's not supposed to have any contact with me," she explained.

Baggot asked Connie if she wanted to sign a complaint,

and she said she would. Baggot radioed in the information and in minutes a call came back saying that the order had expired.

"No, no," Connie said. "That was the emergency order. We renewed it."

"They don't have it," Baggot said.

Connie shook her head. "You mean you can't charge him with anything because the order is not in your computer?"

Connie did not have the new order with her. She knew that if she wanted any swift police action on Wayne's latest attempt to contact her, she would have to drive to Chicago to get it, missing a day's work. She was beginning to feel that her life was in the hands of machines and that the machines were not reliable.

The next day Wayne Chaney was in court. Connie's attorney asked the judge to sign a new order of protection, which he did. On her way out of the court, Connie was greeted by Wayne's lawyer, who handed her an envelope.

"What's this?"

"Summons," the lawyer said. "Fourth Circuit Court of Knox County. You have been served." He walked away.

In the meantime the complaint against Wayne had come under the scrutiny of Detective Bob Schultz, who had dealt with Wayne in the past. When he called Connie she told him that Wayne had gone back to Tennessee. Schultz explained that people were not extradited for violation of a protective order in another state. He advised Connie to drop the complaint and use the incident as ammunition for her divorce.

Soon Wayne, back in Tennessee, began leaving vulgar messages on Chris's answering machine. Connie kept track of all the calls.

Connie continued to work at the deli and socialize with her friends, and there were times when she could push back her fears about Wayne. She continued to feel better about herself, and before long her female friends were trying to match her with some of their single male friends. Donna Rubenstein, from the deli, knew a guy who was single, good-looking, and liked kids. "And he's thin like you are," she said. Connie was hesitant, but finally agreed to a blind date.

Connie often bought her clothes at second-hand stores but now she got herself a new silk blouse, a long skirt, and makeup. On a Saturday night Connie and her date, Patrick Carlson, along with Donna and her husband, went to the dog track for dinner. Connie later raved to friends about how handsome Patrick was, with his black wavy hair. "And he is such a gentleman," she told them. "Unlike Wayne," she added. Patrick had held her chair for her at the track, had opened doors, had done all the gracious little things that Connie was not used to. Best of all, he loved children. "He's still a kid himself," she said.

Patrick was as charmed by her as she was by him. The chemistry was instant and obvious. Donna and her husband might as well have been alone. Connie smiled throughout dinner and seemed happier than anyone had seen her in a while. When she won a race she easily threw herself into her date's arms. She was so smitten with Patrick that when he asked her to stop by his place on the way home, she agreed and ended up spending the night. For a few hours in Patrick's arms she felt safe and childlike. She felt that she had escaped from the world of Wayne Chaney which had possessed her for so long. And it was wonderful to wake up with someone who smiled and was happy that she was there and wouldn't yell at her.

Chris, meanwhile, was unnerved that Connie had not come home. More and more Chris was put on edge by this entire affair. No longer just worried about Connie and Max, she had begun to worry about her own safety and that of her family. Wayne was a dangerous person. When Connie hadn't called, Chris's mind was filled with pictures of Wayne hurting her.

"I'm okay," Connie told her when she finally called. "I spent the night at a friend's house."

"Who?"

"I'll tell you later."

God, Chris thought, after she hung up. Not a man. Chris didn't even want to think about what Wayne might do if he found out Connie was sleeping with another man.

Two weeks later in Des Plaines, after a scheduled weekend visit with Max, Wayne went to Boomer's. As he sat at the bar, sipping beer and recalling better days with Connie, he was joined by an old friend, Lee Baker. He began to tell

Baker how he would win Connie back, but Baker saw it differently.

"Connie's got a new man."

"What are you talking about?" Wayne asked.

"Saw her right here on Saint Patrick's Day," Baker said. "They had their arms around each other, dancing close."

Wayne was ready to explode. "Hell, we've only been separated two months. I guess that makes her an adulteress. You know who this guy is?"

Baker did not know Patrick's name, which was probably just as well for Carlson. Wayne left Boomer's that day in a jealous rage.

At the next court date Wayne was still furious. He tried to talk to Connie, but his lawyer stopped him.

At this court appearance Judge Carol Bellows ruled that Connie was an Illinois resident and that her Illinois divorce filing was valid. Wayne was ordered to pay her twenty-five dollars a week in the meantime.

The following weekend, after his visit with Max, there were no lawyers to stop him, so Wayne drove to Chris's house to confront Connie about the new boyfriend. The confrontation soon became a shouting match.

"It's none of your business who I sleep with," Connie yelled.

"Yeah, well I'll make it my business," Wayne said. "And I hate all this bullshit of me seeing Max just when you let me. I'll see him whenever I want. I'm his father, not some stranger."

Max sat nearby, quietly playing with his trucks.

The screaming continued. Chris had had enough. Finally, she started screaming, too. "Stop it," she cried. "Stop it. I'm going to call the police. There is an order that says you are to keep away from Connie."

"Fuck you, bitch, fuck you," Wayne shouted. Chris reached for the phone. Wayne stormed out, slamming the door behind him, and sped off.

A few days later a troubling letter arrived from Wayne.

When I say I love you, when I say you keep my heart beating, when I say I don't want to live without you and Max, I mean it. You two are my family. I have nothing without you. If you were in my place (alone) you would die. This isn't easy. You don't realize what you have, or who, until it is gone. I think if you are smart . . . which you are . . . at least the Connie I knew was, you would do the following.

1. Return home and seek counseling together for a week.

2. Return and do the same for a short time.

3. Try . . .

Wayne wrote sweetly about the beauty of Knoxville. But he also wrote, "Don't test me, Connie. Be smart, think and act on your own. When I called your house Chrissy hung up on me for the last time. There's no reason for that piece of shit sister to do that. I have nothing to lose. I feel that I have lost it already, so be smart. Max needs a father as well as a family."

At the end of his letter, Wayne wrote, "I'm not a bad guy. I was. I could be. Don't make me famous." He underlined the word "famous" and drew a smiling face, adding the words, "This is it, Connie Rose. Think."

The letter was enough to set Chris off. She had been growing more and more tense about the possibility that Wayne was a threat to her family, and she was angry with Connie for increasing the danger by dating Patrick Carlson. And she was annoyed because Connie had often lied to her about when she came home at night.

"That's it," she screamed at her sister. "Wayne is crazy and he isn't going to come here and hurt anyone in my family to get at you. He calls a hundred times a day. I've had to unplug my phone. I do not want him picking up Max here anymore. Call your lawyer about this letter, and then I want you out of here."

On April ninth John Collins filed an emergency petition with Judge Bellows, noting the harassing phone calls and the implied threat of "don't make me famous." The judge gave Wayne and his lawyer a month to respond to the charges that he had violated the order of protection.

"Can you believe it?" Connie said to a friend. "He calls

me, nearly runs a woman down in the parking lot, and shouts at a police officer as he is leaving a letter on my car. Then he sends me threatening letters. And he gets a month to respond!''

April, 1991

Connie pulled up in front of Wayne's parents' house. It was a warm April morning and she had to leave Max there for one of the court-ordered visits. Though the thought of leaving Max depressed her, as always, she was in a good mood. It was her first week on her new "dream job" as a receptionist at an advertising agency in nearby Mount Prospect.

Suddenly the door to her car was pulled open. It was Wayne. He climbed into the car with her. "Let's go," he yelled. "Drive." He looked wild-eyed. Connie was frightened.

"Wayne, I have to go to work," she cried.

"I said drive."

Connie started the car and began to move forward. Then she shoved her foot on the brake. "I said no."

"I'm not kidding," Wayne said. From his pocket he removed a white handkerchief that seemed to be covering a gun. He pointed it at her. Connie started screaming. Wayne, rattled, reached into the back seat and unbuckled Max. He pulled the boy into the front seat. Connie grabbed the boy by the waist, but Wayne held on, and they began pulling at their son from different directions. Max screamed.

"Please, Wayne, let him go," Connie cried.

"Fuck you," Wayne yelled, but when he saw a neighbor coming to help, Wayne let go of Max and bolted for his car.

Within a week Connie and her lawyer were again standing before Judge Bellows. Bellows issued another order of protection, but Wayne was still not put in jail. Connie was livid. "Now Wayne knows we are serious," Collins told her. "Maybe now he will leave you alone."

Bob Schultz was assigned to follow up Connie's complaint that Wayne had pulled a gun on her. When he talked with Wayne and Donna Chaney, Donna told him, "It's not unusual for Connie to overreact. Her whole thing is to have Wayne continually arrested, to minimize his privileges for seeing Max.''

"We had an argument," Wayne explained to Schultz. "At the time I had one of Max's toys, a Mattel plastic revolver, in my hand." He got the toy gun and showed it to Schultz.

When Schultz called Connie and told her Wayne's side of the story, he said, "I don't see how Wayne violated an order of protection."

"Forget it, then," Connie said. She slammed down the phone. She was becoming as disgusted with the police as she was with Wayne.

In early May Connie and Max moved in with Connie's sister Jane. They shared a two-bedroom apartment on Western Avenue, ten minutes from Connie's job and five minutes from her babysitter. Despite everything, Connie was feeling as if she was gaining control. She had an apartment, a good job, and a new life without Wayne.

Wayne continued to see Max, though. He played on the floor with Max's trucks. He took Max fishing on the Des Plaines River, where they would dig for worms with their hands in the wet soil. He took Max to Boomer's, and taught him how to shoot pool. These were joyous times for Wayne, but he always ended his visits with Max feeling angry and victimized because Wayne had to keep to a schedule and bring Max back at a certain time, as if Max were not really his son.

Wayne also continued to stalk Connie. He often identified with characters in movies, and one morning he called Connie at work to ask, "Have you seen *Sleeping with the Enemy?* You should. It's about an abusive, deranged husband whose wife must fake her disappearance. But, you see, he tracks her down."

After one court appearance, when Connie won the small victory of a child support increase to fifty dollars a week, Wayne walked up behind her and said, "You have only three days left to live," then he rushed down the hall to an elevator.

Connie tried to file a report, but she was told that if nobody else heard the threat she as wasting her time.

In early July Wayne walked up to Connie when she was picking up Max.

"Connie, come back to me," he said, turning on his pleading routine. "Let's be a family again. I am making five hundred dollars a week and I could support Max in grand style."

"Wayne, no, forget it," she said. She hurried to get Max strapped into the car so she could leave.

"My mother said she would buy us a new mobile home if you come back to me."

"No," Connie shouted. She remembered the house they had to give up, the tuition money that never came. "No, no. Do you understand English? No."

Suddenly Wayne changed. The crazed look rushed back into his eyes. He reached into his pocket. Connie wanted to jump in her car and speed away, forever, when Wayne pulled out a loaded black ammunition clip.

"Look, Connie," he said, "these are nine-millimeter hollow points." He spoke too calmly. "If you don't come back with me, then I will kill you."

That night, and for most of the nights that followed, Connie could not sleep. She lay awake, thinking over and over about those bullets, about Wayne's warning, "Don't make me famous," about all the failures of the court to do anything about him. She became convinced that Wayne was going to kill her.

Connie's other great fear was that Wayne would kidnap Max. One night he was late bringing the boy home. Connie grew panicky, pacing in front of the Chaney driveway. When Wayne finally showed up with Max, she lit into him.

"You're late," she said. "The court order says six p.m."

"Fuck off," Wayne said. "I'll do whatever I please with my own son."

When Connie reported this violation, along with the bullet incident, she was told that Wayne could not be arrested unless she got a judge to sign a complaint for violation of the protective order. Another court date.

Connie was beginning to feel as if she lived in the courthouse. This time Collins told the court there was an emergency.

"What is the emergency?" Judge Bellows asked.

"Mrs. Chaney's life has been threatened."

Judge Bellows seemed unfamiliar with the case. "Do we have an order of protection?" she asked.

Connie wanted to explode. "Yes, yes," she wanted to scream. "Yes, we have a goddamn order of protection. It's been extended four times, you signed them." But she held her tongue while her lawyer explained in calmer language that Wayne was threatening Connie, that she had gone to the police, and that the police had sent her to the judge. Collins read through the list of incidents with Wayne, the letter, the phone calls, the late returns of Max, the gun under the handkerchief, the bullets, and the threats in the courthouse.

Wayne's lawyer, Shapiro, of course was available to deny every incident, or make it sound like much less than Connie claimed.

Judge Bellows, finally noting, "We can't take these death threats lightly, we've lost too many people," ordered a psychiatric evaluation of Wayne Chaney. If appointments were made right away with the Psychiatric Institute, she noted, it would probably take three and a half months.

Three and a half months, Connie thought. A lot of tragic things could happen in three and a half months. But she was hopeful. Maybe Wayne would get the help that he needed. Maybe at last he would learn how to deal with his rage and give her some peace.

13

"Only God Can Take a Life"

July 25, 1991

Jeff Mills slowly turned his gold Buick into the parking lot of the Dominick's where Connie still worked at night. Being a single mother, she had to hold down two jobs to help pay for Max's day care and baby sitters, and her own expenses at the apartment. Jeff searched the lot for Connie's father's blue Chevy van which she would be driving, and when he finally spotted it he pulled into an empty spot nearby. He glanced at his watch. It was 10:00 p.m.

Mills, a former law student, now a process server and private detective for the Argus Agency in Des Plaines, had been hired by Wayne to keep an eye on Connie. And it was a job that troubled him.

He'd been on many cases, most of them involving divorcing couples. But something about this one got to him. He'd met Chaney a week earlier under the innocent golden arches of a nearby McDonald's. Chaney, affable enough, had also seemed deeply wounded. He had given Mills a snapshot of his wife and son. "My wife left me," he explained. There was a custody battle and a fight over jurisdiction. This was pretty routine stuff for Jeff Mills. Wayne knew where Connie lived and worked. What he didn't know, and what he wanted to know, was who her lover was and where he lived. Sure, Wayne had seemed upset, Mills thought now, as he waited in the dim yellowish light of the shopping center, but most husbands are upset when they hire a private detective. Then what was off about this one?

A few nights later Mills had strolled into the deli section where Connie worked. He had stood right in front of her at the counter, to get a good look at the woman he would be following. Even then, he had seen fear in her eyes, and she had looked back at him almost as though she knew. Does she look at everybody that way? he wondered. The next night, when he followed her, she had veered suddenly from her route, onto a side street. She knew she was being followed and he had sensed that she was afraid.

Now, he sat in his car waiting for her to leave work. He felt sorry for her. But this was his job. After a few minutes, Connie came out of the store. She was holding Max, the boy. Two of the store's security men were accompanying her. Connie looked around cautiously. About twenty feet from the van she stopped and handed the keys to the security officers. She held tightly to Max, who was asleep. One of the officers stood outside the van, while the other opened the passenger side door. Both men climbed in and looked around.

Mills, watching from his car, felt strange. What was Connie so afraid of? This was supposed to be routine. Why did she have people walking her to her car and searching it? Finally the men stepped out of the van. One handed her the keys and seemed to tell her that everything was okay.

He watched the van back up and headed to the exit. Mills waited a minute and then started his car. He wanted her to be at least five car lengths ahead so Connie would not notice him.

It was immediately clear to Mills that Connie knew she was being followed, or she was taking no chances. She quickly changed lanes without signaling. Mills, afraid of losing her, also changed lanes. He knew that his quick movements were probably being noticed, but he had no choice.

Connie, a few car lengths ahead, was frightened. For days she had sensed the presence of a shadow in her life. She had told many people that she thought she would die soon at the hand of Wayne Chaney, but no one had believed her. Now, as she approached River Road, she gripped the wheel hard in her hands and swerved, then turned again quickly into a gas station. The car behind her, the one that seemed to be following, moved suddenly, but couldn't slow in time to turn with her.

Connie's heart was pounding. Now she was sure. She wasn't paranoid. She really was being followed. She had to escape, had to protect her son. She looked around her. There was no traffic either way on the street. She took a deep breath, stepped on the accelerator, swung the car around, and headed north in the southbound lane, knowing that he must endanger his own life to follow her. In minutes she had escaped.

A block away Mills was cursing himself. Damn it, he thought, she did it again. She's going to her lover and I've lost her.

The following night Jeff Mills met Wayne at the McDonald's.

"Did you find out who her lover is?" Wayne asked.

"No, I keep losing her. She knows she's being followed." Mills studied Wayne's face. He seemed okay, but something was wrong. Mills wanted some answers.

"Wayne, why is your wife so scared?" he asked.

"Scared?"

"Why does she have guys walking her to her van? What happened? Did you ever threaten her?"

Wayne looked puzzled. "I don't know," he said. "I once told her I would kill her, but that was nothing, just talk. We were fighting at the time."

Mills believed him. He had been involved in a lot of divorce cases, and he had seen how couples often had hot tempers. Wayne didn't look to him like a man who would hurt anybody.

"Look, tomorrow is Sunday," Wayne said. "She will be picking up Max at six o'clock from my mother's house and maybe she'll be going to her lover's."

The next evening Mills drove a van and wore a disguise in case she had remembered his car or him from a previous tail. He parked his van a half block from the house and lifted the hood to make it look as though he was working on his engine. When Connie came out of Donna Chaney's house with Max, Mills took up the chase again. He knew she would watch to see if she were followed, so he drove along a road parallel to hers, a block away. He kept track of the car by watching it pass the intersections after stop signs. This time, he vowed, he would not lose her.

His persistence would pay off. He followed her south of Fifth Avenue, until she turned east on Thacker/Dempster, then south on Graceland/Lee, a middle-class neighborhood of aging bungalows, south on I-294 past the forest preserves and scattered factories, then east on I-90 into an area of Chicago that is mostly Korean and Polish neighborhoods comprised of wooden apartment townhouses and framed homes.

Finally, around six-thirty, Connie parked in front of the apartment building at 5049 Argyle. Mills watched her as she went around to a rear entrance, then came back a few minutes later with a young man. They went to Connie's van and started unloading clothes and small pieces of luggage. After Connie and Max and the man had gone back inside Mills went into the building and read the names on the mailboxes. The name for the third-floor rear apartment, where Connie and the man had gone, was Patrick Carlson.

He smiled. He had gotten what he wanted.

It was raining when Mills met Wayne at a gas station later that evening. Wayne got into Mill's car and they drove down the block to a side street. Wayne handed Mills an envelope with his payment in it. Mills gave Wayne his typed report. Wayne was quiet as he read the report.

"This can't be," he said when he finished reading. "I don't even know this guy."

"That's the guy," Mills said. "She had overnight bags. I know it hurts, but that guy is her lover, he has to be."

Twenty-four hours later Wayne sat in his brown Ford Galaxy, parked a few houses from the apartment building. He had come by earlier to check it out, and spot the third-floor rear apartment. He knew where the door was, where the stairs were. He was waiting for Connie to come to her lover. When she did, he would kill them both. He was like a commando, a kind of one-man SWAT team. He would deal with whatever came up. If he concluded that Connie was already there, he would go in, confront Connie and Patrick at gunpoint. If Connie wasn't there, but showed up, he would hold a gun to her head while Patrick buzzed them both in.

Then he would kill them.

Then he would take Max and raise him properly, just as he had promised Gramps.

Wayne had already packed another car with sleeping bags, camping supplies, fishing gear, cooking utensils. He'd parked the car at a friend's house, and he would use it to get away. He had bought this brown Galaxy for the murder, and he had never told anybody. He didn't want to involve any of his friends in what he had to do.

Sitting in the car, waiting, Wayne no longer cared about what would happen to him. He was full of pain, thinking about Connie lying naked in the arms of another man. He remembered her face, the expressions she made during love-making. The idea of another man causing those expressions enraged him. He had to see what this Patrick guy looked like. He pressed his lips together. He tensed his fingers around the cold steel of the gun. It made him feel better. He was sure that revenge would be sweet, that it would take away his bitter pain.

Obsessively, he thought over and over about his promise to his grandfather. Raise Max right. Raise Max right. Those were the words and they had become a mantra to him. "Raise Max right." And is this right, he thought, the boy's mother with some stranger, holding a child hostage from his own father. No, Wayne thought, it's not right. Raise Max right. That was his promise and he would keep it, and anybody who tried to stop him from keeping it, he would take care of.

Wayne had a pistol tucked under his belt. He had loaded two shells into his shotgun, and the pouch around his waist contained a box of shells. In a tattered green duffel bag he had another revolver, along with a bulletproof vest and a gas mask. Wayne was ready for anything. He felt that once he killed Connie, the police would be searching for him, and the gas mask would help if they trapped him and started lobbing tear gas canisters. By this time Wayne had begun to think of himself as the Terminator. He had seen *Terminator II* the week before, and identified strongly with Arnold Schwarzenegger's role. In this movie the Terminator, now working for good and justice, had come back in time to protect the child who would become the rebel leader of the future. He was an android, invulnerable and incredibly power-ful, in the form of a man who would not die and who would kill anyone in his way. Nothing, his programming dictated, would harm the child, not even the more powerful Terminator sent to stop him. Like the good Terminator, Wayne was the underdog here, his child the potential victim. In his mind he ran and reran scenarios of himself shooting people. Cops, people who had slighted him over the years, all were blown to bloody pieces by the avenging guns of Wayne Chaney, the Terminator. These fantasies seemed to free him, at least for a while, from his pain.

As he waited for Connie to show up, Wayne saw that his life was slipping away from him. The once idyllic days in Tennessee were gone forever now. His boat was gone, his mobile home was gone. He had sold them, but most of what he owned had been given to friends or tossed out. Tossed out, he thought. That's probably what Connie had done with the tapes and letters he had sent. She and her boyfriend had probably read the letters and laughed at him.

Connie had been warned, he thought. He had shown her a gun and bullets. He had even warned her, "Don't make me famous."

Every time a car came down the block he felt his body tense. This could be it. He was fed up. She'd been playing games with him, and all the time sleeping with some guy named Patrick. Well Patrick was in for a surprise. They both were.

Wayne dozed off a few times, but always woke up suddenly, alert. By midnight Connie had not shown. Maybe the private detective had been wrong. Maybe this was not the lover. Maybe this was the wrong address. As he became more sleepy, his rage began to subside. She could wait to die, he thought. Yes, she could wait a while longer and it would be all the sweeter. He pulled the pistol out of his waistband, put it back inside the carrying case, and zipped it up. He turned on the ignition and headed back to Des Plaines from the Chicago address. He would rest before he would try again.

The next day, as she drove home for lunch, Connie was feeling better than she had in a while. There seemed to be cause for optimism. The sun warmed her face. The country and western songs on the radio lifted her spirit. Her new job was going well. And earlier, she had called her new love,

Patrick, and they had made a date for that night. Plans were under way for Wayne to have a psychiatric evaluation. She had no idea how close she had come to being murdered the night before.

Though she felt the fear of sudden violence from Wayne was as close as her skin, she had learned to live with it. Two weeks earlier she would have predicted that she would be dead by now. She had told many people that she was afraid Wayne would kill her, but people had scoffed. It was too crazy a thought. "Wayne wouldn't do something like that," they said. "Wayne's not *that* bad," they said. Even when she told them she was being followed they often looked at her as if she were making it up. And here she was, working and enjoying much of life. She had set up therapy sessions at Life Span, the local group that worked with battered women. Though she had written a farewell letter to her friends and family, she had never shown it to anybody, and by now she had folded it up and put it with her divorce papers. She was, for the moment, no longer certain that she was going to die.

As Connie drove down Rand Road, past the McDonald's restaurant, Wayne was just a short distance behind her, at the wheel of his brown Ford Galaxy. He had been hiding in the parking lot by her office, and had followed her. He watched as Connie pulled in behind her building and parked. He watched her walk into the building. He reached for the .38 caliber revolver he had brought with him.

He picked up the duffel bag that contained the shells, the bulletproof vest, and the gas mask, and from the back seat he grabbed the canvas case that held the shotgun and another gun. He took a deep breath. He felt calm. He was the Terminator, and he had a mission. He had to get his son back. Connie had put him through too much. Now she would have to die.

The front door was propped open because of a resident's furniture delivery. He walked in unnoticed.

Wayne carried the weapons to the apartment building. When he reached the door to Connie's apartment he looked around carefully to be sure he was alone. Then he placed the duffel bag on the floor next to her door and rested the shotgun case against it. With his hand over the grip of his gun, he put a cautious ear to the door and listened. He could hear her walking from room to room. She would eat her lunch, he thought, never knowing she was going to die. Then she would have to go back to work. She would open the door. And then he would kill her. Connie, Connie, he thought, I didn't have to do this. He waited.

Twenty minutes later, he heard her footsteps moving closer to the door. This is it, he thought, now you will pay for what you have done. The door opened. As soon as he saw her he threw himself at the door. Connie's face was full of fear. He liked that. "No," Connie screamed. She lunged forward, slamming her body against the door to keep him out, but Wayne was too strong for her. He surged forward, snapping the door wide and bouncing Connie back across the room. She smashed into the refrigerator, hitting her head, and collapsed to the floor. Wayne stormed in with his weapons, slamming the door behind him and locking it.

Connie scrambled to her feet. He's going to kill me, she thought, he's going to kill me. She tried to dash for the bedroom. If she could get inside, she could lock the door, buy a few precious minutes on the phone. But as she bolted, Wayne reached out. His hand snapped around her arm like a metal trap. He flung her down. When she smashed into the floor, she knew she was going to die. She felt warm blood trickling down her face. Her head throbbed. She squirmed around and looked up at him.

"Please," she cried.

"Shut up," Wayne shouted. He came down on top of her suddenly, holding her hands down, pinning her to the floor. "Shut up," he said again, his voice low and ominous. She could see that he was out of his mind. She cried out again. He slapped her face hard. "Shut up," he said. "I'm not going to hurt you. I just want to talk."

Connie was hysterical. "Please," she cried, "please." She couldn't stop herself.

"Shut up, shut up, shut up," Wayne shouted. He punched her face, then spun her over and slammed her head to the floor to muffle her cries.

Connie, now frozen with fear, said nothing. Soon she would be dead, she was sure of it. Wayne straddled her to hold her down, then he reached into his duffel bag and pulled out a roll of duct tape.

"I just want to talk to you," he said. "But I don't trust you, so I have to tie you up."

First he gagged her by laying a strip of the tape across her mouth. Then he grabbed her arms. Connie didn't struggle. She understood that it was over and that the more she fought him, the more pain he would cause her. She went limp as he pulled her hands up behind her and taped her wrists together.

"What is going on?" Wayne demanded, though Connie could not answer.

"I know about your boyfriend, Patrick Carlson," he said proudly, as if he had been some clever private detective. "I was waiting for you last night at his apartment. I had my revolver and shotgun. I was going to kill both of you."

Connie gagged on the tape. Out of the corner of her eye she could see the pistol tucked into Wayne's belt. That's the gun that will kill me, she thought. Wayne shoved the roll of tape into his pocket and pulled out the gun. No one believed me, she thought, no one believed me.

Slowly, Wayne opened the barrel of the gun and began to slide bullets out of the chamber. Connie tried to moisten the tape so she could talk to Wayne. Maybe if she could talk to him she could calm him down.

"You have to pay for what you've done," Wayne said. "You can understand that."

Wayne's statements were as confused as his feelings for her. One minute he was saying he wasn't going to hurt her, the next he was going to kill her. He loved her, he hated her.

Slowly he lowered the barrel of the gun to Connie's head. Connie looked into the slender barrel of the gun. This was the power of life and death that Wayne had always wanted. This was his moment, but if he killed her, it would be gone. He squeezed the trigger. Connie thought this was the end of her life. There was a click. She could almost feel the bullet rushing through her head. She wanted it to end. But it didn't. She was still alive. Her body was soaked with perspiration. Her heart pounded furiously. Another click. Her mouth was dry from the fear, but somehow she was able to signal Wayne that she wanted to talk. He stopped. He put his gun aside, and slowly peeled back the tape from her mouth.

"Wayne, listen to me, just listen to me," she cried. "It doesn't have to be over."

It was a desperate, frightened attempt to reach him. Connie knew it was her only hope. "I thought it was over, I did, but it doesn't have to be." As she spoke she knew that each word would be her last. Say the right things, she told herself, say the right things.

"It can't be over," Wayne said. "It can't be."

"You're right," she said. "You're right. Maybe we could go to counseling." Her mind was racing. If you say the wrong things, you are dead. Just distract him, get him talking, get him thinking about the good things, about Max.

"Do you still love me, honey?" he asked. The question was not as bitterly ironic as the situation would suggest. Wayne was serious. He wanted her love, and Connie knew it. He placed the gun to her head.

"Of course, I do, Wayne," she said. "You know that. I never stopped loving you."

For a moment his thoughts seemed to drift. He stared off in space, forgetting, it seemed, that he was straddling her, that he was trying to kill her. For a moment Connie thought he might let her go. But soon he looked at her again, differently this time.

"I'm in this loving way about you," he said. He smiled. He raised the gun. "Let's go into the bedroom."

He yanked her onto her feet. Below her she could see the blood that had oozed from the gash on her head from hitting the refrigerator. The tape tugged against her wrists as he pushed her toward the bedroom. At the phone she stopped.

"I have to call work," she said. "They'll wonder where I am."

"Call them," Wayne said. "Tell them you aren't coming in." He thought about it. "Tell them you had a car accident. That you are at the hospital." He held the gun near her face. "I will dial the number."

Wayne held the phone to Connie's mouth as she spoke into the phone.

"Hi, this is Connie," she said. "I'm not coming back to work this afternoon. I'm at the hospital. I got into a little accident, but I'm okay."

Wayne hung up the phone. He smiled. Connie was doing everything he wanted. He was pleased. Now she would give him what he wanted. When he got her into the bedroom he pulled a white blanket from the closet. He tossed it onto the bed. Then he pushed Connie down onto the mattress. Still holding the gun in one hand, he reached down and grabbed the pink top she wore. With one ferocious yank he ripped the top from her, tearing at it as it bit into her flesh. When he had the garment free he tossed it aside. Connie lay helpless on the bed, wearing only her bra and a pair of long flowered pants. Then Wayne plunged his fingers under the wire frame of the bra and snapped it off her chest. He glared at her. "I don't trust you," he said. He reached into his pants pocket and pulled out the roll of duct tape. "I am going to gag you again."

"Wayne you don't need to. I won't—"

"Shut up," he said.

He ripped off a length of tape and pressed it over her mouth. He pulled off her shoes and unbuttoned her pants and slipped them off. Connie felt his hard fingers pulling down her underpants. She heard the sound of him unzipping his pants. She felt his weight on top of her, so familiar, yet suddenly so alien. He pushed her legs apart. As he forced himself inside of her, Wayne slowly placed the barrel of the gun against her head. Then he placed the gun next to her head on the bed so that if she turned she would see the barrel pointed at her. He pushed himself up and down inside of her. Connie closed her eyes. She tried to block out the experience. This isn't happening, she told herself, this isn't happening. Just get it over with.

Wayne came quickly inside of her. She opened her eyes. He looked nervous, shocked, confused.

"Sorry I came so soon," he said, apologizing, as if he had been making love to her instead of raping her. "But what do you expect, I'm so confused."

"Let's talk Wayne, please," she begged when he had removed the tape.

"We have to clean up, Connie," he said.

"What?"

"A shower," he said. "I know you always like to take a shower after sex."

By this time Wayne had decided that he was not going to kill Connie, at least now. The blanket on the bed and the shower were an attempt to hide the fact that the rape had taken place.

"Yes," Connie said. "A shower." She was beginning to see hope, to sense that Wayne was trying to erase evidence of the crime.

Wayne held her at gunpoint while Connie got into the shower. Then he went into the bedroom and looked through desk and bureau drawers for letters and cards from her lover. When he found them he stuffed them into his pockets. Then he went to the refrigerator, looking for something to eat, and came back with just a glass of water.

"I see you still have the same nothing in the refrigerator," he said, laughing at his own joke. He picked up the torn bra and blouse and stuffed them into a plastic grocery bag. He handed Connie some paper towels and told her to wipe the blood off her face.

Still holding the gun on her, he followed her around while she wiped up the blood on the floor, and wiped his prints from the phone and the glass counter top in the bedroom. She wiped everywhere he asked her to. Then Wayne put all of the towels and duct tape into the grocery bag.

The mood of violence seemed to be seeping out of him like a battery that was losing its charge. More and more he was careless about where he stood in the room, whether or not he trained his gun on Connie. It was as if she were not his prisoner, as if she could leave at any time. But Connie did not dare.

For a long time they sat on the couch. Wayne cried. He tried to express to her how much he was hurting inside.

"We could go to counseling," Connie said. "We really could. We could start tomorrow." Say the right things, she thought.

Wayne, hearing what he wanted to hear, believed her. Soon he was smiling. "Oh God," he said. "We're going to be family again, you and me and Max. I know it will work this time."

Later, after they talked about how things could be good again between them, he told her, "You know, I even wanted to kill your sister, Chris. I was going to drown her in the bathtub."

They talked some more. Finally, he said, "I guess it's too

early to get Max. Let's go to my mom's house and tell her the good news, and then we'll get something to eat.''

Connie was willing to go anywhere, just to leave the isolation of the apartment. She wanted to be out in the open, maybe he wouldn't kill her where there were witnesses. She had to keep him convinced that everything would be okay now, that they would be a family.

Wayne shoved the grocery bag containing her ripped clothes and bloody towels into his duffel bag with the handgun. He even handed Connie the shotgun in the case, as they walked out. Connie was still shaking. In the car she asked Wayne to get her a pack of cigarettes and a Coke. He ran to a nearby gas station to get them. But still, she could not bring herself to run. If he caught her, there would be no second chance.

When they got to Donna Chaney's house, Wayne's brother Steve was just pulling out of the driveway. Connie wanted to scream for help. "Your brother has gone crazy!" she wanted to say. "He's going to kill me!" But when she had the chance, all she said to Steve was, "Wayne is acting a little strange." She didn't know if she could trust Steve. Since the breakup, the Chaney family had turned against her.

Donna Chaney was, of course, shocked to see Wayne and Connie together. "Everything is going to be okay," Wayne told his mother.

Connie went to the bathroom. There she tossed cold water on her face and dabbed at her scratches and bruises with a wet cloth, while downstairs Wayne was telling his mother that he and Connie and Max were going to be a family again, that they would go for counseling.

Donna was skeptical. She told Wayne, "I don't trust her," but Wayne assured his mother that everything was going to be fine.

After a short visit, Wayne drove Connie to lunch at a small pub in the neighborhood. Connie drank beer to calm her nerves. Connie knew it was unwise to drink, especially now when she needed to be alert for every nuance of Wayne's behavior, but it was all too much. She also had a cigarette. Right now a cold beer seemed like her best friend after what she had just been through.

She tried to act calm. She didn't want to do anything that

would upset Wayne before they saw Max. Max was all she could think of now. She had to do whatever was best to protect him. She could not let Max fall into the hands of this monster.

While Wayne went on and on about how happy he was that things were normal again, and how he was looking forward to seeing Max, Connie thought about Patrick, and how Wayne had planned to kill Patrick and her the night before. She knew that what had happened in the apartment could happen again. Wayne was a ticking bomb, and she didn't know what might set him off.

Wayne told her that he had sold his boat and the mobile home.

"But don't worry," he said. "I'll be able to make enough money so we can move back there in a year."

"Great," Connie said, but saying the right things was losing its ability to comfort her. If she were disagreeable, Wayne might get angry. However, if she were too agreeable Wayne might know she was lying.

Next they drove to the home of Yolanda Blair, the babysitter. When they got to the house, Yolanda's husband George was outside, washing his car. He talked to Wayne while Connie went in to get Max.

Yolanda looked up from packing toys when Connie entered. "Jesus, what happened to you?" she said. "You're all bruised and swollen."

"I'm with Wayne," Connie said. "He beat me and raped me."

"I'll call the police."

"No," Connie said. "Please. He has a shotgun. He'll take Max. Call the police after I leave."

From Yolanda's, the family drove to a park near Connie's place. She sat quietly on a bench while Wayne pushed Max on the swings. When she saw a Des Plaines cruiser drive by, she wanted to run to the police, screaming bloody murder. But she was afraid. Wayne had Max. And he had taken the duffel bag containing the weapons over to the swings with him.

After a few minutes Connie spotted Letty Pacheco, an old friend from high school, who had come to the park with her daughter. Letty, a stocky Latino woman, sat a few benches away.

Connie called to Wayne, asking him if she could sit on the other bench. She felt like a prisoner. She was a prisoner.

"Sure, honey."

She walked over to the bench where Letty was sitting. Letty could see that something was wrong. Connie stared straight ahead, her face like stone. "Wayne broke in and tied me up and held a gun to my head," she told her old friend, without looking at her.

Letty offered to help, but Connie was afraid. She didn't want to get somebody else killed. "He has a gun," she told Letty. "I'm so scared for Max."

Letty said she could distract Wayne while Connie grabbed Max and ran. Connie glanced over at Wayne. He looked at her. He suspects, she thought. "No," she said, "I don't want to get you involved. Call Tammy, tell her what happened."

In a few minutes Connie went back to Wayne. She asked him if they could go home to her apartment now.

"Sure, honey," Wayne said. He was agreeing to everything now. When they got to Connie's building Wayne carried his son upstairs. He kissed Max good-bye and then he kissed Connie. He smiled. "I'm really happy about this," he said. "Call me tomorrow."

"I will," she said, and as soon as he was out the door she bolted it and began sobbing hysterically. The full force of what had happened fell upon her. She felt faint, nauseous, dizzy. Max, crying, came to her. She held him in her arms and they wept together.

After a few minutes the phone rang. It was Tammy. Letty had called. Already, word of Connie's ordeal was circulating through the network of female friends. After she hung up on Tammy, Connie called Chris. Chris told her to call the police and then go to the hospital. She would meet her there. Right after she hung up, Kathy Hoshell called. Connie's friends were reaching out to her. Connie cried as she told Kathy what had happened.

"Call the police now," Kathy said. "I'm coming over, I'll take care of Max until the police are done with you."

By the time Connie called the police, they had already heard from Yolanda. The officer who responded to Connie's call was Ron Sharin, a veteran of the Des Plaines force who, like many of his comrades, had come upon the name Wayne Chaney before. He had arrested Wayne years earlier for burglary and drug charges. Sharin had his own ideas about Wayne. He saw Wayne as a man who thought the world was dumping on him. He knew Wayne was dangerous and he thought that Wayne could explode anytime and wreak a good deal of havoc. Clearly Connie had been beaten, but Sharin also knew that it was often hard to get a rape conviction when the rapist was the husband. Connie told him about how Wayne had made her wipe up the prints and the blood. Sharin called in a report on Wayne. When Kathy arrived to take care of Max, Sharin took Connie to the police station.

A three-man team known as Delta, a special tactics unit of the Des Plaines police, was dispatched to the Chaney house. Trained in surveillance, the team was formed mainly to deal with gangs and narcotics dealers. But the team happened to be in the vicinity of Donna Chaney's house when the call came in. They parked across the street from the house to watch for Wayne.

At the police station Connie met with Officer James Prandini, a man who had always known that he and Wayne Chaney would cross paths again. Prandini had never forgotten Wayne's rage of years ago, nor his threat: "I'll get a gun and blow you away. Don't forget what Manson did." Though it had been ten years since Wayne had been arrested, Prandini had always suspected that the rage inside of him would someday erupt. It seemed now that the day had come.

Prandini urged Connie to press charges of battery, home invasion, and rape. He could see that she was afraid. "We can put him away for a long time," he promised.

"He's going to kill me," Connie said. She began to cry.

"No, you don't have to be scared anymore," he said. "I'll protect you." Her hands were trembling, and he knew she had come inches from death. How could he make her believe that this time it would be different?

"I'm only alive now because I convinced him that we would go to counseling," Connie sobbed. "But you can't protect me. I've had three orders of protection, and what good did they do?"

Prandini felt frustrated. He knew it was true. If Wayne was

absolutely determined to kill Connie, there was no piece of paper that would stop him. Only the walls of a prison could do that.

Prandini took Connie to the hospital, telling her along the way that he would bring in someone from the state attorney's office to get the charges approved right away. Connie agreed. She would accuse Wayne of raping her.

Wayne, meantime, was celebrating. He went to his mother's house. He placed the bag with Connie's torn clothing and the blood-soaked paper towels in his room downstairs. Then he shaved, took a shower, and put on some fresh clothes. He was all smiles when he came down to talk with his mother and father. Things were working out just great, he said, he couldn't be happier. His mother was still skeptical, not because she thought of her son as a violent psycho, but because Connie had left him once, and couldn't be trusted not to do it again.

When he left the house a few hours later, however, he sensed that something was wrong. He backed his car out of the driveway, then he stopped and got out. He walked around for a few minutes before climbing back into the car.

Delta team had seen him and already they were calling for a backup.

Wayne pulled out of the driveway and headed north on Fifth Avenue. Soon he was at a stop sign. He didn't like the looks of the car waiting on the other side of the intersection. Wayne had been around cops enough to know undercover police when he saw them. Here were two grungy-looking guys in a clean and sleek car with an antenna on the trunk. They might as well have worn a sign that said, "Unmarked Police Car." They waved him on. "No, you go," he signaled.

As they drove by, they seemed to stare at him and he realized immediately that Connie had turned him in. He had to get away. He made a quick left turn towards Wolf Road. Up ahead in the Delta team car office Randy Akin pulled out his pistol. "This is Delta," he called in. "He's speeding towards Wolf Road. He's spotted us."

Wayne was panicky. He heard the shrieking of sirens in the distance, and he knew they were for him. Max, he thought, what will happen to Max, if I go to jail? He pressed harder on the accelerator, running through stop signs. Suddenly a car appeared ahead of him in the middle of an intersection. It stopped there and he realized it was one of the police cars, trying to cut him off. He took a sudden right, thinking he would circle back to his mother's house. His family would protect him. Now another car came at him from his left, and he saw that he was being surrounded. He slammed on the brakes. The sirens wailed, doors were thrown open, and cops with weapons drawn crouched behind them.

Akin called out to him, "Police. Get your hands off the wheel now, and put your hands up." Wayne did as he was told. "Now climb out of the car and put your hands on the roof . . . now."

Wayne was enraged. They couldn't do this to him. He would kill these cops, every last one of them.

"Get out of the car, Chaney," he heard again. One of the cops, holding his gun steady in front of him, moved toward Wayne.

"Get out now," he said. He stood next to Wayne.

"Hey, what did I do?" Wayne yelled.

Now there was a whole cluster of cops around him. One of them pulled open the door. Wayne kept his hands high. The cop reached in, grabbed him by the shoulder, and pulled him out. In seconds, Wayne Chaney was on the pavement being handcuffed and listening to his Miranda rights.

Jim Prandini was on his way to Holy Family Hospital when he heard Akin on the radio saying that Wayne Chaney was in custody. He smiled. Connie would be okay now.

Though Prandini had only known Connie for a short time, he had taken a special interest in her case, partly because of his own run-in with Wayne Chaney. Prandini was deeply bothered by what had happened to Connie. The image of her, bruised and trembling, had affected him more deeply than the ordeals of other victims. Her pathetic words, "He's going to kill me, he's going to kill me," echoed in his mind, and he could visualize Wayne dry-firing the gun at Connie's head, gagging her, raping her. He could not imagine living in so much fear. He promised himself that he would protect Connie, and that he would do what he could to keep Wayne Chaney in jail.

14

Deals Made in Fear

July 29, 1991

Though the physical beating was over, Connie Chaney now had to endure an emotional and psychological one. During the days following her rape, Connie was questioned endlessly, it seemed, by police and lawyers from the state attorney's office. Step by painful step they dragged her back through the events of that dreadful day, forcing her to relive the attack many times.

Connie was a modest person and when they would look her in the eye and ask, "Did Wayne insert his penis into your vagina?" or "Did you respond sexually to him in any way?" she would hesitate and squirm before finally answering. But those were not the worst questions. The worst were questions like, "Why didn't you run away?" They made her wonder if they believed her at all.

Connie also had to face the equally insistent questions of young Max. Max had been brought to the hospital after the attack and had cried uncontrollably when he saw bandages, bruises, and scratches on his mother's swollen face.

"Mommy, what happened?" he had asked, his eyes wide with fear.

In the past, when Wayne had abused her, Connie had lied to Max. "I fell," she would say, or "I bumped into a door." But now she had run out of lies. She held her boy in her arms and said, "Daddy hit Mommy, and Mommy had to go to the hospital."

"Does it hurt?" he had asked, and, with tears rolling down her face, she had told him. "Yes . . . oh yes, it does, Max."

In the days after her release from the hospital the questions from Max had been unrelenting, and all Connie could do was tell the truth, and promise Max that they both were safe, though she knew they were not.

Wayne, meanwhile, had fallen into the unsympathetic hands of Jim Prandini. After Wayne was captured he was charged with aggravated criminal sexual assault, home invasion, and residential burglary. Prandini himself took Wayne to a bail hearing and told the judge what Connie had told him about Wayne beating her, tying her up, holding her at gunpoint, and raping her. This testimony added fuel to Wayne's growing obsession about the officer. Wayne believed that he and Connie really had been on the verge of becoming a family again, but instead, Prandini had convinced her to press charges against him. The way Wayne saw it, this cop was turning Connie against him. Now it was Prandini who was responsible for his problems.

Based on Prandini's testimony, the judge set Wayne's bond at three hundred thousand dollars. Wayne was enraged. There was no way his family could come up with that kind of money. He glared at Prandini, who was smiling. You'll pay for this, Prandini, he thought, you will pay for this. I am the Terminator and you will be terminated.

Wayne told his family that he was worried about spending time in the Cook County jail. It was, he knew, a far cry from the suburban jails he had known, with their fresh sheets and clean toilets. The county jail had over thirteen thousand inmates, and a lot of them slept on blankets on the floor. Furthermore, most of them were black, and Wayne hated and feared blacks.

Two days after the attack Connie went to a court hearing. John Collins, shaken by what had happened to his client, was asking for another order of protection and a termination of Wayne's visitation rights. Connie's greatest fear, he said, was that Wayne would be released on bond and kidnap Max.

In a crowded courtroom before Judge Carol Bellows, Collins argued his motion. He was angry, he said, that Wayne had never been charged with violating the previous orders of protection. Certainly his client, still bruised and scratched, was evidence enough that Chaney was a danger.

Wayne's lawyer, Wayne Shapiro, put quite a different spin on Connie's day of terror.

He told the judge, "The parties were together that day. They went out to dinner that day—there is a plot by her to get my client in trouble."

Shapiro was merely repeating the party line from the Chaney side of things. Donna Chaney and the Chaney brothers continually put forth the story that Connie was making up incidents in order to deprive Wayne of visits with his son.

Connie, whose faith in the legal system had already been badly shaken, could not believe what she was hearing from Shapiro. Wayne was telling people that he never broke into her house, never held her at gunpoint, never raped her. They were saying that she had lied, had made the whole thing up. Connie began to protest. Collins signaled her to keep cool.

Collins fought back. He argued that if Wayne were set free on bond he would almost certainly try to grab Max.

When Connie took the stand she was shaking. Her voice wavered as she described the events of that day. "Wayne was going to take Max and me," she told Judge Bellows. "He couldn't live without me and he would kill me. He almost killed me. He had a gun to my head." She stopped in mid-sentence. What else could she say, she wondered? How could this be made up? How could anybody even think such a thing? She wanted to scream. Couldn't they see that she was afraid for her life?

If Connie was looking for sympathy, she certainly was not going to get it from Wayne's lawyer. Shapiro came at her with a barrage of questions.

"Did the police ever find those weapons?"

"No."

"Did they find the ammunition?"

"No."

"Wayne didn't even know where you lived?" Shapiro asked.

Connie glared at him. She couldn't believe what was happening.

"He knew where I lived. He had me followed," she said. "It's all on paper. There was a private eye who was following me."

Shapiro, apparently taken by surprise about the private detective, looked up from his notes.

"No further questions," he said.

Collins spoke again. He reminded the judge of a threatening letter Wayne had sent, the letter in which Wayne wrote, "Don't make me famous."

In the end Judge Bellows agreed with Collins's contention that Wayne was a threat to Connie and to their son. She canceled Wayne's visiting privileges, until arrangements could be made for visits in a supervised setting.

With Wayne locked up Connie began to live again. There were moments of doubt, certainly, and she worried constantly that Wayne would get out of jail and kidnap Max. At the apartment she found it impossible to sleep in the room where she had been raped. She had terrifying flashbacks of Wayne pressing the gun to her head, pulling the trigger. Sometimes Connie was swept by a feeling of helplessness.

But she still had her friends. They called the jail every day, just to be certain Wayne was still locked up. And when word came back, "He's still there," Connie felt free. She began to believe that her ordeal was over. Wayne would be convicted. More and more she and Max avoided the apartment. They stayed much of the time with Patrick and his family. The summer, despite the painful memories, became a happy time. No longer did she have to watch every doorway, suspect every shadow.

It was as if some emotional wiring had been reconnected for Connie, and soon she felt closer than ever not just to Patrick, but to Loretta, Cathy, and Tammy. At work she became close with several other women, too, especially Jill Jozwik who was, for Connie, not just a confidant, but a role model. Jill, a slender young woman with flowing, shoulder-length hair, was a marketing and media director at age twenty-five. Connie wanted to be like Jill, but more importantly, she had reached a point in life where she believed that she could become like Jill.

Indeed, the potential was there. Connie was a quick study

on the computers and she was constantly updating files for the company. Jill would always ask for Connie's opinion on copy and artwork for ads. Soon Connie felt more and more that she was a professional, that she was part of something.

It was fortunate that Connie had a good relationship with her employers, because during this period she often had to skip work to make court appearances. Maybe it was because she worked with women and they understood her fears and the importance to Connie of keeping Wayne in jail.

In the months that followed Connie kept in almost daily touch with Prandini. She required constant assurance that Wayne Chaney was in a prison cell and would stay there. Her friends continued to call daily to make sure Wayne had not come up with the three hundred thousand dollars bond. Prandini warned her that there would be a hearing for reduction of the bond and that it was imperative that Connie be at the hearing. No date had been set, but he assured her that the state's attorney would tell her when to be in court.

Wayne, in the meantime, was sleeping on a tattered woolen blanket with an inch-thick pillow on a concrete floor with thirty other inmates in the overcrowded Cook County jail.

Wayne was the only white man in his section, and he made the mistake of telling his jail mates that he lived in Tennessee. They called him "John Wayne" and "Tennessee Wayne," and constantly challenged him. But Wayne, wisely, did not fight with black men who could sense his racism when there were thirty of them and one of him. If they asked for food off his plate, he gave it, or traded it for milk. And he learned quickly to make friends by keeping his mouth shut. He learned that the way to survive was to sleep during the day when the lights were on and the guards were watching, and stay awake all night, which wasn't difficult, because the sounds of gospel music and jazz always echoed through the jail until 4:00 a.m. At night he worked out with plastic bottles filled with sand. During his first month in jail he lost fifteen pounds.

In August Wayne got his first visit from Dennis Born, a former public defender and a well-known defense attorney who often handled high-profile murder cases. Born, a youthful-looking man who wore wire-rimmed glasses, had been hired by Donna Chaney.

Born could see that his client was depressed. Wayne's first bond reduction hearing had not gone well. Wayne told Born about battles in jail, how "nigger" inmates tried to corner him so he would have to fight them.

Born could also see that Wayne did not fully appreciate the mess he had gotten himself into.

"I want to get back together with Connie," Wayne told him.

"Wayne, that is the least of your problems," Born told him. "You could serve up to six years in prison on these charges. Forget about Connie for now."

It was the same advice that Wayne was getting from his divorce lawyer, Shapiro. "End it now," Shapiro had said, "And begin a new life." Shapiro had urged Wayne to stop fighting with Connie over relatively worthless items they had stored in Tennessee. But Wayne had not listened to either lawyer. Connie and Max, he said, were all that mattered to him.

Not wanting to see his client killed in jail before he had a chance to get bonded, Born got Wayne transferred to a high-security area where guards checked more frequently on the inmates. There, Wayne had a black cellmate whom he got along with, and a cell. He no longer had to sleep on the floor with sixty inmates.

On the walls of his cell Wayne hung pictures of men fishing, and woodsy landscapes clipped from the fishing magazines that Donna brought when she came to visit.

Wayne was still obsessed with communicating with Connie. He had to let her know what he was thinking. He knew that a kind word from her would get his bond reduced. So he began writing to her friends, Loretta mostly, hoping that what he said would be passed on to Connie.

He began one letter to Loretta, with: "WRITING LIVE FROM THE COOK COUNTY JAIL ... ARE YOU READY? SIT DOWN GRAB A COKE, OK? GO ...

"Lori, Lori you're a good girl and I'm still Wayne," he wrote. "I'm not crazy. I'm just going through some difficult times. I love Connie very much and would still give my left nut to have my family back—but it is now over."

He described his days. Often he wrote humorous comments, or deeply emotional passages, after which he drew smiling faces or frowning faces.

As Wayne expected, Loretta turned the letters over to Connie. Connie read them at Loretta's kitchen table and her response was always the same. "This is shit," she would say, tossing the letters to the table. "I don't want him out. If he gets out he will kill me."

On September thirteenth a bond reduction hearing was held for Wayne in front of Judge Sheila O'Brien. Connie's advocate at the bond hearing was Toni Ann Winninger who, at thirty-five, was a seasoned assistant state's attorney and very much an advocate for the rights of her clients. Though Winninger sometimes had a hard appearance about her, Connie found her easy to talk to. Connie liked having a woman representing her. It made it less difficult to talk about the details of the attack.

Unfortunately, though Connie had described the graphic details of the attack to Winninger, she had not told Winninger much of the history of her abuse at Wayne's hands. Later Connie explained this strange omission to a friend, saying, "Why should I? No one ever took me seriously before, not even the police." In some logic, peculiar to Connie, there was no point in telling Winninger about all the things Wayne had done while she was under an order of protection. She had told Collins, of course, and he had told Judge Bellows. However, this information had not been passed along to Judge O'Brien.

O'Brien was a woman who might have been particularly sympathetic to Connie's plight if she had been told more about it. O'Brien herself had been a stalking victim when she first became a judge. Her tormentor was a man with mental problems who fantasized that he was engaged to her. He wrote to her and called her constantly. Then one day the man just stopped calling and writing. O'Brien never knew the man, but she knew the frustrations of feeling watched everywhere she went, of not knowing who the stalker was or how dangerous he was. She knew what it was like to live in fear.

Winninger had Connie sit way in the back of the courtroom so Wayne could not see her. Donna Chaney sat quietly a few rows in front of her. Wayne, wearing a tan-colored Cook County jail uniform, was led in and had his handcuffs removed. He did not see Connie, but later wrote in his diary: "She was there but not in view because she feared for her life. She knew of the weapons that were never found and that I'd be out to kill her—she's right!"

Wayne's lawyer for this hearing was James Kissel, a partner in the same firm with Born. Kissel, in his late forties, was a former public defender. He began by telling Judge O'Brien that Connie and Wayne were in the middle of a divorce and child custody battle. He wanted to minimize the severity of the charges by saying that what occurred was not battery but Connie's way to get at Wayne. Winninger listened with disgust as she planned how to turn his words against him. To Connie it sounded as if Kissel was hinting that she made up the rape story to get at Wayne. Kissel told Judge O'Brien that if Wayne was released on lower bond he would go back to his mother's house and have no contact with Connie.

"She is not in danger," he said. "She is not in danger. I don't believe so at this time." Winninger repeated his last words softly. The court reporter looked at her as Winninger darted a look at O'Brien.

Judge O'Brien heard everything but was not convinced. What does "at this time" mean? she wondered. And she wondered, too, why the first judge had set bond so high in the first place. There had to be something more, she thought.

Winninger then described the attack, reading from the complaint. Next she read into the record of Wayne's criminal history. O'Brien waited for more, but that was it. Winninger could not tell the judge about the four protective orders and all the other threats and attacks that had occurred, because Connie had not told her about them.

Kissel asked that bond be reduced to fifty thousand dollars, and told Judge O'Brien that Wayne's mother would be putting up the bond. But still, Judge O'Brien was not swayed. She was troubled by the fact that high bond had been ordered in the first place.

"Motion denied."

Connie, thinking she had seen the end of Wayne Chaney, smiled with relief. She looked at her watch. It was almost

11:00 a.m. and she had to get back to work. She slipped out the back of the courtroom and waited for Winninger.

What she didn't hear was Kissel responding quickly to the judge's ruling.

"Your Honor is going to deny my motion to reduce the bond," he said. "Would Your Honor entertain an option of having him evaluated by pretrial services for home monitoring?"

O'Brien, having been a public defender, sympathized with Kissel's position. After all, Wayne had not killed anyone. She thought about it. "Sure," she said.

Winninger thought little of the request. Wayne already had had two bond reduction denials, so it all seemed routine. She caught up with Connie outside. She told Connie about the request for pretrial home monitoring for Wayne, but explained that the chances of that being approved were very slim. "Everything from here on in," she told her, "is just paperwork."

The next day, September eighteenth, was Wayne's thirtieth birthday. Donna visited Wayne, and told him that Kissel would ask the judge again on October third for a bond reduction.

Connie was being given more responsibility at work. There was a trade show coming up, and she was asked to help set up the company's booth. Her boss gave her money to buy a new suit and to get her hair done. For months Connie had been buying her clothing at second-hand stores, so the idea of a new outfit and shopping with cash in hand thrilled her. The next day she walked into the office with a tan, tailored two-piece suit and cream-colored silk blouse. Her hair was cut at her shoulders and styled. She wore lipstick and eye shadow and her nails were manicured. Everything matched, even her shoes and purse. To Jill, Connie looked as if she had just stepped out of a fashion magazine.

At the Cook County jail Wayne was looking a little less fashionable. One inmate witnessed an incident in which Wayne almost found out what it feels like to be raped. Wayne was taking a shower, when he turned around and saw four men standing behind him. Alarmed, he quickly shut the water off and turned towards them. He looked for a guard but didn't see one.

"What do you want?" he asked quickly.

A husky black prisoner smiled. He was a dangerous-looking character who had had most of his front teeth knocked out in fights.

"Hey Tennessee Wayne, you are pretty tough, I hear. I understand you hate niggers, is that true?"

Wayne said nothing. Another black man, this one about six feet tall, with a close-cut Afro and a gold earring, was swinging a pillowcase that looked as if it had a can of soda in it. A third black man, a teenager, held a ripped piece of blanket that could be used as a rope. A white man who was there looked on and laughed. The four men moved closer.

Wayne knew the drill. He had heard about other men being attacked in the shower, held down on their stomachs, while a gang of guys took turns butt-fucking them. It was a way of seizing power, of degrading a prisoner who had insulted the wrong person.

Three of the men grabbed Wayne's arms and held him back while the man with the pillowcase swung it wildly and smashed it against the side of Wayne's head. Wayne was knocked into a daze, but with his body still wet and slippery from the shower, he was able to wrestle one arm free. Like a madman he began to punch wildly at the men, but they threw him to the hard floor of the shower. The pillowcase containing the can kept swinging at him. He fought off the blows with his forearm.

They might have killed him, but one of them spotted a guard and the men scrambled to their feet and ran off as Wayne laid in pain on the shower room floor. The guard came rushing up to him but Wayne would not tell him anything. He knew if he did then they would kill him for sure the next time.

The next day Wayne appeared again in front of Judge O'Brien. Now his face was swollen and he was covered with bruises and scratches. Anyone could see that he had been in a serious fight. He told Kissel what had happened and Kissel listened intently. The lawyer knew how valuable this information was.

First, he brought Wayne's mother up to stand next to her

son. He told the judge that Donna had raised the money for a lower bond by mortgaging her house. He said that if Wayne were released on lower bond, he would have a job waiting for him and he would live in his mother's house.

Fred Musser, the man from pretrial services, gave his report to the judge. Wayne had been living with his parents before the incident, he said, and confirmed that Wayne would get work as a landscaper. Musser also testified he saw no drug or alcohol problem with Chaney.

"Upon what do you base that?" O'Brien asked.

"Upon what he said, upon what his mother told me," Musser said.

When Musser described Wayne's arrest record as minimal, Toni Winninger joined in.

"He's a convicted felon," she said.

Wayne, beaten and weary, almost dozed off while the attorneys argued about just how much of a criminal he had been. O'Brien, observing Wayne, asked the attorneys to pipe down.

"In this, I'll be frank with you," she said. "Mr. Chaney looks glassy-eyed, and doesn't look like he's tracking real well."

Kissel saw his chance.

"There was a problem in the jail yesterday which I'm not at liberty to go into unless Your Honor wants to have that heard in chambers," he said.

"Do you think it bears any relevance to the hearing?" O'Brien asked.

"Possibly," Kissel said, excited now, but not wanting to overplay his hand.

In chambers Kissel told O'Brien, "I think Wayne is having a problem in the jail. I didn't really want to say that on the record because his mom was in the courtroom, and Wayne didn't want his mom to know that he was having problems in custody. He said he was beaten up and there may have been sexual overtones."

There was little that Toni Winninger could say. It was clear to everybody that Wayne had been roughed up. O'Brien took a deep breath. It was a hard decision. Being a judge, she had often thought, is like being an umpire in a baseball game. No matter what the call, somebody is going to be unhappy. She knew what sort of crimes occurred inside jails.

She knew that prisoners were sometimes hanged by other prisoners. She had to look to the future of a child, who might depend on the support of his father.

Finally, she turned to Kissel.

"Does he have a drug or alcohol problem?" she asked. The word of a mother was hardly unbiased.

"I don't know," Kissel said.

"If I did release him on bond one of the conditions would be that he gets counseling and that he is not allowed to have a drink or a drug. How do you feel about that, counsel?"

"I have no problem with that Your Honor," Kissel said. He turned to Winninger. They both could see that O'Brien was rethinking her position on Wayne.

"Okay, let's go back in," O'Brien said. She still was not convinced.

Back in the courtroom O'Brien was thorough. Noting that Connie was not present, she asked Winninger if the state attorney's office kept Connie informed. And, she asked, if this was a major case of a battered woman where was Life Span? They almost always sent representatives to court when a batterer was trying to get out on the street. O'Brien asked the questions, but Winninger didn't always have the answers.

(As for Life Span, perhaps there was a reason they were not present. Connie had walked out of a Life Span counseling group when one woman showed up excited because she had acquired a protective order. The whole idea of "protective orders" was a hot button for Connie. Wayne had attacked her and threatened her numerous times while she was under their eyes, and the orders had become to Connie powerful symbols of society's failure to protect her and women like her. The idea that Life Span would give any credibility at all to protective orders was more than Connie could take.)

With neither Connie nor Life Span present, O'Brien was faced with the fact that relatively little opposition to Wayne's release had appeared in her courtroom. Connie never knew about the court appearance, let alone the bond reduction. She had already missed so much time from work because of Wayne that she could no longer appear at every hearing unless she was told to. Winninger was there, of course, doing her job. But, as she saw it, there was a good deal of weight on the side of releasing Wayne. There was the danger of him being injured or killed in prison. There was the promise that he would not drink or touch drugs, and the assurance that he had a job. Furthermore, O'Brien was touched by the fact that Wayne's parents had mortgaged their house to come up with some bond money. She was getting close to a decision.

"Do you want to put anything else on the record?" she asked the attorneys.

Winninger stood forward. "Judge, I don't think we have on the record at this point in time the seriousness of the allegations."

Winninger then began to read into the record the counts of the indictments.

O'Brien listened, but she was thinking: "Tell me something I don't know Ms. Assistant State's Attorney. Give me something to hang my hat on. Don't tell me what he is charged with. Where's the victim, the family, the advocacy group? I can only rule on what is being presented to me here and now." She shook her head. There was nothing new.

When O'Brien began to question Wayne about where and when he would work, Winninger knew she was losing. Winninger pushed harder. "Your Honor, we're strongly, strongly opposed, just on potential safety for the victim in this case. Not only the allegations in this case, involving two weapons, but the fact he's a convicted felon. There was supposedly a no-contact order in effect from the divorce. It was apparently meaningless."

Kissel, knowing he was on the verge of victory, was calm. He promised there would be no contact.

O'Brien gave Winninger a final chance, but Winninger was nearly out of ammunition. She had used all the information from the police. Most of Wayne's past misconduct had been kept from her, so Winninger's hands were tied. She knew that legally she could not order the civil files of a pending case to introduce them into court. No matter what Wayne had done, Judge Bellows never made a ruling on Connie's allegations in the case and never held Wayne in contempt of court. All she could get to introduce into court was the half sheet that listed court dates and judges' orders. The only thing granted to Connie were protective orders—three that she knew of. For now, she had nothing more to offer O'Brien.

O'Brien, presented with greater reasons to reduce bond

than to deny the reduction, said, "Over the objection of the state I will grant the defendant's motion to reduce bond. Bond will be reduced to one hundred thousand dollars."

Winninger shook her head. It wasn't the fact that she lost that bothered her. It was that Connie would again be living in fear of Wayne.

Wayne looked up. He smiled, and turned to his mother. She smiled back. He could see the tears. Everything would be okay now, he knew it. He and Connie and Max would somehow get back together.

O'Brien believed that the promises would be kept. Nonetheless, she was cautious. She wanted to make Wayne's freedom as restrictive as possible.

"The special conditions of your bond are the following," she said. "You are to have no contact with the complaining witness, you will have absolutely none. You can't call her, write her, see her, go by her place of business, home, nothing, as if she doesn't exist. You have to work, you have to follow all the recommendations of the drug and alcohol group that is going to evaluate you. You have to appear at all court dates. You have to call pretrial services three times a week. You have a curfew of 8 p.m. to 6 a.m. . . . You cannot drive. I don't want you driving any motor vehicle. I want to cut down the possibility of your going by her house. Somebody will drive you to work and somebody will pick you up and bring you home. You can't use alcohol or drugs. You have to set aside funds for the support of your child. You have to live with your parents at 668 South Fifth Avenue in Des Plaines and that's the only place you can live until you petition the court."

She then leaned over her desk and looked directly at Wayne. "Mr. Chaney I'm being frank with you. My concern is that you not get near your former wife. I'm trying to cut down the possibility of that occurring. If you can't get in a car, it cuts it down pretty well. That means you would have to walk over there. If you were walking over there the police would probably pick you up. Pretrial services will be checking up on you. . . ." She took a deep breath. "And it goes without saying, you know what happens if you violate any conditions of the bond. Do you know what happens?"

"Yes," Wayne said. His altercation with the men in the shower had put the fear of jail in him.

"You come back to the county jail," O'Brien said. "Do you know that?"

"Yes I understand that," Wayne softly said.

On her way out of court a frustrated Toni Winninger ran into Detective Bob Schultz. She asked Schultz to tell Jim Prandini about Wayne being released, and the restrictions.

Connie was at her computer working when she got the call from Winninger. She had just returned from a smoke break in the parking lot. She was feeling good. And then the lawyer told her, "Judge O'Brien lowered the bond on Wayne. He's going to be released as soon as his mother pays a bond."

Winninger went through the long list of restrictions, but Connie hardly listened. She felt sick. Wayne. Out. She began shaking. Then she cried.

"I'm sorry, Connie," Winninger was saying. "I tried, I really tried."

Connie hung up.

Jill Jozwik walked in and found Connie with her head down on the desk, sobbing into her hands.

"Wayne is free. He's going to kill me, I know it," Connie cried.

Jill could see that Connie was terrified. She put her arms around her. "We will do whatever we can for you," she said. "Take some time off to get yourself together."

The Des Plaines police was notified by the sheriff's office. Jim Prandini was at his desk when the news came in—he was angry. The state attorney's office had assured him that Wayne Chaney would stay in jail. If he had known this would happen, he thought, he would have gone to court. He called Winninger and raised hell, then he called Connie. She was distraught, saying that Wayne was going to kill her. Prandini explained that Wayne wasn't on the street yet. "He's going to kill me," she kept saying. Prandini knew from Connie's tone that she felt he had let her down.

"I want you to take precautions," he said. "Do you have someplace to stay? You can have somebody drive you to work. We will monitor Wayne and see if he starts to follow you . . ."

"It doesn't matter what you do," Connie said. "He is going to kill me and take Max this time." The fight that had often pulled her together since Gateway, had all but abandoned her.

After he hung up, Prandini, normally a man to hold his feelings inside, banged his fist on the desk. "Shit," he said. He paced across his office, repeating the curse with every hard step.

Three days later Wayne was released. His brother Ken drove Donna to the jail, where he paid the bond. Wayne was uncuffed. Doors were opened. Wayne and Ken walked outside to the car, where Donna waited. When Donna saw her son she got out of the car and hugged and kissed her boy. Tears streamed down her face. Wayne held her close. Later in his diary he described the moment, and recalled his words to his mother: "Mom, Mom, I am out from a place I call hell." Wayne also noted in his diary that he was taken with two thoughts: One was to get home and call pretrial services to check in, because he was so afraid of going back to jail. The other was to have a hamburger.

Life at home was not blissful. Wayne had never gotten on well with his father, and now Tom Chaney bristled at having Wayne in the house, as the judge had ordered. Donna worried. She knew that things could get tense between the father and the son.

Steve, though, was thrilled to have his brother home, and he razzed him about the weight loss. While Wayne was shaving on his first night home, Steve saw the scratches and bruises on Wayne's arms.

"Hey, what happened in jail?" he asked. Wayne went very quiet and serious. He looked at Steve coldly.

"Never ask me that again," he said.

"Okay, Wayne," Steve said. He was hurt. "No problem."

"You never want to go there," Wayne said, trying now to be brotherly. "Okay, that's all. I am never . . . never going back."

While Wayne was thrilled to be out of jail, Connie felt as if she had been thrown back into one. Worse, she'd been sentenced to die. All the calls from friends and all assurances of the courts and police did nothing to release her from her prison of fear. Connie knew that she was alive only because she had tricked Wayne into believing that she wanted to go back to him. Wayne would not forget that. And now he was free to get his revenge.

For the moment Wayne did not know where Connie lived. She was staying with Patrick, who had been forced to move into another apartment because his landlady did not like having Max around. Patrick was Connie's protector. She felt safe when he was around. If he left town on business, she would stay with someone else. She had decided never to be alone with Max again.

Patrick gave her a gun. It wasn't much of a weapon, just a little .22 with chipped handles that had to be held together by rubber bands. And it brought its own worries. She had to keep it loaded, or it would be worthless, but then she had to keep it in a high place where Max could not get it. To Max any gun was a toy.

Tammy and some of her other friends tried to tell Connie that her fears were exaggerated. "With all those restrictions, Wayne will be okay," Tammy told her one morning over coffee. "He doesn't want to go back to jail." Tammy was afraid that the gun would do Connie in long before Wayne did.

The only hope Connie had was that the psychiatric evaluations that had been ordered by Judge Bellows in divorce court would lead to Wayne getting the help he needed. However, even that hope was dashed one afternoon when she received in her mail a copy of a letter that John Collins had gotten from the Psychiatric Institute. The institute would not be examining Wayne, the letter explained. "Since there are serious felony charges pending against Mr. Chaney involving Mrs. Chaney, we feel that it would be inappropriate for us to engage in an evaluation. It is our policy in examining any criminal case not to do an evaluation unless we receive a court order from the criminal court judge . . ."

Connie added the letter to her growing file of court documents, each of them, it seemed, more worthless than the next. More and more she was becoming convinced that the only person who would do anything to help Connie was Connie.

She made it her habit to take a different route to work

every day. She checked her rearview mirror for cars following her. One day, at a shopping mall, as she stood outside the car strapping Max into his car seat, she left her purse, containing the gun, on the curb and drove away. It was never recovered.

Connie felt safer at her office. Wayne knew where she worked, but it seemed unlikely that he would come for her in front of other people. Nonetheless, she heeded Prandini's warning to take precautions.

Connie showed pictures of Wayne to her workmates, so they would recognize him if he showed up. She said that if she saw him she would shout his name.

One day in the office a panel fell from the ceiling and a bird came flying in. She told her workmates that if Wayne came she would run to the back of the office and pop one of those panels and climb in. Jill told her she wouldn't have time because Wayne would be running after her. Connie came back with a different plan. She would run around the office and run back out the front door. She worried constantly, and she was always coming up with plans for what she would do if Wayne came for her there.

One day Jill Jozwik found Connie sitting at her typewriter, writing out a list of people to be contacted if she was murdered at work. Connie talked about what would happen to Max if anything happened to her. She felt bad that she really didn't have anything to leave him. All of her belongings were in Tennessee, she said, and she couldn't get any of them. She handed Jill the piece of paper with phone numbers on it. She said, "If anything happens to me, these are the people you need to call and they are in the order of importance."

"Connie, this is really morbid," Jill said. "I can't believe you are doing this."

"He is going to kill me and I want to have everything prepared," Connie said. "The first number on the list was Max's school. If anything happens to me, before you call anyone, call the school, tell them if anyone tries to pick Max up, don't let him go, and make sure the police are there first."

At home Connie worried about the effect her fear was having on Max. Believing that she would be leaving her son soon, she smothered him with attention. Connie would brush his hair back at night and dress him in his Batman underwear and pajamas. She would hold him until he fell asleep in her arms. She never wanted him to forget his mother.

Wayne also wanted to hold his son. One day Kathy Hoshell, who was babysitting Max, found Wayne standing outside her door. He looked tired and wild-eyed. He pleaded with her. "Kathy, I know you babysit Max, and I beg you, if I come one day and he is here, please, please let me see my son. I love Max. Please don't shut the door on me. Let me see and just hold my son for a minute or two." Then he turned and left.

While Wayne's divorce lawyer prepared motions for visitation rights, Wayne tried to anticipate what Connie would do. He knew that Connie would say he was crazy. He wanted to prove to Judge Bellows that he was mentally fit to see Max. On October twenty-ninth Wayne went to a mental health clinic in Park Ridge for an initial intake and psychiatric evaluation. He wanted to be evaluated for the November twentieth hearing on visitation. With a counselor he talked mostly about the pain of not being able to see his son. His lawyer, however, had advised him not to talk about the rape incident.

In the three-page report of this visit, Wayne's counselor wrote, "He experienced sorrow, pain, confusion, and anger, yet these were all within the limits one would expect when seeing a helping professional. There was no evidence of delusions or hallucinations. Though there appeared to be a paranoid flavor to some of his thoughts, this was not excessive."

This report was placed in Shapiro's file.

Connie, disgusted with all the legal wrangling, felt as if she had been caught in some bizarre trap. Right and wrong didn't matter; only what a judge said. If the judge felt in August that Wayne was a danger to her and Max, why would she think Wayne had changed in three months? Why did she have to face Wayne in court again, why?

Wayne did not abide by all the restrictions that the court had put on him. His diary shows that he had a car hidden at a friend's house. Sometimes he would sneak out and go to the car and drive it to the Arlington Race Track. He hated the restrictions. At Donna's house he stared out the window for hours. Sometimes he was sure that Jim Prandini had driven by the house, checking up on him. He hated Prandini.

On November seventeenth Wayne and his lawyer went to Judge O'Brien, requesting that Wayne be allowed to drive a car, so that he could return to Tennessee to get some property, and also so that he would be able to drive a plow in wintertime to make money. O'Brien, concerned about easing her restrictions on Wayne, asked an assistant state's attorney to call Connie Chaney and get her opinion. A few minutes later the assistant state's attorney came back and reported, "Connie said she does not want him to drive a car, and doesn't want him to go to Tennessee. She wants him back in jail. That's all she kept saying, 'I want him locked up again, I want him in jail.' "

O'Brien sighed. "Jail is not an option now." She gave Wayne permission to drive to and from work, and to drive to Tennessee. She also ordered Wayne to keep a diary of his jobs and where he went every day. He was to send the diary to the state attorney's office. She added, "I may call you on the phone myself, because you're under a bond ordered by me."

Again, speaking sternly to Wayne, O'Brien looked down at him and said, "You understand the complaining witness wants you in jail. She thinks this whole thing is goofy. My original gut reaction was, you're staying in jail. So I went out on a limb. If this thing falls apart and you violate this bond you're going back to jail. Do you understand that?"

Wayne looked at her. "Yes."

During this same period, in divorce court, Judge Bellows appointed Lee Howard as attorney for Max. Howard, who had raised four children of his own and had eleven grandchildren, was considered an expert on child custody. He was usually brought in by Judge Bellows on cases where visitation has been terminated. Howard lived in a spacious suburban home. In his basement he had a special area set up with pinball machines, doll houses, and boxes of cowboy and Indian action figures. There were shelves lined with toy trucks and cars. There, parents with restrictions such a Wayne's could have supervised visits with their children. Howard would observe the interaction, and report back to the court.

In November Wayne was allowed his first visit with Max

since the rape. Connie arrived at Howard's home with Max first. She would stay upstairs with Howard's wife, while Howard would stay in the basement with Wayne and Max. Then Wayne showed up with Donna. It was a deeply emotional moment for both Wayne and Max. Max had missed his daddy terribly and his face lit up when he saw him. He giggled and ran to Wayne and hugged his knee. Tears flowed freely down Wayne's face as he gently lifted the boy in the air above his head and hugged him. Max put his arms around his father's neck and hugged him back as Wayne kissed him on the forehead.

For an hour, with Howard sitting at a discreet distance, taking notes, Wayne played with his boy. There was a box of toy trucks, and Max took endless delight in them. "Zoom zoom," Wayne would say, "this is Daddy's landscaping truck." Howard noted that the boy was thrilled to see his father, and Wayne was thrilled to see Max.

The parting was difficult. Max fought against it. But Wayne promised that he would see him again, soon.

Howard ordered Wayne to stay downstairs as he took Max to Connie, who had spent the time upstairs with Howard's wife. "Mommy, why can't Daddy come home with us?" Max asked.

"Because Daddy has other things to do," Connie told him. It pained Connie to keep Max from Wayne. She knew that enormous love flowed between father and son, but to put Max in Wayne's hands without supervision would be to lose control of her life, and she knew it. Max loved Wayne, yes, but she knew that Wayne was not good for either one of them.

Wayne, of course, did not see things this way. To him, Connie was keeping Max away out of spite, just to hurt him. He wrote in his diary:

"The lawyer for Max in this divorce said and told the court that he doesn't see any problems with having me see Max for weekends. Well Connie wouldn't let up—she wanted me to suffer. You'd figure she'd be cool about this, knowing of what I'm capable of doing. She just wasn't using her brain in doing this to me. It only put me in a more serious murdering state."

Wayne did go to Tennessee. Later he wrote in his diary

of how free he felt, being able to drive legally, tooling down
the highway with the wind rushing through his hair. In Tennessee he picked up some clothes. Then he bought a used
truck, a new nine-millimeter pistol, and ammunition. He came
back with a loaded U-Haul trailer and pulled up at Boomer's.
He looked around for police. Seeing none, he entered the bar
for the first time in months. He got high fives from his friends
and a hearty welcome all around. He drank beer until 5:00
a.m. He toasted freedom. He said it gave him strength.

Connie worried that Wayne was getting too much freedom.
She continued to take precautions. When she left work she
would always ask someone to watch from the window as she
walked to her car. Connie always told somebody where she
was going, and she would call that person when she got there.
When she left after a visit with friends, she always left Max
inside while she ran to her car and started the engine. Then
she would run back and grab Max. At work she often got
frightening calls. She would say hello and the caller would
hang up. She knew it was Wayne. But he never stayed on
the line long enough to trace the call. Sometimes Connie
worked in a conference room because from there she could
see who was coming up the stairs.

Though Connie often seemed fatalistic during this time,
there was a more optimistic part of her that made plans. For
example, she continued to plot a future with Patrick. Patrick
was bonding closely with Max, and Connie knew he could
be a good father to the boy. The couple agreed to officially
move in together in May, and they would get married as
soon as Connie's divorce was final. More and more Patrick
spoke boldly about Wayne, about how he would take care of
Wayne Chaney if he ever showed up.

At a December court date Wayne handed Howard a letter
for Connie. In the letter he wrote, "I still love you very
much, and think of you daily. There's nobody alive that I
care more about than you and Max—I still say I will take
you back in a second. I would and you know it—remember
you left me! It's hard living alone. I'm dying and I need to
live and be free."

He begged her to come back to him, to stop the divorce,
drop the charges, and to call his lawyers and "make it go
bye-bye."

Though the letter was a violation of Wayne's bond condition to avoid all contact, Connie did not turn him in. She had little faith that anything would be done about it.

Soon after that, she later told her friends, Wayne called her at work. He said, "I am not going back to jail. You will die before I got back to jail. I will die before I go back to jail."

Again Connie didn't report the violation. It would be her word against his and she didn't expect to be believed.

The death threats never left Connie's mind. At the office Christmas party Connie sat with a co-worker's boyfriend, who was an insurance agent. "I want to know about life insurance," she said. Visiting Loretta during the holidays, she talked about making out a will. Should she add Patrick to the policy? she asked. Someone would have to take care of Max.

"Connie, stop it," Loretta said. More and more, Connie's friends were losing patience with this preoccupation she had with being murdered. They didn't want to talk about it. It scared them.

Wayne's allowed visits with Max grew longer. He was granted eight-hour visits with his son at Wayne's parents' house. When Max came home from these visits he was always overexcited. Connie would try to calm him down. Topic A with Max always seemed to be Arnold Schwarzenegger, his father's movie hero.

One troubling incident came in January after a visit. Max, using his finger as a gun, pointed it at Connie and said, "Bang, bang, Mommy you're dead." When Patrick came into the room Max began to spit. Connie stopped him. "Daddy said to spit on Mommy's boyfriend," Max said.

Connie held Max and tried to explain that spitting was wrong and that Max didn't have to do what Daddy told him. She held the boy and cried. But it was the image of Max shouting, "Bang, bang, you're dead," that stayed with her and frightened her.

This incident, it seems, was crucial in creating a major change in Connie's attitude. More and more she was thinking that Wayne would kill her if she went ahead with the rape charges, and that she could avoid his wrath by dropping the charges. This was a complete turnaround for Connie, inspired, no doubt, by the belief that the court system simply could not do anything right, and could not save her.

If her mind was not made up yet, her dream a few nights later pushed her into the new decision.

In the dream something was not right. Connie saw the red and white marquee of the Des Plaines Theater. The American flag in front of city hall flapped in the wind. In front of the police station next door there were no people. Now she saw that there were no people and no cars anywhere, just the buildings and the flapping flag, all enveloped in an eerie silence.

Connie, dressed in black slacks and a black sweater, walked along the sidewalk, Max by her side, clutching her hand. Suddenly Max let go of her hand and began to run down the empty street. Connie's heart was pounding as she ran by the empty theater, screaming Max's name. Just as she was about to turn a corner, Connie saw Max. He wore jeans and a white t-shirt under a black jacket. He was wearing dark sunglasses, trying to imitate Arnold Schwarzenegger. As she turned her head, she saw Wayne darting from an alley.

Wayne looked massive. His hair was a mess, and his face was dark with an unkempt beard. He was also wearing a white t-shirt and jeans, and he held a sawed-off shotgun in his left hand. He stopped as Connie ran past him to Max. Connie stretched out her arms and picked up Max. Pressing the child to her chest, she turned towards Wayne. He said nothing. Quickly, he lowered the gun toward them. Holding the gun with one hand, he pressed two shells into the chamber. Connie looked at Max and then Wayne. She screamed, "Max, Max."

"Wake up, Connie, wake up." It was Patrick, shaking her awake. Max, hearing his name called, came running into the room and onto the bed. Connie bolted up, soaked with sweat. She took deep breaths to steady herself.

"It was just a dream," Patrick said. "Just a dream."

"Oh God," she cried, "it was awful." She pulled Max close.

Connie called Winninger and said she wanted to drop the charges.

"Why?" Winninger asked. She was shocked. For months,

Connie had been complaining about Wayne not being in jail, and now she was proposing to set him free permanently.

"I'm afraid he will kill me," Connie said.

"I can't honestly say that is a good reason to drop charges," Winninger said. "Let me talk to his lawyer. Maybe we can make some deal to get him out of Illinois."

After Kissel heard from Winninger, he called Wayne at his mother's with the proposal. Wayne leaned against the kitchen wall as he listened, his eyes closed in relief and pain. He told Wayne that a deal could be made if Wayne would join an antiviolence counseling program, plead guilty to lesser charges, and agree to leave the state of Illinois for a year or two. Wayne opened his eyes, but still saw Max in his mind. "That means," he said, "not even seeing Max."

"But that's my son," Wayne pleaded, his voice cracking.

"Yes, we could be talking about six years in jail," Kissel said. "You wouldn't see much of Max in there, either."

"I don't know," Wayne said.

"You don't have to decide now," Kissel said. "This is their first offer. I'm obliged to tell you what is going on, that's all. I'm trying to make a deal with the state to avoid a trial for you. Wayne, you don't want this to go to a jury. Think about it. It's not forever."

Wayne hung up and his body began to shake. He gritted his teeth and clenched his fist against his tears but lost the fight.

Later Wayne wrote in his diary, "This was great. I have no plans to blast my wife—I just want to be free. I couldn't wait—this was a deal I thought would never happen."

On January 19, 1992, Wayne had a visit with Max. When he returned Max to the police station, which was part of the arrangement, he was with his father. Connie was waiting inside the police station, and Patrick, who had been advised to avoid Wayne, was parked outside with his brother, waiting for Connie.

While Wayne's father took Max inside, Wayne stared across the way at Patrick. It irked him to see Connie's new lover, the man who would be with both his wife and his son tonight. Wayne got out of his car and walked to Patrick's.

"Haven't you done enough?" he said to Patrick. "Why

do you have to be right out in sight of me. You are a real asshole. You'd better stay away from me or you are dead.''

Patrick, over the months, had built up a pretty good hate for Wayne Chaney and now he felt his fist clenching. He wanted to lash out at him, but he held himself back.

"You're going to jail!" he shouted.

The men were about to get physical when Wayne's father emerged from the police station and pulled his son away from a battle he couldn't win.

"Get into the car. Now," he said. "You want to go to jail? Let's get out of here."

Patrick went directly into the police station and made a report of the incident. The next day Patrick got a call from detective Norman Klopp, who wanted a formal statement so he could get an arrest warrant for Wayne. Patrick made an appointment with Klopp, but never showed up. Klopp put the report aside. There was nothing he could do if Patrick didn't press charges.

Patrick finally showed up on the thirty-first, offering no explanation for why it took him so long to come in. He and Klopp drove to the Skokie courthouse to have Patrick testify so that a warrant could be issued. Prandini, aware of the incident, asked Klopp to inform Winninger about it.

Winninger didn't press Klopp for details. Connie certainly hadn't called her about it, and she didn't even know the name of Connie's boyfriend. After the judge signed the warrant it entered the legal system by computer. Klopp tried to serve the warrant on Monday but Wayne was not home. On Tuesday Wayne was in Judge O'Brien's court to go over the terms of the plea agreement but another judge, Joan Corboy, was on the bench. Winninger, recalling the warrant, asked a sheriff's deputy to check it out. He came back and told her he could not find any warrant for Wayne Chaney in the computer.

Winninger walked over to Kissel, who was just entering the courtroom with Wayne and Donna. Privately, she whispered to him, "There is some sort of warrant out for Wayne."

Winninger knew that there would be a problem concerning the warrant. Judge Joan Corboy was a personal friend of Jim Kissel because of his association with her husband—he had been the best man at their wedding and the godfather to one of their children. And Judge Corboy always made it her policy never to hear any contested matters concerning Kissel regarding which she would have to make a legal judgement.

Off the record, the attorney informed Corboy that she intended to take his client into custody, which meant that it would be a contested matter. Corboy would either have to continue it or seek another judge to hear the matter.

Kissel then gave an out. He looked at Winninger.

Since Winninger did not have the warrant in her possession, she agreed to a one-day continuance and hoped that Kissel would be good to his word and make Chaney come back to court. If Winninger did not agree it would mean that she would have to leave the courtroom and hand search for the warrant, which could be anywhere.

"Look," Kissel said, "we can clear this up tomorrow. I will bring him back. Let's get a continuance." Since Winninger had a full court call and could not leave to do the search anyhow, Kissel's word seemed good to her. He had always been a man of his word. They agreed to ask for a one-day continuance. The judge granted it.

On the way out of the courtroom Kissel told Wayne that there was some sort of warrant out for his arrest.

Wayne went white. His hands started trembling. His greatest nightmare, ever since the incident with the black inmates in the shower, was that he would end up in jail. Donna tried to calm him.

Kissel got a copy of the warrant from the warrant book and made a copy.

"It's a warrant taken out by Patrick Carlson for assault," Kissel said.

Wayne had gone into some kind of shock. He pulled his wallet and change out of his pocket and placed them on a chair.

"What are you doing?" the lawyer asked.

"I'm going to jail," Wayne said. "O'Brien warned me. She will send me back to Cook County jail. I'm going to jail."

Kissel, who can be quite calming to his clients, put a hand on Wayne's shoulder.

"Now listen," he said, "we will come back tomorrow. A

judge will set some bond, and we will explain this. Be here at eight a.m. sharp. The judge will understand. This isn't a major thing, Wayne. This is verbal assault, okay. Just relax, calm down.''

Kissel told Donna to take Wayne home and try to get him settled down. But Wayne was still shaking all over, and at home he wept.

"I'm not going back to jail," he kept saying. "I'm not going back to jail.

Through the afternoon Donna Chaney tried to comfort her son. She told him she would raise more money if the bond were raised. She told him things would be all right. But the fear of jail had pushed Wayne over the edge. His eyes were red from crying when he went to his room. Later he asked his mother to drive him to the home of a friend on Prairie. Donna didn't ask why, she just took him. When he got out, Wayne gazed for a long time at his mother's face. He hugged her and kissed her and then dashed from the car.

Donna Chaney didn't know that Wayne had a car at his friend's house, packed with clothes and provisions. It was Wayne's escape car. And she didn't know that earlier in his room he had taken the new gun, a nine-millimeter automatic he had bought in Tennessee, along with the ammunition, and placed it into a pouch. He had also taken the copy of the arrest warrant, containing Patrick Carlson's new address. And he had taken his old birth certificate and whited out his name, and replaced it with Thomas Arnold Matrix. Thomas was his middle name. Arnold was for Arnold Schwarzenegger, the Terminator, the man who could kill without feeling, a man who was a machine—getting ready for Judgement Day. He took the last name from the character John Matrix, played by Schwarzenegger in *Commando*. Matrix was a man on his last mission, a mission to take back his child.

As Donna pulled away that day she didn't know that in his own mind, Wayne no longer was Wayne Chaney. He had become Thomas Arnold Matrix—the man who was not afraid to die nor afraid to kill anyone who tried to stop him.

15

On the Run

Wayne did not show up for his court appearance. He had, it seemed, vanished. His disappearance wreaked havoc with Connie's emotions. Haunted by images of what Wayne might do, and especially by the memory of her dream, she sought the company of friends. The dream, she said, had been too real. It was a terrifying glimpse into the future.

"I can find no peace in my life," she told one friend. "Even in my sleep, he is there."

Connie called Jim Prandini often. Had Wayne been found? Had he been seen? She must have hoped at times that Prandini would tell her, "Yes, he was killed in a high-speed auto chase." The death of Wayne, it must have seemed, was the only thing that could prevent her own. But no such luck. Prandini told there was no sign of Wayne, but that he would personally go out and look for him. "If he is here I will find him," Prandini said.

He went first to Wayne's parents' home, along with his partner of six years, Terry McAllister, a tall, round-shouldered man with bushy graying hair and a large moustache.

The two detectives sat with Donna Chaney in her living room. She was shaken by her son's disappearance. "He was scared," she told them. "He didn't want to go back to jail." The skin around her eyes was red, as if she had been wiping away tears for days. "That's all he kept saying. He didn't want to go back. He just left and he never came home."

Donna lost her grip more than once during the visit and the detectives waited patiently for her to pull herself together.

"He just couldn't take it anymore," she said. "I don't think he is ever coming back."

It was possible, Prandini knew, that Donna Chaney was lying to protect her son, that she knew exactly where he was hiding. But his instinct was to believe Donna. She seemed to be a strong woman, and she seemed to be grieving. She truly loved her son, he could see that, and it was probably impossible for her to accept the truth about just how dangerous Wayne Chaney was. Prandini knew, too, that Donna Chaney was probably right about Wayne not coming back. She might have seen her son for the last time, he thought, and he felt sorry for her.

After the two men spoke to Donna, Steve Chaney took them aside. The court battles and the visitation battles were taking their toll on his mother, he said. She had a bad heart and he was afraid that this latest turn of events could bring on an attack.

The detectives also called on old friends of Wayne, guys who had been involved with him back when they were all teenagers into drug dealing and big plans. Ironically, Wayne Chaney looked positively respectable compared to some of his old pals. Many had drifted along for years, in and out of jobs, in and out of jails, hooked on drugs or alcohol or both, while Chaney had gotten married, fathered a son, and built up a successful business.

At Boomer's Prandini and McAllister got lucky. At the bar Prandini flashed the black and white mug shot of Wayne at patrons. One man, whom Prandini had arrested for battery a few years earlier, signaled the detective that he wanted to talk privately. McAllister stayed at the bar to distract the other patrons while the two men stepped into the side room where the pool table was.

"Wayne's got a buddy, Norb, from the bar," the man told Prandini. "Wayne had a car stashed there with clothes, so he could take off if he had to. I heard last Saturday that he just got the fuck out of here. He's gone man. You know where Norb lives, on Prairie?"

"Yeah, I know Norb," Prandini said. "Thanks."

"It's the house with the black iron railing in the middle of the block," the informant said. "Hey, don't forget me, man."

"I won't," Prandini told him as he left.

It was close to 10:00 p.m. when Prandini and McAllister walked to the back door of the Prairie Street house owned by Norb and his brother. With their guns drawn, the detectives approached cautiously. There was a bright light in the back window. McAllister stood on his toes and peered in. Norb was asleep on the couch. The television was on.

When Prandini rang the back doorbell Norb sat up, came to the door, and pulled back the shade. Norb recognized McAllister and Prandini. He opened the door. Prandini and McAllister slipped their guns back into the holsters and walked in.

Norb, a painter by trade, was a man in his late thirties. His face was drawn, and his brown hair had streaks of gray in it. The house smelled of fresh paint.

"We're looking for Wayne Chaney," Prandini said.

"Yeah . . . so?" Norb said.

He was the type of man who didn't volunteer information.

"I know he had a car hidden here and now it's gone. Do you know anything about that?" Prandini asked.

"Yeah, saw him on the fourth. He was really upset because Connie's boyfriend set him up on a warrant. Connie didn't have the guts to sign it, so he did," Norb said. He sat on the couch and lit a cigarette. Prandini and his partner stayed by the kitchen counter. It was obvious to Prandini that Norb thought Wayne Chaney was the victim here.

"Did he say where he was going?" Prandini asked.

"No. He came to my door in the afternoon and said, 'Norb, this is the last time I am ever going to see you. I'm leaving for good.' Hell, he didn't want to go back to jail. He knew they would kill him there. I imagine he went back to Tennessee."

"Can we look around?" McAllister asked.

"Sure, go ahead. Wayne isn't here. He is long gone. He had clothes and camping stuff in that car. He was here by noon and out with the car by 1:15. That man was so upset he cried. Heck, he was so happy with the charges being dropped, then that damn warrant shit screwed everything up. That damn boyfriend . . ."

Norb stared down into his hands. "I'm going to miss Wayne," he said. "He was a friend."

The detectives took a quick tour of the house, looking for signs of Wayne. The place was well kept. There wasn't a lot of furniture but what there was, was in good condition. Even the beer cans had been crushed and stuffed into a bag for recycling.

The detectives thanked Norb and left. It was past quitting time, but Prandini was worried about Connie. If Wayne was still in the area, finding him was urgent. He and McAllister stayed up later, showing the mug shot to bartenders around Des Plaines. No one had seen Wayne Chaney.

The next morning Prandini called Connie. He was feeling confident that Wayne had left the state.

"We are still looking," he told her, "but I think he is gone for good now. He's just scared."

But Connie did not share the same feelings. "No Jim, he's out there. He's going to kill me," she said.

Connie was right. Wayne was out there.

In Chicago the area around Belmont and Sheffield is a place where people can lose themselves in many fantasy worlds, from punk bars to gay bars to biker bars. There is a massive steel el train structure dividing the two streets, and beneath that structure, if you know who to see and when to see him, you can buy drugs, guns, sex, or anything else that the law has made precious. It was this world that Wayne Chaney entered as Thomas Arnold Matrix. At the Diplomat Hotel he rented a small hundred-dollar-a-week room that looked out onto the street and the el.

Wayne chose this location because it was just a few blocks from Patrick Carlson's new apartment, an address he had gotten from the arrest warrant. Wayne, in his new identity, was adrift in paranoia. He slept with his nine-millimeter pistol gripped in his hand. He tucked the gun into his waistband when he went to the bathroom. If he went out for food or cigarettes, the gun was concealed on him. He let his beard grow. He wore a navy cap that covered much of his head, dark sunglasses, a well-worn olive-green army jacket, and his faded jeans. He might have stood out as a felon on the lam in one of the better Chicago neighborhoods, but here he fit right in.

He drove very little, knowing that even something as small as a parking ticket could lead him back into the arms of unfriendly black inmates. Also, his car had stolen plates, which he had taken from a junked Chevy in a Des Plaines junkyard.

Mostly he sat in his room and wrote in his diary, in the section called "Escape": "Was I really free? What if I got pulled over by a Chicago cop? What do I do? Start blasting? I don't have any plans to hurt or kill anybody—I'm not a crazed killer. But I am not going to jail. I have to use it."

He also wrote, "I was a walking potential killer, hoping not to use it on anyone other than Connie FIRST." From an entry in Wayne's diary we know that at 7:00 a.m. on a cold, wintry day, February tenth, Wayne drove to Patrick Carlson's Kimball Street address. There he hid behind a brick wall in a driveway between Patrick's apartment building and the one next to it. He held his hand against the pistol tucked in the pocket of his jacket. Though he had insisted in his diary that he was no mad killer, he noted in this entry that his plan was to kill Connie and Patrick as they left for work. He had no second thoughts about it, he said. The killings had to be fast, and without warning. Hiding behind the wall, he felt his body grow tense with excitement, his biceps swell like Schwarzenegger's inside his coat. Arnold had no emotion when he killed, Wayne thought, and neither will I.

The front door of the apartment building opened. Wayne tensed. When he saw Connie's face as she came through the door, he gripped the gun harder and began to slowly draw it out of his pocket. He flicked back the safety. All he had to do was press his index finger and the gun would fire one shot after another. He had a clip of eighteen hollow-point bullets that, upon impact, would mushroom inside the victim's body, ripping quickly through flesh, bones, and organs. He smiled. That was what he wanted.

Then he saw Max following behind Connie. She stopped and reached out for his tiny hand. Max still looked sleepy. He held onto a stuffed green Ninja Turtle. Max took one hand off the toy and placed it into his mother's hand. Patrick Carlson came out right behind them.

Wayne pressed himself up against the brick wall. What to do. "Max, Max," he whispered. The seconds passed by. He watched as Connie and Patrick went to separate cars. Patrick opened the door to his car and Max crawled into the back seat. Connie kissed them good-bye and walked to her car. Wayne slipped the gun back into his pocket. "So, so lucky Connie," he whispered. "I'll be back."

Later he wrote in his diary: "Max was there. I couldn't kill her and Patrick in front of Max. It would leave me to take Max with me in the state of excitement and shock that I'd be in."

Wayne watched the taillights of both cars disappear in the distance. Then he ran to his car, and began to follow. When he exited onto Belmont he spotted both cars ahead of him. At the expressway Patrick turned west towards the suburbs. Wayne figured that he was taking Max to day care. Where? he wondered. Wayne followed Connie north on the expressway until she got off at Cicero.

Connie had glanced often in her rearview mirror, a habit she had developed, but she had not seen Wayne. Connie pulled into a parking lot next to a seven-storied office building just a block off Cicero, at Peterson. Wayne quickly parked across from the lot. He put his sunglasses on and got out of his car. He watched as Connie left her car and began walking toward the building, looking around for police and holding the gun in his pocket. I am not afraid to die, he thought, and that gave him a sense of power. He felt that with this revenge he would do his son some good. He knew that his grandfather would approve. Later he noted in his diary that he laughed out loud when he thought, Maybe Connie's not afraid to die either.

Wayne was not nervous. He felt his fingers closing around the handle of the gun, inching their way down to the trigger. He was no more then forty yards away from Connie, watching her. He could hear her heels clicking on the pavement. She never turned around—she didn't know he was there.

But he didn't kill her. He looked up at the large building looming over him and decided there were, he later wrote in his diary, "Too many windows, too many witnesses," and "I would have died quickly by police."

He released his grip on the gun and turned back towards

his car. It was then that he made the decision to kill Connie in Des Plaines or at her office, just over the line in Mount Prospect.

"This would be ideal to me"—he wrote in his diary later that day—"being able to get to Des Plaines easier—would put me in the opportunity of a shootout with police—they'd love it! And so would I!" After those words he drew a smiley face and added, "I'd get them good, but if I didn't . . . you can't say I didn't try."

Wayne felt that he needed to rest up for his "mission." He wanted to take a trip, but he needed cash. Afraid that police might be tapping his mother's phone, he had arranged to leave messages on the answering machines of his mother's friends. Also, he could reach his brother Ken by calling a pay phone at the business next door to the car dealership where Ken worked.

On this particular day he made one of his phone calls, and it was only a few hours later, in a doughnut shop at the corner of Belmont and Clark, that he received an envelope containing twelve hundred dollars, along with a hug from the deliverywoman, a friend of his mother.

Connie, in the meantime was, in her own words, "hitting bottom." Recently, she had turned again to Life Span, the abused women's support group, which matched her with a counselor, Vicki Poklop. She felt as if she was getting to the end of the line, she told Vicki. She was torn. She wanted to change her name and run away with Max. "But why," she asked the counselor as she had asked her friends, "why should I have to leave? All I did was divorce him."

For her first visit with Vicki, Connie dressed fashionably in a suit she had bought at a local second-hand store: olive-green slacks and a tan suit jacket over a free-flowered silk blouse. Max was with her. He was just getting over a cold and he was irritable. Connie held him gently on her lap to calm him.

Vicki could see how deeply Connie loved her son. Connie seemed to melt when she held him. Max had just gotten a haircut the day before and his hair was frizzy. There was an innocence about him as he laid his head on his mother's lap. Connie gently bent down and gave him a kiss on his forehead as she talked to him.

"Honey, Mommy has some toys for you. I have to talk to this lady for a little while and then we go . . . okay," Connie said. "Please Max, help Mommy out . . . okay?" Then she opened up her purse and pulled out some toys that she got in children's meals from McDonald's.

Connie told Vicki about Wayne, the divorce, the rape, the gun to her head. Vicki had heard many stories like this one, but still she was touched and horrified. Connie also told her that she had found another man, and how their lives had been put on hold because of Wayne.

Vicky had seen many emotionally upset women, but she knew that she was looking at something more severe. Connie, she could see, was terrified.

"I don't know why it is taking so long for them to find him," Connie kept saying. "I don't know why it is taking so long."

Vicki offered to talk to a Life Span attorney about Connie's situation.

"I feel," Connie said, "that he is definitely going to kill me."

"There must be something that somebody could do," Vicki told her. "I'll find out and let you know."

It was the night of that meeting, after Max had gone to bed, that Connie signed for a one-hundred-thousand-dollar life insurance policy naming Patrick Carlson as beneficiary with Max.

On Valentine's Day, 1992, Connie got a call from someone saying that he had a delivery for her from a florist. Frightened, she called every florist in the area. They all said they had not called.

After that, she froze with fear every time the phone rang. Later that day she called Vicki, hysterical. Vicki tried to calm her down by telling Connie that she had spoken to Toni Winninger. Everybody was optimistic that Wayne would soon be in custody.

Vicki then called the Mount Prospect police and had a special bulletin issued. The bulletin, which was issued to all officers, had Wayne's picture on it, along with Connie's address. It explained that the Chaneys were going through a bitter divorce, that Wayne had made death threats, that he could be violent.

"Chaney is known to own guns and carry them on his person," the bulletin said. "Chaney is also known to fight with police. There is an active warrant for Wayne Chaney's arrest from the Des Plaines police department. Connie Chaney has a current order of protection against Wayne Chaney. Officers should use extreme caution if Chaney is located."

In the small hotel room about twenty miles away, Wayne Chaney was planning not a murder, but a vacation. He had decided to take a train to Flagstaff, Arizona, where he had a friend. But this was not to be his getaway. He bought a round-trip ticket. It was Sunday, and after he was packed and ready to leave, Wayne put in a call to his brother Ken. He was sure that Prandini had probably tapped Ken's line . . . he had heard that Prandini was looking for him . . . but he knew he would be out of town long before the cops could reach the hotel. He told Ken where to find his car. Then he hung up and headed for the train station.

From the section of his diary called "On The Right Track," we get a fairly clear picture of Wayne's paranoia during this trip.

He took a cab to the station. The station was empty. As he walked in he could feel the heavy, loaded gun in the pack about his waist press against his leg. With one duffel bag on his shoulder and another dragging behind him, he made his way to the steps that led to the train platform. As he looked up he saw a man staring at him. He eased the duffel bag down and quickly put his hand over his pack, where the pistol waited. "A possible law enforcement officer," he later wrote. The man moved forward and Wayne watched him carefully. Wayne had no fear as he picked up the bag and made his way up the stairs. The men stared at each other, or at least that is how Wayne perceived the moment. He wasn't a hundred percent sure, he later noted in his diary, but the way the man looked at him made Wayne think he was a cop.

Once he was on the train, Wayne felt better. There were women and children aboard, so Wayne figured that if the man was a cop he wouldn't risk other people's lives with gunplay. As the train began its journey, Wayne opened the duffel bag and took out his diary to record what he was feeling and what had already happened that day.

The next day, while he ate breakfast in the club car, Wayne watched the man he had become fixated on. He heard waiters talking about some teen smoking pot nearby. Suddenly the man got up and was joined by another man, and they rushed out of the car with the waiters. Wayne smiled. "Cop," he thought.

At the first train stop after breakfast, the man got off the train. Wayne was relieved. But then he began to think, "Is there another one to take his place? Am I still in a threatful state? Am I free?"

The fear imprisoned Wayne. His paranoia deepened. He became very suspicious of an attendant who tried to carry on small talk with him about where he was going. Wayne told the attendant that he was ill and wanted to get off at the next stop. But when they got closer to the stop, Wayne was sure there was a police force waiting for him there, so he told the attendant that he was feeling better and would not be leaving the train. As the train pulled away from that stop, Wayne was content. He had outsmarted the attendant and the police. Then he began work on another plan to trick his enemies. He would get off somewhere unexpectedly. As the train moved closer to Albuquerque, New Mexico, he changed his clothes. At Albuquerque he climbed off the train, but left his luggage on the train, figuring he would pick it up in Flagstaff. Then he walked to the bus station, and bought a ticket. Fifteen minutes later he was on a bus for Flagstaff, feeling that he had again outsmarted the police. Matrix was free. He pulled out his diary and wrote some more.

While Wayne was heading west on the train, Connie was staying part of her weekend with Kathy. They spent long hours at the kitchen table while Max played on the floor with Kathy's boy, Travis. Connie talked about running away, about changing her name. Patrick had a cottage in Michigan but Connie did not want to be in the woods alone. She knew she would jump at every sound.

Shortly after Wayne went west Connie got her own chance. Jill, feeling that Connie needed a break, asked her to go to California to set up a display for a trade show for a client. Connie was first excited, then depressed, when she realized it would mean her first long separation from Max. But a trip to California would mean getting away from her fears for a while.

Connie felt a sense of relief as the plane took off from O'Hare. It felt good to see Chicago disappear behind the clouds. She kept thinking of Max, her family, and her close friends, of happy times. She was in a mood of retrospection and she took the time to write letters to many of her friends, telling them how much they meant to her.

Connie missed Max and she called from the hotel as soon as she arrived. Max went through a hard time with his mother gone, and when she returned it was a tearful reunion at the airport. There Patrick and Max were waiting for her by the gate. Max broke away from Patrick and ran down the ramp where Connie knelt down to catch him. The boy wrapped his arms around her, saying "Mommy . . . Mommy." She quickly opened her arms, dropping her purses and bags of gifts for Max on the ramp. They embraced. Softly he whispered into her ear, "Mommy, Mommy, never go away again."

Connie, crying, whispered back, "I will never leave you, Max."

He looked at her, "Promise, Mommy."

Connie recalled this moment often for friends, explaining why she had decided not to work on trade shows outside of Chicago.

March 7, 1992—Friday

When Connie reunited with her friends, Tammy and Cathy Sullivan, at Boomer's, they could see that the trip had not freed her of her fears. Her constant talk about Wayne killing her made both women uncomfortable.

"They say Wayne is gone," Connie said, "but I know he is still around."

Her friends assured her that Wayne was weird but not so far gone that he would commit murder. Often in the past, when Connie talked about Wayne killing her, she would smile and pass it off as a joke. But tonight Cathy and Tammy could see that there was no humor left.

"What can we do for you?" Tammy asked.

"Nothing. Let's get another round of beer."

A few nights later Connie and Patrick went to a bowling alley, where they met some of Connie's co-workers from Dominick's, where Connie still worked part time. To Donna Rubenstein something seemed strange about Connie on this particular night. Connie's mind was elsewhere. Connie hugged many of her co-workers and was cheerful, but Donna would later think, "It was as if she came to say good-bye to everyone."

After bowling Donna and her husband went out for dinner with Connie and Patrick at a Mexican restaurant. Donna asked if Connie had heard anything from Wayne.

"Oh Wayne," Connie said. "He's going to come and go boom, boom, you're dead." There was an awkward silence at the table, then Connie raised her fork and repeated it, "Boom, boom, you're dead."

By the second week in March Wayne had packed his clothes and left Arizona. Things had not worked out well in the Southwest. The friend he had stayed with turned out to be undependable and a drunk. Wayne gave the guy sixty bucks from his own dwindling funds and bought a ticket out.

He stopped in St. Louis to visit his old friend Chris. Chris had a girlfriend, so the three of them went out drinking until all hours. To Chris, Wayne seemed happy, laughing and drinking just like in the old days, but he became morose when Chris's girlfriend showed Wayne a picture of her little girl. The photo got Wayne thinking about his own child, and he showed them a photo of Max. He talked about how much he missed his son. He talked about Connie, too, and his mom and dad and brothers, and the promise he had made to his grandfather to raise Max right. It was typical late-night maudlin beer talk.

But later, in the dark of 4:00 a.m. back at Chris's place, with a winter storm rattling the windows, Chris found Wayne wide awake, writing maniacally in his diary. Wayne had had a dream, he told his friend. He had dreamed about Max, something he had not done in Arizona. In Wayne's dream, Max was running towards him. Wayne tried to get to him to hug him, but he couldn't. It had awakened him. He'd sat in bed and cried, and then gotten up to write in the diary.

In his diary he wrote that life on the run had not been quite the way it was in the movies. He was concerned about his identification. He had the dummied birth certificate with the name Thomas Arnold Matrix, but he wanted more. He wanted a fake driver's license.

Of Max, he wrote, "His presence triggers my mind to react. I miss my son always, but I feel that when I think of Connie right away, it prevents me to think or remember the past or Max. This puts me in a hate/violent state of mine."

Wayne wrote of his loneliness and of his fears of being caught one day. He didn't want Connie to win.

"I couldn't let her think it or do it. No way," he wrote. "What about Max? My gramps? Myself? My feelings? And what she's done to me. I was to be a free man with probation and to live in Tenn. But NO she couldn't stop Patrick's anger.

"I feel she's at fault [sic] just as well, 'Yes'! I couldn't live with myself thinking or knowing she won or she got me. No! This is war! She wants to play—then let it be—we'll play—I'm getting upset I need to quit and go back to sleep. This chapter is to be about being on hold, meaning waiting—waiting—ha! Ha! Here I am getting into the final chapter so soon." A circular smiley face is drawn at the end of the page.

The next night he wrote, "I was actually so flattered by my life, I didn't realize what was happening. I AM so filled with life that if I do die, which I am sure will happen—I know that I'll still be here. 'I'LL BE BACK.' 'YES' I'll still be as popular and talked about after I'm gone. My son is very special to me and as I always know . . . He will be me. I'm sorry for what's happening—but it's not my fault. This shouldn't be! . . ." He ends it with "I find that having a son is more stronger than life."

When Wayne got off the bus in Des Plaines he took a cab from the el stop to the house of his friends, Fred and Diane Leone.* Before he went in he first walked past the house, watching for police. Fred and Susan had known Wayne's family for years. They knew Connie too. After Wayne told them everything that had been going on, they invited him to stay for dinner. They told him he could spend the night, but they urged him to turn himself in to the police the next day. Later, when Wayne unpacked, Fred noticed the pistol, but decided not to get involved.

That night Wayne sat in the dark living room, looking out the window at the dimly lighted street. He made plans. After he killed Connie, he would steal a car; he would kidnap the driver.

March 17, 1992—7:30 a.m.

Connie left the apartment with Patrick and Max, whom she was dropping off at the day care center. She had plans to pick him up later. Patrick would meet her at Loretta's house, where the two couples planned on having a typical Saint Patrick's Day dinner of corned beef and cabbage and beer.

When Wayne woke up at Fred's house, he asked Fred to drop him off at a hotel on Higgins Road. Fred noticed that as they drove toward the hotel, Wayne seemed concerned about the weather.

In the hotel room he showered, put on clean clothes, and checked his gun once more to be sure it was fully loaded. He slid it into the belt of his pants. Then he wrote in his diary about what had happened the day before. On a separate piece of paper he wrote to his family. "I'm sorry," he wrote. "When someone asks where your son or brother is, just say for me, 'He is With His Gramps,' I love you all."

Then he smiled as he took another piece of paper and wrote: "JAMES PRANDINI IF YOU'RE STILL ALIVE YOU ARE A LUCKY S.O.B."

In his room at the hotel Wayne left the diary, a map of the western United States, and his identification, including the false birth certificate. He took a cab to 2350 Carboy, the circular, two-story office building where Connie worked.

He stood outside the building, looking for signs of cops. Once inside the building, he walked past the numbered doors. Unable to find the office, he began to panic. What if they moved, he thought. Finally, almost ready to give up, he walked into one of the offices of another advertising firm.

"Is this G&S Advertising?" he asked.

"No," an elderly employee told him. She pointed out toward the hallway. "It's up those steps."

Wayne smiled. He was in the right place, after all. Matrix had planned correctly.

It was 11:00 a.m. Four women were in the office, all working at their desks, writing and laying out an ad campaign for a client. Connie had just finished discussing her plans for the evening on the phone with Loretta. After Connie hung up, Jill walked over to her and handed her some paperwork for the computer. Jill turned the music on her radio. It was a song by Eric Clapton, "Tears in Heaven."

Wayne moved quickly up the seven steps to the next landing. He drew his gun out of his belt and held it down by his leg. His plan was to point the gun at Connie and ask her to come outside the office.

Connie saw Wayne before he got to the office. She spotted him on the stairs. "Wayne Chaney," she screamed, and bolted from her chair. Wayne yanked open the door, gun in hand, to find her already running. She was shouting, "Call 911, call 911," as she dashed through the maze of desks. Wayne took up the chase.

The other women in the office rushed from their desks. Connie did not look back. She kept running and yelling, "911, 911."

Wayne clicked off the pistol's safety.

The door to the staircase flew open as Connie hit it with her hand. She made it to the first stair. Wayne had paced her step for step. He held his hand out in front of him and quickly pressed his index finger onto the trigger.

Connie stiffened as the bullet ripped through her sweater into her back, the hollow-point bullet mushrooming out as it severed her spinal cord. She fell forward down two stairs and collapsed onto the carpeted landing.

The bullet paralyzed her instantly and she could not feel anything in her legs or arms. Her back was against the wall and she lay, helpless, on her left side. She felt no pain. She couldn't even turn her head, yet she was alive.

Wayne could see that she wasn't moving. He moved closer to her and yelled out, "This is for Valentine's Day 1991," followed by other holidays that he had missed with her and Max. Then he fired at her six more times.

As four bullets ripped through her body, Connie gasped for air. She was in a daze. She could hear the gun but she could not feel the pain of the bullets. Wayne's last shot was to the back of Connie's head. Its impact ripped through the top of her skull. It all ended so quickly. Connie lay bleeding on the stairway. The look on her face now was one of peace, not terror. She was dead.

16

Reality of Fear

It was noon when Jim Prandini heard the sound of squad cars in the distance from his home. He had slept late, after a four-to-eleven shift and now, while his wife was out, he was making lunch for their kids, two-year-old Mark and five-year-old Anthony.

Prandini lived not far from the ad agency, and as he dashed about the kitchen, trying to throw together bologna sandwiches while keeping an eye on two rambunctious boys, he thought little of the police sirens wailing in the area. As a cop, he was curious. As a father, he already had his hands full.

He was spreading mustard when the phone rang.

It was Detective Tim Veit. "Jim," he said, "Wayne Chaney just killed Connie Chaney over at the office on Carboy."

Prandini felt dizzy, as if he had been slugged. "Did they catch Wayne?" he heard himself say.

"Not yet. It just happened," Veit told him. "I wanted to notify you as soon as possible. Is there anything I should do?"

Prandini could not answer. Emotions rolled through him like thunder. He felt grief. He felt the adrenaline; he wanted to join the hunt, track down Chaney. He felt guilt; if only he had done more for Connie, if only he hadn't been so sure that Wayne had left the state. In his mind suddenly he could

206

see and hear Connie Chaney, pleading with him in the hospital emergency room: "He is going to kill me." And he felt fear; Wayne Chaney had sworn to kill him also. Though it had been many years ago, Prandini had never forgotten the moment when Wayne Chaney glared at him, yelling, "I am going to get a gun and blow you away. Remember what Manson did." Prandini's instinct was swift and powerful: Protect yourself, protect your children.

"Jim," he heard Veit say. "Jim, are you there?"

Children, he thought. Max.

"Listen," he told Veit. "The Chaneys have a three-year-old boy, his name is Max. Wayne is going to go after the kid, I can feel it. I'm coming in as soon as my wife comes home."

He gave Veit the name of Max's day care center, then he hung up. He pulled his boys away from the patio door that looked out onto the street. Then he went into the bedroom and got his .38. It was his practice to keep the gun and the ammunition as far apart as possible. Now he ran into a closet and, reaching to the back of a high shelf, found some rounds. He loaded the gun, then shoved it into his belt.

"Hey guys," he told his boys when he came back into the kitchen, "you and your mother are going to Grandma's for a couple of days." He moved toward the glass doors of the patio and scanned the street below. As a detective, he was used to being the hunter. But now he felt like the hunted.

When his wife Donna came home, Prandini made arrangements to get his family to his wife's mother's house. Then he went to the police station where he used the computer to call up the names of everybody Wayne had ever been arrested with. He knew that criminals often rush to the homes of friends after their crime. To get current addresses, he ran the names for recent traffic tickets or arrests.

Next, he and Terry McAllister, wearing bulletproof vests, drove an unmarked car to Connie's Western Avenue apartment. It was one place Chaney might run to. Prandini said little on the way. He couldn't get the image of Connie out of his mind.

McAllister knew his partner was angry at himself for what had happened. "Sorry, Jim," he said. "There was nothing we could do. We did our best to find him."

They circled the apartment complex twice before parking

the car and approaching the building, revolvers drawn. Slowly, they made their way up the stairs, suspicious of every shadow, nervous about every noise. When they got to the apartment door, they stood on either side of it. Prandini reached across with his left hand and knocked on the door. Nothing. He knocked again. Nothing. He rapped the door hard a third time and it moved. The door was open. Somebody was in the apartment.

Prandini took a deep breath. There was no time to call for backups. If Wayne was in there, he could have his son or a hostage. In one well-practiced motion the detectives pushed open the door and rushed inside, holding their guns with two hands, and keeping low to make themselves smaller targets. "Police," Prandini shouted. "Freeze!"

"Oh my God," they heard a woman cry. It was Jane. Still shaken from just hearing the news about her sister's death, she was hysterical. In a moment she fell into Prandini's arms, sobbing. Later a police car would be posted in front of her apartment building for her protection until Wayne was caught.

Chris Musetti was in the auditorium at the hospital when she heard the news. She was standing at the podium, getting ready to speak to a crowd of a hundred people. She was adjusting the microphone when her beeper paged her.

"Well, I guess these things are good for something," she said, getting a big laugh from her audience.

The beeper paged again. "Well," she said, "I am an administrator, and this is a hospital, so I guess I'd better have someone fill in for me until I return."

She headed for the door. On the other side of the door was her secretary, Ann, calling to her. This was odd and disturbing. Ann would never call her out of a meeting unless it was something important. Chris's first thought was of her children.

"It's your husband," Ann said. "He's on the phone, and he says it's very important."

Now her heart was beating. She got quickly to a phone. "Al, what is it, what happened, are the kids okay?"

"The kids are okay," he said. "It's . . . it's Connie."

"Oh my God, has she been in an accident, is she okay?"

"She hasn't been in an accident," Al said.

He didn't have to speak again. Chris knew. She could feel it. "She's dead," Chris said. "He killed her."

"Yes," Al said.

The phone fell from her hands as she collapsed to the floor. Ann grabbed her. "Oh God ... no, no, no," Chris cried. "Oh God, oh God. My sister is dead. He killed her."

For John Krauser, the news of his daughter's death came at the customs office where he worked. He got the news as his daughter Chris had, from Al Musetti.

The news numbed him. His first question: "Where's Chris and Jane?"

After he hung up, the grief poured out of him. He put his head on his desk and wailed pitifully. "Connie, Connie," he cried. "My baby."

John Krauser had understood for some time that Wayne Chaney was a threat, not just to Connie, but possibly to the whole Krauser family. And so, when he pulled himself together enough to go to Chris's house, his fellow agents would not let him go alone. Three of them, armed with automatic machine guns, went to Chris's house with him. Once inside, they moved up to the roof of the house.

Chris, still terribly shaken, was home by this time. She looked around her. What was happening? Her sister was dead, and now men with machine guns were standing on her roof.

"Dad," she cried, "What is this? Why the guns?"

John took Chris in his arms. "Chrissy," he said, "don't you know, he is going to come after us next."

Later that day a Des Plaines police car was assigned to Chris's house. The family was put under police protection.

Patrick Carlson was at work when the police called him. They had found his name on Connie's list. The police told him that Connie was dead, but he refused to believe it. A few minutes later when Al called with the news, Carlson told him, "I don't believe it. She must be in a hospital."

"Connie is dead," Al kept saying. "She is dead."

"But I love her," Patrick said. "I was going to marry her," as if his plans made death impossible.

Max was picked up immediately at the day care center and put under police protection with a foster family so Wayne could not find him.

Prandini and McAllister, in the meantime, were still searching for Wayne Chaney. They went to visit a man named Clyde Johnson*, who lived in an old apartment building in nearby Palantine. Johnson had been arrested on drug charges along with Wayne ten years back. When they got to Johnson's building Prandini and McAllister rang the apartment bell, then pulled out their guns and made their way up the poorly lit stairway. Johnson, a tall, bearded man, held his door open just a crack, enough though for Prandini to show him his badge.

"We want to talk to you," Prandini said.

"About what?"

"Wayne Chaney. You used to hang out with him."

"So?"

"He killed his wife today."

"Heard it on the news," Johnson said. He opened the door and let the cops in. The place smelled of unwashed diapers and marijuana. "Ain't seen the guy in months."

"Mind if we look?"

"I don't give a shit," Johnson said. "Just don't mess the place up."

Prandini and McAllister moved slowly around the apartment. It was nerve-wracking work. They knew that holding a gun in your hand didn't necessarily offer much protection if some lunatic with a weapon leaped out of a closet or crawled out from under a bed. McAllister had once found a suspect hiding under a kitchen sink. Now, recalling that moment, McAllister signaled Prandini to aim his gun at the cabinet under Johnson's sink. Prandini braced himself. McAllister reached down, grabbed the knobs on the cabinet and quickly swung the doors open. Both men jumped back. Nothing. The cabinet was filled with kitchen supplies.

Johnson, sitting in an easy chair, shook his head.

"Wayne's got you guys spooked," he said.

Yes, Prandini thought, spooked. And it would be like this for a while. He and McAllister would go to a lot of seedy apartments, open a lot of kitchen cabinets. And before each one revealed its collection of Ajax, Joy, and roach baits, there would be a moment when the cops would know that Wayne might be there, that he might shoot, and that they might die.

Outside, in the car, Prandini pulled out a legal pad. He

wrote down the time and the place, and Johnson's relationship to Wayne. This began his journal of the search.

Shortly afterwards, Prandini got a radio call from a Sergeant Gibson of the Mount Prospect police. Wayne had called the switchboard at the Elk Grove Chalet Motel, told the operator what room he was in, and that he had just killed his wife. The motel then called the police. Gibson and his partner had gone there and found a baseball cap, shirts, the birth certificate, an auto registration, a map of the western states, and Wayne's diary in the room.

"James Prandini?" Gibson asked.

"Yes," Prandini said.

"Why would Wayne Chaney want to kill you?"

"What?"

"We found his diary," Gibson said. "He wants to kill you."

Tom Krauser was at work at Rockwell International in Georgia when Chris called him. From the tone of his sister's voice, he knew immediately that something awful had happened.

"It's Connie, isn't it," he said.

"She's dead," Chris said. "Wayne killed her, and he is still out there."

Toni Winninger heard the news on the car radio when she was driving home from working as a poll monitor. It was election day.

"Police are still looking for a man who shot and killed his estranged wife early this morning at her work in Mount Prospect," the radio said. "The couple was in the middle of a bitter child custody dispute and criminal actions were pending against the husband for allegedly stalking and raping his wife."

Winninger rushed home. Bitter custody dispute, she thought. She hadn't heard the names, but she had an awful feeling that it was Connie. She felt sick. When she got home she turned on the television news. Her hands were shaking. In minutes, her fears were confirmed.

WBBM-TV reporter John Duncanson was doing a live shot outside the Des Plaines police station. There was a shot of the building, then the video of Connie's body being taken out. "A terrifying few minutes here in this office complex about 11:20 this morning as a husband chased his estranged wife down a hall, then finally fired five or six shots into her. She is now dead. The woman apparently feared her husband enough to have ordered a court order of protection against him. Police are aware of prior death threats made by the husband against the wife. All that did little to stop the tragedy here today. Twenty-six-year-old Connie Chaney of Des Plaines was gunned down in her advertising agency. She was running, and fell just before reaching a stairway. Police are looking for thirty-year-old Wayne Chaney of Des Plaines. He is listed as six feet two inches tall and two hundred pounds. He has blond hair and was last seen running . . .''

Winninger clicked off the TV. She was numb. Damn the system, she thought. Damn it, I want to get out of it. She wanted to call Judge O'Brien and scream at her, ''See, see what you've let out on the street.''

Judge Sheila O'Brien had also taken an interest in the primaries. As a federal court judge, she had many friends who were running for reelection and she had gone downtown to watch the election returns at Democratic headquarters. On the way back she stopped at the courthouse to pick up some files. Though she knew nothing of the Chaney murder, she was feeling edgy. As she moved through the dark and silent courthouse, she felt as if somebody were there, watching her. It was a feeling she sometimes had, because she had once been a stalked woman.

''Hello, is anyone there?'' she called. There was no answer. She turned to her office, then she looked up suddenly and saw a man standing in the shadows. She was momentarily frightened, until she realized it was a friend, another judge who had stayed late after a trial.

He walked over to her. ''Sheila,'' he said. He looked troubled.

''You scared me,'' she said.

''Sheila, didn't you handle a case where a man raped his wife and then you lowered his bond. Chaney?''

''Yes,'' she said. ''Why?'' She had a bad feeling.

''He killed his wife this morning,'' the friend said.

''Oh my God.''

''Sorry,'' he said. ''The police are still looking for him.''

''Oh God,'' she said. ''Oh God. I was the judge.''

Steve Chaney had just gotten home when he learned from police about the murder of his sister-in-law by his brother. He was still outside the house when an unmarked police car pulled up. As he walked over to the car, another unmarked pulled up. Steve leaned into the first car. It was Larry Zumbrock and Bob Schultz. "Hey guys, what's happening," Steve said cheerfully. He knew the men, he had gone to school with their kids.

"We're looking for Wayne. He is in a little bit of trouble," one of them said.

"Has he gotten into it with Connie?" Steve asked.

The officers, afraid that Steve would clam up if he knew the truth, avoided the question. But Steve's answer came soon enough, when his brother Ken roared into the driveway.

Ken stormed out of his car. One of the cops, Zumbrock, went to him to ask questions. "Get away from me," Ken shouted. He slammed the door of his car. "Steve, come here," Ken shouted.

"Hey, we're looking for Wayne," a cop called. It was Tim Veit, who had come in the second car.

"Why? What did he do, blow the bitch's brains out?" Ken asked. He already knew that Wayne had killed Connie. Wayne had called a friend and asked her to tell Ken about the murder.

The officers were floored. "Well, as a matter of fact, that is exactly what he did," Veit said.

"Well I'm glad he blew the bitch's brains out," Ken said. "What she was doing to him, it serves her right. *I* would have killed her a long time ago."

The officers, who had seen plenty of hard cases in their time, were stunned. Steve was doubly shocked, first by the terrible news and then by his brother's reaction. He felt Ken pushing him toward the door. "Come on Steve, we're going in," Ken said.

"We have to find him before they do," Steve said. "They'll kill him, I know it."

"Is Wayne in there?" Schultz called as the brothers entered the house. "We need to search the house."

The police officers gave the Chaneys a few minutes alone in the house. Tom Chaney arrived and the boys broke the news to him. Then Bob Weirick, Veit's partner, went to the door. Weirick seemed like the best choice to keep the Chaney boys calm. He had arrested Wayne once on a disorderly conduct charge, but Wayne had never held it against him, and always said hello whenever their paths crossed.

At the door he met Tom Chaney. "Look," Weirick said, "we don't want trouble. But we have to search the house."

"Donna's not here," Tom Chaney said. "I don't want her to hear this on the news. I have to go tell her. Just finish searching by the time I get back."

The four officers drew their guns and moved into the Chaney house. Ken, angry at the cops, who he saw as constantly harassing Wayne and the family, stood back against a wall and watched them.

"Why are you doing that?" Zumbrock asked.

"I'm just getting out of the line of fire. Because he ain't going to shoot me, fellows," Ken said. "He will shoot you." He laughed. He wanted the cops to feel afraid.

Though Ken Chaney had built up a powerful hatred of the police, Steve Chaney understood that the police were the family's best hope of keeping Wayne alive. The sooner Wayne was in custody, the less the chance of further disaster.

Steve knew that Wayne admired Arnold Schwarzenegger and he knew that Wayne had a lot of bitterness toward the police. He was afraid that Wayne might steal a car or truck and ram it into the police station—as Schwarzenegger did in the first Terminator movie—just to get into a shootout with the police.

Steve called Zumbrock and asked him to meet him in an empty parking lot. He wanted to tell the cop everything he knew about how Wayne might act, and get Zumbrock's word that they would try to take Wayne alive. But despite his good intentions, to the cops, Steve was still a Chaney.

That night at the rendezvous, Zumbrock had another squad car waiting out of sight in case of trouble. He climbed into Steve's pickup truck. If anything went wrong, he would open the car door, signaling for backup.

Steve told Zumbrock his theory that Wayne might be in some kind of crazed Arnold Schwarzenegger mode and looking for violence.

"Don't underestimate my brother," he told the cop. "He has nothing to lose. He's not afraid to die or to kill. He is not going back to jail. He doesn't want to go to jail. I don't know where he is but I don't want him to die."

Zumbrock promised to help. He told Steve that there would be psychiatric help for Wayne if he could be captured. He gave Steve his home phone number.

"I have to get to him first," Steve said. "He'll listen to me."

Steve had a plan for finding Wayne first. In his truck he had a police scanner, and every day he listened to police frequencies. He would know where Wayne was almost as soon as they did. As much as possible he stayed in his truck, listening for Wayne sightings. He figured Wayne was in a room alone somewhere, wanting to call for help but unable to out of fear that the phone was tapped.

The next day there was a dispatch that a citizen had seen Wayne in a trailer court on the west side of town. Steve got there shortly after the police. He arrived in time to see squad cars lined up, shotguns being pumped, revolvers being cocked, all the deadly resources of a police department being marshalled for just one reason: to capture, or possibly kill, his fugitive brother.

Nothing came of this sighting. Soon Steve followed the police to another address, a two-story apartment complex where a resident had supposedly spotted Wayne in a vacant apartment. Here Steve found cops wearing bulletproof vests, with their guns drawn. Some had helmets and body shields. He could hardly believe his brother had created such fear. A crowd gathered. Steve was afraid. He half expected to see his brother running out, guns blazing like some scene out of a movie, only to be cut down by a barrage of police fire. He watched. He waited.

While he waited he thought about Connie, whom he loved. She was dead. Wayne, whom he also loved, was being hunted. He could hardly process it all. He just wanted to find Wayne, somehow talk to him, keep him alive. He thought about how his life would be changed by today's tragedy. Already it had begun. Earlier that day he had walked into Boomer's, thinking that he could somehow get a lead on where Wayne was. The bar had been empty. Someone said that people were staying home because they thought Wayne might come there and they could get caught in a shootout.

As he was leaving Boomer's Steve passed a few men at a table. He didn't know their names, but they looked familiar. He heard one of them say, "That's the brother of the killer." I'm the brother of the killer, he thought now, staring at the apartment complex, with its ring of cops and gawkers.

In a moment a police officer came out of the building. "Not here, he yelled." Steve was relieved. But there would be another sighting and another. And, just as James Prandini would go from house to house searching for Wayne, knowing that each place could be where he took a bullet, Steve Chaney with the help of his police scanner, would follow police teams from one sighting to the next, knowing that at any time he could see his brother being killed.

Wayne's flight from justice began right after he shot Connie. With her lifeless body sprawled before him on the stairs, Wayne turned away and ran out of the building and across the street. He had been smoking heavily in recent months and he ran out of breath quickly, so he stopped at a nearby gas station. Though he had left his diary behind in the hotel room, he would begin another with a section called "Hostage" during this period of his flight, and from that diary we can get an idea of what he was thinking at the time.

When Wayne got to the gas station he didn't have a plan because he hadn't expected to get away. He had envisioned a shootout with the police, and hadn't really thought about the fact that he would have time to run before the police even arrived. Now, he stood in the parking lot by the pumps, feeling proud of himself. He kept his word. He had killed Connie. It had happened fast, the automatic had fired perfectly, everybody had been terrified, and he had gotten away.

Quickly he plotted his next steps. He would kidnap someone who was getting gas and drive off in their car. The only problem was that nobody was getting gas. The gas bays were empty. He would wait, he decided. Someone would pull in for gas in a minute. His mouth was dry. With his gun tucked out of sight, he walked into the gas station, and picked out a pack of gum. As he placed it on the counter and paid for it, he heard the shrieking of police sirens coming closer and closer.

He stared out the window while waiting for his change,

and noticed that at the end of the gas station there was a drive-up pay telephone. At that moment a 1990 gray Oldsmobile Cutlass pulled up. A young man reached out the window and began dialing a number. Wayne knew what to do. He left the gas station and walked over to the Cutlass. He opened the passenger's side door and climbed in.

"Excuse me, sir," Wayne said, "can you give me a ride?" Then he showed the man his gun. "I just shot someone. Do as I say or I'll blow your brains out. Now move it."

The young man, a twenty-eight-year-old advertising salesman named Steven Wielock, dropped the phone. Nearly paralyzed with fear at the sight of the gun, he put the car into gear and began to drive slowly out of the gas station. "Faster," Wayne said. He shoved the gun into Wielock's ribs. A squad car rushed by on the way to the crime scene. "Move it," Wayne hollered.

Later Wayne described his getaway in his diary: "It was like clockwork. No police."

After they had been driving for several minutes Wayne could see that his hostage was terrified, and that made him unpredictable. Wayne began to talk to him in a more soothing voice. He put his gun down beside him. "Everything's going to be okay," he promised. "Just keep both hands on the wheel. Don't speed. Just be cool, and I won't hurt you."

He began to chat with his hostage. He asked Wielock if he was married, where he lived, how many kids he had. Wielock, more frightened than he had ever been, answered each question minimally, like a court witness, not knowing what extra word or phrase could set this lunatic off. Wayne's impression of Wielock, later recorded in the diary, was, "a guy who really thinks he might die. I can see him sweat and his legs are shaky ... he stared straight ahead studying the roadway."

When they came to a toll booth Wayne shoved the gun in Wielock's ribs again. "If you try anything," he said, "I have nothing to lose. I'll kill you sure as shit."

"I understand," Wielock said, as he pulled up to a toll booth. "I'm going to roll down my window now, okay?"

"Yeah," Wayne said.

After they got through the toll booth Wayne asked for Wielock's wallet. The wallet contained only twenty-seven dollars in cash, but also an ATM cash card. Wayne told his hostage to drive until they found a bank machine that would take the card.

"I know how it is to have to pay bills and all," Wayne said, "but I need, well, about four or five hundred dollars."

At the ATM Wielock quickly gave his code number to Wayne, but there was a daily limit on withdrawals and Wayne was only able to get $200. Wayne was beginning to trust his hostage.

They picked up hamburgers at a Burger King drive-through window, then Wayne directed Wielock to a forest preserve outside of Des Plaines. There they ate lunch at a picnic table. Wayne, now much calmer, talked about his mother and his family. He had to be sure that his mother was okay, he told Wielock, he had to be sure there was somebody there to comfort her. He told Wielock he had plans with a friend for that night, but that now he would have to cancel the date.

After they ate Wayne took Wielock back to the car and turned on the radio. He was eager to hear about his crime. They sat there for a while, listening to the news reports and Wayne correcting them as they went along. "I shot her in the hallway," he said to Wielock, "not outside her work, and I shot her eight times, not six." His prediction that Connie could make him famous had come true, and he was very proud.

Later they stopped again, this time at a pay phone in a nearby gas station. That's when Wayne put in the call to Ken's friend, with the message: Tell my brother I killed my wife. Then he called the hotel where he had stayed, and he told them to call the Mount Prospect police.

"Tell them I just shot and killed my wife," he said. "Tell them I was in a room there under the name Matrix."

Wayne wanted the police to search his room at the hotel. He had originally planned to drop his diary off at a local newspaper, but decided he didn't have time. So he had deliberately left his diary in the room. It was, he felt, his side of the story. Also there were threats in the diary against Patrick Carlson, Chris, and Jim Prandini. Wayne wanted those threats to prey on their minds, to make them all the prisoners of fear. And Wayne wanted to play games with the police. By leaving behind a map of the western United States, he believed the police would then think that he was headed back to Tennessee. The logic is not easy to follow, but it meant something to him. And he left his false birth certificate, with the name Thomas Arnold Matrix on it. Wayne thought all of this would somehow catch the police off guard, and he would be able to come back and kill everybody who had caused his pain.

Later Wayne and Wielock checked into a Red Roof Inn off of I-94 and Waukegan Road, about twenty miles north of Des Plaines. Fearing that Wielock's picture had already been shown on TV and he would be recognized, Wayne made his hostage wear sunglasses. When they got into the motel room, Wayne told Wielock to lay on the floor on his stomach, with his hands cupped behind his back and his feet pointed to the bathroom. Wayne stepped over him to use the bathroom. Later, in his oddly thoughtful way, Wayne used an ice bucket to urinate in, so that Wielock wouldn't have to lie on the floor every time Wayne went to the bathroom.

Though Wayne was very tired, he was eager to see the TV coverage of his crime. He turned on the television and saw Connie's wrapped body being taken down the stairs by police. He smiled and turned to Wielock.

"I would love to kill my sister-in-law," he said. Then he turned the gun on Wielock. Wielock had been numb with shock ever since the moment Wayne had appeared in his car. Now, he stared into the barrel of Wayne's gun, thinking he had done something wrong and would die for it. Wayne continued to point the gun at him.

"Prandini," Wayne said, waving the gun. "James Prandini. If it's the last thing I do, I'll get him. I want you to say his name."

"James Prandini," Wielock said.

"Spell it," Wayne demanded.

Wielock spelled out the name. He felt as if he would faint from the fear.

"Good," Wayne said. "Remember that name." He tossed Wielock the briefcase that Wielock had carried with him all day. "Here," he said, "work on something, keep yourself busy. I'm going to get us some pizza. It's on me."

That night on his way home, James Prandini stopped at his mother's house to pick up her dog. He would take the dog home to the empty apartment; an extra warning device. When he pulled up in front of his building he looked around for a Mount Prospect squad car. He had asked for one to meet him at his house, to look the place over before he settled in for the night, but none had arrived. He turned off his headlights and waited in the dark a moment so his eyes would adjust before he opened the door. At least he had gotten his wife and kids out of harm's way, he thought. He stared constantly into his rearview mirror. From the front seat he picked up a sawed-off shotgun that he had taken from the station. He pumped a shell into the chamber and slid the gun under his arm. He unsnapped his holster, so that he could quickly draw his handgun if he needed to. Then, slowly, he climbed out of the car. He let the dog out. He listened. No sound. He drew his pistol and walked slowly around his house, checking for broken windows or doors jimmied open. His heart was pounding, his hands were sweating. He knew something of what Connie must have felt. He unlocked his door and called quietly to the dog. He knew she would bark if there was anyone in the house. At the threshold he waited a few seconds while the dog raced through the house, but the dog ran back to him, without barking. Prandini quickly entered, closed the door, and bolted it. Before he drew the drapes closed, the Mount Prospect squad car pulled up in front of his house. He waved to the officer in the car, who flashed his headlights at him.

The Terminator, Prandini thought. Chaney thinks he's the Terminator, which means he will stop at nothing. He shoved a chair in front of the door, jamming it up under the knob. The chair wouldn't stop Chaney, but it would sure as hell add to the noise if he broke in.

As he slipped into his dark bedroom, Prandini suspected everything. He put on a light and was alarmed by the fact that a closet door was ajar. Was it like that before? he wondered. He put the shotgun on the floor and held his automatic in front of him as he moved toward the door. Taking up a position to one side of the closet, he yanked the door open. There was nobody there. Then he remembered that he had not closed the door after he pulled out suitcases for his wife that afternoon. Got to get a grip, he thought. Wayne's threat had infected him like a poison. He was startled by every noise, every shadow. He lay on his bed, still fully clothed, still wearing a bulletproof vest, still holding his pistol across his chest, and with the shotgun nearby on the floor. He lay awake for a long time, picturing the moment when he would have to face down Wayne Chaney. And he understood that there was something more severe than fear eating at him. It was regret, a feeling of responsibility. He kept seeing Connie Chaney's face, kept hearing her words, "He's going to kill me, Jim, he is going to kill me."

17

Putting to Rest

Chris Musetti did not sleep that night. She lay in her bed and cried. And when she wasn't crying she stared helplessly at the ceiling. She could hear the sound of her police guard downstairs walking around or turning the pages of a magazine. Every time the headlights of a passing car cast shadows on her bedroom wall, she tensed. Was this it? Was this the moment Wayne would break into Chris's house to kill her and her family?

When her mind was not filled with the horror of what had happened and what could happen, it was alive with images of her baby sister. She saw Connie at age seven, laughing and holding her pet cat, Sinbad, or running joyously with Pepe, the dachshund. She saw Connie playing with dolls on her bedroom floor. She saw Connie smiling, and she felt Connie's small trembling shoulders as the sisters stood at their mother's funeral. There was Connie in a coma at the emergency room, Connie announcing her pregnancy, Connie in a wedding gown. The sad images flowed by all through the night. Most poignantly, Chris remembered Connie saying, "Please, if anything happens to me, take care of my son." It was a promise Chris had not been able to keep. At least not yet.

Even after her death, Connie's world was being manipulated by the court system. The Department of Children and

Family Services had stepped in and taken custody of Max because Connie had not made any written provisions for him. Max, in protective custody, had been put into a foster home, its location kept secret. Not even Chris had been allowed to see him. She had talked to him earlier that evening, when the foster parents called her.

"Where's Mommy?" he had asked. Chris could hear that the boy was confused. He didn't have his toys, he said, or his stuffed turtle, and he didn't understand why he wasn't being allowed to watch television.

"Mommy is okay," Chris had told him, her heart nearly breaking as she spoke. "She is on a business trip and she will be back on Wednesday." And then Chris had been so overtaken with a wave of grief, and the tears had flowed so quickly from her, that she'd had to hand the phone over to Al.

How, she wondered now, do you tell a three-year-old boy that his daddy has murdered his mommy? It was a question that troubled her all through this sleepless night. Who would tell Max?

In his room at the Red Roof Inn Wayne Chaney was finding sleep less difficult.

Earlier he and his hostage had watched the Chicago Bulls playoff game and eaten pizza. When it was time to turn in, Wayne ordered Steve Wielock to put a mattress and sheets under the sink, which was built into a counter of the bedroom just outside of the bathroom. Wielock did what he was told and stretched out on his makeshift bed. Wayne told Wielock to lie on his stomach and then, using strips from a sheet that he had packed for bandages in case he was wounded, Wayne tied Wielock's arms to the leg of the sink, and bound his legs together. Wayne's knots were not tight and Wielock knew that he could easily wriggle out of the bandage, but he had no intention of trying. Wayne was polite, as he had been throughout much of Wielock's ordeal. He notes in his diary that when he was done tying up his hostage, he said to him, "Please don't try to escape. Please. I need my sleep, plus I'll kick you practically to death if you try, so please don't."

Wayne took additional precautions. He pulled the boxspring from one of the beds and pushed it against the sink, next to Wielock. Then he pushed a dresser on top of that, and topped off the whole obstacle with soda cans that would tip and alarm him if Wielock got free. Now satisfied with his alarm system, he laid down on his bed, cocked his pistol, and placed it on his chest, and went to sleep.

March 18, 1992—5:30 a.m.

The next morning Wayne rose early and left the motel in Wielock's car. He knew that Wielock would be found by the maids when they came in to clean, and that would trigger a search for Wielock's car. So Wayne drove to a junkyard, where he stole new license plates for the vehicle. He stopped off to pick up a screwdriver to fasten the plates, then he got breakfast at a restaurant and read the stories about Connie's murder in the morning newspaper. Recalling that Susan Hay*, a friend from high school, lived in the area, Wayne decided to drop in on her. After breakfast he drove to her neighborhood to look for her house.

Steve Wielock, in the meantime, waited fearfully for Wayne to return. As the minutes, then hours, passed, Wielock grew more hopeful that his trial was over. After two hours he was confident that Wayne would not return. He wriggled free of the bonds, crawled out from under the sink, and called the police.

Wayne drove to Susan Hay's street in a neighborhood of mostly ranch houses with large backyards. He parked down the street from her place and carefully scanned the area. No sign of police. He pulled his pistol from its pouch and stuck it under his belt so that his jacket would hide it. With his newspaper tucked under his arm, he walked across the front lawn to Susan's patio door.

Susan Hay was in the kitchen at the time, making breakfast for her two-year-old daughter. Her husband had gone to work. She was startled to see a strange man standing outside her patio door. He had a beard, gold-rimmed glasses, and wore a baseball cap. It took her a few seconds to realize it was her old friend Wayne. She had already heard about Connie's murder on television. Suddenly, she was afraid that she and her daughter would be in danger if she let Wayne in. But she was even more afraid of what might happen if she did not. She went to the patio door, snapped the lock, and slid the door open.

"Hi, Susan," Wayne said. He seemed nervous, but not threatening. He acted as if he were just an old friend dropping by for a visit. He strode over to her kitchen counter and put down his newspaper, somewhat proudly, it seemed to her. "I did it," he said, "and she deserved it. I was looking at twenty years for something I didn't do."

Susan, her motherly instincts aroused, now stood protectively near her daughter while Wayne calmly described to her how he had taken a hostage, and his night in the motel. While he was talking, Susan's phone rang.

"Go ahead, answer it," Wayne told her.

Susan moved to the phone. Be careful, she thought, don't get him riled up.

The caller was Diana Leone*, the woman whose house Wayne had slept in two nights before. Diana had called to tell Susan about the murder and to warn her to be on the lookout for Wayne.

"Yes," Susan said, her voice hollow and cold.

Diane sensed that something was wrong.

"What's the matter? Is he there with you?"

"Yes," Susan said.

"Okay, stay calm," Diane said. "I'm calling the police."

"Yes. Thank you," Susan said. She glanced into the kitchen at Wayne. He seemed unconcerned, as if he could not imagine that one of his friends would turn him in to the police.

When Susan came back into the kitchen Wayne asked her for writing paper and an envelope. He wanted to write a letter to his mother and he wanted Susan to deliver it.

"No," she told him. "Wayne, just leave, get out of here."

It was a risk, but she realized that she and her daughter were at far greater risk if the police showed up while Wayne was still in the house.

"Okay," he said. He looked hurt, not angry. "But I need a shower first, and then I'll go."

While Wayne showered, Susan sat in the kitchen with her daughter. She was torn. All she had to do was grab her child and rush through the patio door to safety. But she was held in place by fear. Wayne had left the bathroom door open. He would hear her, he might see her. She could imagine him chasing her and her daughter down, shooting them while they ran, as he had done to his own wife less than twenty-four hours ago.

Diana Leone had in the meantime called Bob Schultz at Des Plaines police headquarters.

"Wayne is at my friend's house in Wood Dale," she said. "I just talked to her."

Schultz, who had just come out of a strategy meeting on Chaney, rushed back in to give the word. Suddenly the station came to life. Assignments were made. Bulletproof vests were donned by the officers who weren't already wearing them. Weapons were readied. Schultz put in a call to the Wood Dale and Mount Prospect police to tell them the situation and to warn them about how dangerous Chaney could be. Minutes after Diane's call, two Des Plaines squad cars were on the way.

As the police cars raced toward Wood Dale, Wayne Chaney was finishing up his shower. He dried himself, got dressed, and went back into the kitchen. "Thank you," he said to Susan. "Please don't call anybody for at least two hours."

He went out the patio door and then he stopped and paused. He turned and looked at Susan and her daughter. "The next time you see me," he said, "I will be dead." Then he left, literally seconds before the police arrived.

The news that Wayne Chaney had been spotted but had gotten away irked Jim Prandini. The police station, he had found, offered no sanctuary from fear.

Even as he sat at his desk reading the teletype with the distressing news about Chaney, Prandini became aware of the doorway that faced him. If Wayne Chaney stood there holding a shotgun, Prandini would be the proverbial fish in a barrel. Suddenly edgy, he began moving his desk at different angles. All of them looked fatal. Finally he shoved his desk clear out of the doorway's path, and put McAllister's in its place.

"Great, Jim," McCallister said when he returned. "Thanks. Let Chaney kill me."

Though McAllister was good-humored about it, the fact is

that Prandini and McCallister and many other members of
Des Plaines's ninety-eight-man police force were suffering
with something that never seems to afflict the cops on television: fear.

Zumbrock's meeting with Steve Chaney had created con-
siderable tension at the Des Plaines police department. Chaney, it seemed, had declared war on the police and the talk
about him coming through the door blasting away like Arnold
Schwarzenegger had taken its toll.

Prandini was moving furniture, everybody was wearing
bulletproof vests. Acting Chief Ken Randall had stayed up
all night reading Wayne's diary and it had given him and
eerie feeling he had not had since his combat days in Viet-
nam. Afterwards, he started carrying a gun, something he had
not done since he became an administrator. The station was a
smoke-free building and normally you could find the smokers
gathered outside the back door. But now everybody stayed
inside, fearing a sniper attack. Vacation days were canceled.
Every squad car was now a two-man car. The Chaney
sightings were coming in at the rate of three an hour. Wayne
Chaney had created a manpower shortage. Not only would
officers be needed to guard Connie's family, but plenty of
extra men would be required to make sure her funeral did
not become the site of a massacre.

A meeting was held in a conference room at police headquarters to discuss plans for the funeral. Al Freitage, commander of the detective division, had to meet with Connie's
sisters, her brother, her father, and Al Musetti. It was an
acrimonious meeting. The family was seething with anger
that the system had let this happen.

"If it wasn't for you guys and that damn warrant, my
sister would be alive," Chris said. The courts, the police,
government, had all merged in the minds of the grieving
family. The system had killed Connie. "I hope," she said,
"that the judge who lowered his bond burns in hell."

There was nothing Freitage could say or do. This was no
time to try to explain the law or the system, and certainly
not time to make excuses for it.

He told the family that they could not have Connie's wake
the following day. The police needed time to make plans and
set themselves up to protect the family in case Wayne tried

to get them at the funeral, which would be held the day after the wake.

Freitage told the Krausers that the man who would be in charge of the police operation at the funeral was Lieutenant John Meese, head of a special operations team. Meese, he said, had taken seriously the message from Steve. Meese had sent out requests to police units of the IRS and the United States Navy for the use of vans, special night vision equipment, and high-powered sniper rifles.

"And," Freitage added, knowing he would make no friends today, "we have to put you all in hiding until we get Wayne. We can't keep you in Chicago. We have to keep you in Des Plaines for now."

He told them they would all stay at Jane's apartment and they would have twenty-four-hour police protection.

"Hell, if everyone did their jobs we would never be in this, would we?" Chris said, as the family was leaving. "And you better make sure that those Chaneys don't show up at my sister's funeral."

Later that afternoon Jane's apartment was filled with family members, any of whom could be next on Wayne's hit list. Chris and Jane took on the somber task of choosing clothes for Connie to be buried in. Patrick, John, and Al drank beer, watched TV, and tried to forget. Tom, ever the businessman, went through Connie's papers. He wanted to be sure that her bills were organized and paid, that all her friends were notified about the wake. In one box Tom found a letter dated July thirteenth. The letter was not addressed to anyone. He opened it slowly, perhaps sensing its troubling contents. It was the farewell letter that Connie had written.

"I'm grateful that I am one of the fortunate ones to be able to have the opportunity to tell you all good-bye," she had written. "Each and every one of you have touched my life in one way or another. We all have memories of each other. Some good, some not so good. I will always cherish our memories. I had some wonderful times that I want you all to know were wonderful only because of you. It is a sad fact that someone could steal another life, yet it is really up to God to make the final decision."

Tom felt the emotion swelling within him as he read on, through a paragraph of farewells to Tammy, Cathy Sullivan,

Jackie Mudd, Kathy Hoshell, Loretta, other friends, and Tommy and Jane. At the bottom of the page she wrote:

"I want to break a minute to ask you all to take care of my baby. Nobody could touch a person's life like a child, the whole world looks different through a child's eyes. Please teach him to be confident, caring, and have morals. I know that he can accomplish whatever he wants. Protect him and love him. He was my life . . ."

Tom slipped the letter back in the envelope. He could not show this to the others, not now. It was too powerful. He put his face into his hands and wept uncontrollably.

While the police were getting ready for gunfire and the Krausers were getting ready to hide, Wayne Chaney was getting out of town.

Feeling proud and free, he headed for Iowa along Route 64, a two-laner that worked its way through rural farm communities. He wanted to stay off the interstates. It was a cold day, gray and foggy as he drove along, listening to a country western station. The songs, with their lyrics about broken loves and starting over, made him sad. His mind wandered and he ran again those movies in his mind of good times with Connie and Max. Wayne knew that the police would be hiding Max, and for him to even try to get his son back could endanger Max's life. He knew now that there was no life for him without Connie, and that there would be no life for Max with him. Max needed a new start with new parents.

Wayne drove cautiously. He kept his seatbelt on, stayed under the speed limit. Now and then he thought he was being followed, and he turned off the highway and worked his way along side roads until he got back to 64. When he passed the sign that said, "Welcome To Iowa," he notes in his diary that he thought, I made it, I made it. I am free.

Wayne pulled off the highway in Cedar Rapids and checked into the Shady Acres Motel. He appreciated the fact that the motel was on a hill and he could see who approached, and he liked the small, individual cabins. He felt hidden there, as he had in his fishing and hunting days. He ordered pizzas from the local Pizza Hut, and read the Chicago Tribune for stories about the shooting. He cut the stories out and pasted them in his diary, along with Connie's obituary. Alongside the newspaper articles he wrote corrections of facts. Then he tuned in a Chicago TV station and watched the stories about the search for Wayne Chaney. Celebrity suited him.

The fear continued to eat away at the police. Kate Couris, a psychologist, came to the station to talk with Prandini. An attractive, slender woman in her early forties with shoulder-length brown hair, Couris had often conducted stress workshops for the Des Plaines police along with Detective Kevin O'Connell. O'Connell had called her and told her how Prandini was acting. She understood what the officer was going through.

"It's not your fault," she told Prandini. "Don't beat yourself up. You know that if someone is bent on killing someone you can't stop them."

Prandini, of course, knew all that. But he was still feeling what he was feeling. To him it felt as if there was only one cure for the guilt that consumed him: track down Wayne Chaney and bring him in. With the threat of a shootout, many officers were now going to the target range for practice. Later that day at the range, where he had gone to release some of his tension, he slipped an eight-by-ten "Wanted" poster of Chaney over the silhouette target and blasted the hell out of it.

He smiled. "Kate said to take care of myself," he told McAllister.

Because Wayne had told his hostage, "I must finish my work by Friday," and "Friday is judgment day," there was a strong belief among the police that Wayne would make his move at Oehler's Funeral Home, where Connie was to have her wake on Thursday and her funeral on Friday. The police had asked the family to postpone the funeral service or change the location, but the Krausers had refused. So security for the funeral was extensive. Drawings were made of all the streets in the area. A diagram of the funeral home was given to every officer. Streets were closed off. Lieutenant Meese established a command post in an apartment across the street from the home. Snipers were placed on the roofs. Surveillance vans and night vision equipment were borrowed from navy intelligence.

One reason for all the security was that an entry in

Wayne's diary had indicated that he might use a truck to bash the door down.

"We'll ring the front entrance with unmarked squads," Meese told his team at a planning meeting. "The vehicle will also act as cover for officers. We will also block the parking lot with unmarked squads. This will force all visitors to walk from the city lot to the funeral home so our undercover teams can get a good look at everybody."

There would be two vans at the front of the building, he explained, which would have ballistic shields. The family would be brought to the funeral home in three unmarked squad cars, by three different routes, and taken in through the garage door. Then a dump truck would be parked in front of that door. Eight men would be inside with Larry Zumbrock. Two more would cover the front. After everyone was inside, an iron rod would be slid into the door front of the funeral home. If shooting began everyone would be pushed away from the windows. One police helicopter would circle the area throughout the day. The coast guard would fly over to check the roof tops. Meese, in his command post across the street, would be accompanied by two marksmen with scoped rifles.

Every possibility was being considered. One informant told the police that Wayne could come, hidden in the trunk of a car.

"Someone could smash through the door in a car," the informant had warned, "and Wayne could come up from the trunk, shooting. He could disguise himself, he could be wearing a wig."

A copy of Wayne's diary, in the meantime, had been turned over to the F.B.I. profile team, in the belief that he was deliberately leaving clues. In a matter of hours, it seemed, Wayne Chaney had been transformed into the bigger-than-life Terminator that he saw himself as.

As the moment of the funeral grew closer and the search for Wayne more intense, Donna Chaney and her family grew more and more desperate. They imagined Wayne being trapped by police and they saw no good end to it. Though they didn't believe that Wayne would kill police officers, they knew that his threat to do so was enough to get him killed in a shootout with the cops. They turned for help to

Bill Spyrison, a thirty-year veteran of the police force and a longtime friend to Wayne and the family. Spyrison cut short a Florida vacation to fly home and counsel the Chaney family. The day before Connie's wake he sat in Donna Chaney's kitchen with the family. Spyrison promised that if Wayne called he would do what he could to keep Wayne alive. But he was not optimistic.

"There is no word from Wayne," Donna told him. "They are going to kill him, I know it."

"Wayne is no cop killer," Steve said, "but he knows damn well that if you say you will kill a cop you have signed your own death warrant. Wayne always said he could not live without Connie and Max. A shootout with the police is one way to kill himself."

"Dear God, no," Donna said. "Wayne isn't like this, he isn't."

The Chaney family was blind to the fact that Wayne had become a killer, and that he was growing more and more paranoid.

At the Shady Acres Motel Wayne paced and constantly glanced out the window. He was afraid that the police would spot Wielock's car. On the morning of Connie's wake, while an army of police officers were preparing to defend the funeral home, Wayne was checking out of the motel, driving to a junkyard, and bolting yet another set of plates to the car. After he scraped off any stickers that identified the car as being from Illinois, he explored the town. In his diary he notes quaintly that he came upon a small area of Czech bakeries, a museum, and a thrift shop. In town he bought used clothes to change his appearance, then he asked about fishing in the area. He was directed to a location off of I-380. He bought a cheap rod and reel, and bait, then drove to the fishing spot. There he walked the nature trails, and he talked out loud to Connie as if she were strolling through the woods with him. "What should I do?" he asked. "I need money in a hurry. Should I pull a job?" By the time he settled down to fishing he had decided he would pull a robbery. After all, he was Wayne Chaney. He had gotten away with murder. Certainly he could get away with a little robbery.

It was a cold day, but it made him happy to once again stand by the shore and cast a fishing line into the still waters.

I can be patient, he thought. I can wait for my prey. They will take my bait and then I will hook them.

March 20, 1992

At 7:00 a.m. Lieutenant Meese opened the front door of the funeral home. Seven members of his special team, all of them wearing bulletproof vests and carrying assault rifles, filed in. Each carried a map of the funeral home. They moved quickly and efficiently through the building, searching everywhere, including the coffins containing other bodies.

At ten o'clock Patrick Carlson arrived with Connie's hairdresser. Though she was reluctant to work on a dead body, the hairdresser had come because Patrick had been insistent. "I want her to look her best for the wake," he had told her. Patrick asked to be shown downstairs where Connie's body was. He was told that he could not do that, by Bob Weirick, who was in charge of security inside the funeral home.

"What do you mean I can't go down?" Patrick asked. Like the other people close to Connie, Patrick was seething with hostility toward the police and all forms of civil authority who had, in their eyes, allowed this tragedy to occur.

"Look, I know this isn't easy," Weirick said, "but no one goes downstairs, okay?"

"No, it's not okay," Patrick said.

"It will have to be," Weirick replied.

"Hey, don't tell me what to do or where to go. My girlfriend is dead and if you cops did your job she would still be alive."

The war of words continued until a supervisor arrived and gave permission for the hairdresser only to go downstairs with the funeral director.

The police formed a three-car motorcade with the family, and squad cars waited for them to pass at each intersection on their way to the funeral home. Chris could not believe all the security when they arrived. The funeral home looked like an armed camp. The helicopter circled overhead, police guards with rifles and walkie-talkies were everywhere. It was overwhelming. She turned to her brother Tom.

"If they were like this when she was alive, we would not have to be here today," she said.

Chris was brought into the funeral home with her husband, father, brother, and sisters. She had only gone a few feet when she saw the name Chaney on the directions board.

"No," she shouted. "She is not going to carry that son of a bitch's name today." She ripped off the plastic letters. Her husband and brother put their arms around her and held her. "She is a Krauser," Chris cried, "not a Chaney. He killed her. I don't ever want to see that name."

John Krauser spoke quietly to the funeral director. "Change it," he said. "It's Krauser," and he spelled out the family name.

The family joined hands as they walked quietly into the parlor where Connie lay. The room smelled sweet. Flowers were everywhere and soft organ music seeped from speakers in the walls. Though they were joined with their hands, each felt pathetically alone, each dealing with his own memories of Connie, each practicing grief in his own style. Soon they were joined by Patrick Carlson.

Meese, at his command post, was on the job. He stood by the window of the apartment across the street, staring through binoculars at the street below. His marksmen were ready. Everyone was tense.

There were false alarms. One officer spotted an old friend of Wayne's. This was a man who had had his own run-ins with the local law enforcers, and it wasn't hard to imagine him taking revenge by throwing in his hand with Chaney. But nothing came of it. Another man pulled the tension cord tighter when he walked along the sidewalk with his head down, wearing sunglasses as if to disguise himself. But he, too, turned out to be uninvolved. Everybody was feeling the stress.

Connie's friends came to say good-bye. Tammy and Loretta came. Cathy Sullivan came with her two sons, telling them, "Say good-bye to Max's mom." Vicky from Life Span came. Connie was wearing the same outfit she had worn in Vicky's office, and it brought back vivid pictures of Connie, distraught, crying, holding Max in her lap and saying to Vicky, "Can't anyone help me?"

Notably absent from the wake was Jim Prandini. Prandini had wanted to go to the wake but for security reasons had been banned from the funeral home. He was, after all, a known target of Wayne Chaney.

On the afternoon of the wake Prandini met with Commander Freitage in an office at the police station. Freitage told Prandini to get out of town until Wayne was caught.

"I'm not going to run," Prandini said. "I'm not afraid of Wayne Chaney."

"No one's saying that you are running, Jim. But this death threat makes everybody nervous. I know you want to help, but that's hard when you are one of the guys Wayne wants to kill. He said if it's the last thing he does he will kill you. We have to protect the family as it is. Having to protect you just makes it too much."

Freitage told Prandini about a place in Wisconsin where he could take his family.

Prandini finally agreed. He, too, had become a prisoner of Wayne Chaney.

Wayne had no intention of appearing at the wake. On the day that Connie's friends said good-bye, Wayne moved into a new room, this one at the Skylight Motel, twenty-two bucks a night. In his diary he noted that the room smelled of disinfectant and cigarette smoke. And the bed, he noted, was lumpy, but he did like the TV satellite dish, which brought in over thirty-two channels.

Wayne, it seems, was living on a steady diet of pizza these days. On this day he went to the local Pizza Hut where, while he ate, he worked on a scheme for robbing the place. As he recounts it in his diary, he would wear a knit cap and a nylon stocking on his head, as well as dishwashing gloves. He would enter the Pizza Hut through the back door with his shotgun an hour before closing time, rob the place, steal a car from the parking lot, drive it to his own car, then go to a bar for an hour or so.

After making his plan and eating his pizza, Wayne went back to catch the television news from Chicago. He liked seeing stories about him on the news. This evening he was surprised and annoyed that they didn't mention the hostage and that they ran an old mug shot of him. In his diary he wrote:

"The police there don't really know what I look like. Why

didn't the news show a sketch of me as I am now? Did Steve Wielock get found later than I planned? Is Steve scared because I have his address? What? Why? He knows that I wouldn't hurt anyone that wouldn't threaten my capture or death . . . but I know for a FACT that there's no way I'll get CAPTURED ALIVE. I'm not afraid to die! I'm not! I know what jail is like . . . I've seen more than enough . . . I'd rather die. I need to stay here for at least 2 weeks or one before going to war in D.P. I'm happy to say that Chicago . . . D.P., etc. believes that I'm in the Chicago area. Ha! Ha! Ha! I MADE IT.''

That night SWAT teams continued to watch the funeral home. A light snow fell over the area, making it difficult to use the special night vision binoculars. Extra lights were brought in to illuminate the streets.

March 21, 1992—10:00 a.m.

More than three hundred people came to Connie's funeral. Some, like Cathy Sullivan, were locked out because they arrived late.

"I'm one of her best friends," Cathy told the police. But there was no reprieve. The doors had been bolted shut, and Cathy was left to stand outside and cry and never say good-bye to Connie.

Wayne sightings continued to come in. Despite the light snowfall, the helicopter circled the area. The police were ready to move, but the Terminator never showed up to test them.

When the funeral service ended Patrick Carlson took one of the red roses that had surrounded the coffin. Chris kissed her sister's fingers, touched the still cheek, and took away the satin pillow to give to Max. John Krauser patted his daughter's shoulder, as if to comfort her as he had when she was a child. Jane placed a rose in the coffin. Tom also laid a rose on his sister, remembering the day not so long ago when they had laid Cynthia Krauser to rest. As he stood silently by the coffin of his sister, he knew suddenly there was something more he had to do. From the area around the coffin he gathered a dozen roses.

"I have to go to the cemetery," he said to one of the police guards.

"You can't," the officer said. "We haven't made the security arrangements."

"I have to," Tom said, his voice cracking as he fought back the tears. "See these flowers. I have to put them on our mother's grave. Connie was her daughter."

"Okay," the officer said. "If it's that important, I'll take you."

While the rest of the family was escorted back into hiding Tom got into a police car that followed two other squad cars to the cemetery. At the cemetery the officer emerged first, holding his gun, surveying the area for signs of Chaney. Then Tom got out. He walked in the fresh snow to his mother's grave. For a long and anguished moment he stood silent, thinking about the days when he had both of them, Cynthia and Connie, in his life, and knowing that for as long as he lived he would hold all the more precious the family that was left to him. He brushed a shallow layer of snow from the gravestone, and knelt on the ground. Gently he laid the roses from his sister's coffin on the cold ground in front of his mother's gravestone.

"Take care of Connie, Mom," he said.

18

The Hunt and the Hunted

The murder of Connie Chaney made waves in Chicago. Hindsight made it clear to everyone that Connie Chaney's husband should never have been released. The fact that his bond had been reduced raised questions about the court's effectiveness.

Local newspapers and television stations milked the story for all that it was worth. Outraged citizens had their say.

Perhaps the most vociferous voice of protest belonged to Leslie Landis, executive director of Life Span. Once she had absorbed the shock of Connie's death, the murder of "one of our own," as she put it, Landis began to beat media drums. What had happened to the orders of protection, she wanted to know. What role had the court and the state attorney's office played in this tragedy? She wanted copies of the court transcripts involving Connie. Landis—believing that the only way to get answers during an election year for the state attorney's office was to go public—arranged a news conference. On Friday she stood before the cameras and microphones at the Skokie courthouse. Connie's death had released Life Span from its promise of confidentiality, she felt, and she talked freely about the victim.

"We find it incredible that in the face of ample evidence and information indicating that Wayne Chaney was an extreme danger to his wife and others, that he was released through a reduction in his bond on some twelve violent felony charges," Landis said. "Wayne Chaney broke into Connie's home, beat her, raped her, and held her at gunpoint. With these facts the judge reduced bond?"

Landis said that the conditions Judge Sheila O'Brien had imposed were "unrealistic and insufficient" to keep Chaney away from his wife.

"We believe," she said, "that there was plenty of information given for her to have reached a conclusion that this was a serious criminal, a dangerous man. The tragic result of this case cries out for some responsibility. You can't have a woman lose her life for a mistake."

On that same day Judge O'Brien fared no better in the newspapers. The *Chicago Tribune* headline read JUDGE HAD WARNED HUSBAND TO STAY AWAY. The *Tribune* reported, "O'Brien's decision to reduce the bond angered prosecutors, who pointed out that Chaney was a felon with a conviction for battery and that he had violated a court order to have no contact with his wife." Bruce Paynter, supervisor of the Skokie branch of the state attorney's office, was quoted, "We tried to impress on her that 'no contact' orders in the past had done no good. This was a volatile situation. It was a mistake in judgment."

Judge O'Brien refused to speak to the press about it because Wayne was still free and his violations of her orders were still a pending case, even though Connie was dead. But privately, O'Brien was furious. "This is crap," she told Paynter. "You never told me about past problems, just the charges in this case."

O'Brien was public enemy number one the next day when more than forty men and women from various advocacy groups gathered in front of the courthouse and marched in the snow, carrying posters that read DOMESTIC VIOLENCE KILLS, VIOLENCE IS A CHOICE, and STOP VIOLENCE AGAINST WOMEN. Many of the protesters, fearing some sort of retribution from Wayne, hid their faces with scarves, mufflers, and sunglasses.

Meanwhile, in Chicago, F.B.I. Special Agent Delbert Dilbeck had completed his profile of Wayne Chaney, based on the diary. Dilbeck reported that Chaney was probably suicidal, and would probably arrange to be killed in a shootout with police. He was inclined to blame others for his problem, which is why he had threatened to kill Prandini. Wayne's only really love, Dilbeck guessed, was Max. Dilbeck, noting that Wayne was in a "progressive state of confusion of events in an almost delusional perspective," believed that Chaney would remain in the area to fulfill some plan, possibly to kill Prandini and Patrick Carlson.

The search continued. Police stopped Frank Allen*, the old Chaney pal who had been spotted at the funeral. They searched his trunk. No Wayne. They staged an early morning raid on the home of Wayne's friend, Norb, with twenty officers from a hostage terrorist unit. Armored in helmets and bulletproof vests and carrying automatics, the specially trained officers searched room to room, using a mirror mounted on a pole to look around corners. In the garage the officers put on gas masks and shot tear gas into the loft area. But they still didn't find Wayne.

The Krauser family was moved into a two-story bungalow on Chicago's north side, near the airport. Patrick slept in one room, Chris and Al in another with their two daughters. Tom slept in a sleeping bag on the floor. Jane had a bed in the basement. Not surprisingly, the stress of Connie's murder and hiding in tight quarters began to show. Chris and Jane started fighting over who would sleep where. Friends and family members became short with each other. At one point Patrick Carlson sported a tattoo that said "Connie, Gone But Not Forgotten," which Chris thought was, to say the least, in poor taste.

Though these tiffs were not significant, a battle of greater import was beginning between the Krausers and Patrick Carlson. It concerned Connie's life insurance.

Carlson was sitting in front of the TV drinking beer one night at the hideaway when he happened to mention that he would help Max financially with the proceeds of an insurance policy Connie had bought.

Chris began asking questions about the policy. It slowly dawned on her that Connie, intending to marry Patrick, had made him the beneficiary of a policy, though clearly her intentions were to provide for her son. Now Chris was worried. Patrick could take all the money and give Max nothing. When she pressed Patrick on the subject he refused to discuss it.

This was all very troubling to Chris because, at least for

now, she saw herself as the person who needed to look out for Max's welfare. Four or five times a day, she was talking to her nephew on the phone. Max continued to ask when Mommy was coming home. It was heartbreaking, and more and more Chris felt that the painful job of explaining to Max would fall on her. That moment, however, was being delayed. Of more immediate concern was keeping everybody safe until Wayne was caught. As long as they were at the house, the Krauser family had to have a police escort when they went outside. While the Krausers grudgingly accepted this invasion into their lives, Carlson bristled. He carried his own gun and told the police, "I don't need you guys. I am a free citizen. I'm not afraid of Wayne Chaney."

After a few days Al, Jane, and John were allowed to return to work, though they stayed in the safehouse at night. Chris and her daughters stayed in the house during the days, and Tom remained there for moral support. Chris, stressed almost to the point of a breakdown, began to talk about changing her name and moving out of the state. Over coffee one morning she told her friend Angela Burton, a police officer who was brought in to protect the family, "I am going to leave. Hell, if Connie did what I told her to do she would still be alive. I am not going to stay here like she did, so he can kill me. Connie knew she was going to die. I am not going to die."

The counselor that Chris and Tom Krauser turned to was Kate Couris, the psychologist who had been brought in by Officer O'Connell to counsel Jim Prandini. O'Connell had told Chris and Tom about Couris, and suggested they meet her. Couris knew something of what they were feeling. At age eighteen she had been married to an abusive husband who had even taken a shot at her through the window of a diner where she worked as a waitress.

Alone in counseling, Tom told Kate about the letter from Connie, which he still had not shared with the family. Kate suggested that the letter be read in front of the whole family. Tom, she could see, had not really done his grieving. He was putting on the strong front. "I haven't had time to grieve," he told her. "Been too busy looking over my shoulder to see if Wayne is there." He told her, "Our next problem will be telling Max what happened, and I am sure we will hear from the Chaney family about custody of Max. The nightmare," he said, "is just beginning."

Kate told Tom and Chris that they could be spared at least one part of the nightmare. She explained that the person who told Max that his mother was dead would be forever branded as a bad person, and for that reason the job should not go to anyone who was part of Max's life. Max should be told the tragic news by a professional counselor, she said.

Hiding was also taking its toll on the Prandini family, secluded in Wisconsin. Jim griped constantly about having to be pulled out of the action. He was afraid that people would think he was running because he was afraid of Chaney. While his wife, Donna, consoled him, she had problems of her own. She hated lying to her children, telling them that men were working on their home. And when her oldest boy became ill it angered her that she could not take him to the family doctor.

While the Prandinis and the Krausers were imagining that Wayne was nearby plotting their executions, Chaney was in fact, concerning himself with the more immediate matter of getting money. He had not robbed the Pizza Hut as planned. However, on the morning after the funeral, wearing a blue nylon stocking over his head and dishwashing gloves on his hands, Wayne walked into the Coastal Mart gas station on 6th Street in Cedar Rapids, Iowa, and shoved a gun into the side of twenty-one-year-old Brian Owen. He handed Owen a brown paper bag.

"Put all the money in the bag," he told Owen.

Owen, terrified, emptied the cash register into Wayne's bag, then stood with his hands over his head while Wayne ran out of the gas station and sped off.

In minutes Wayne was back in his motel room. He pulled off his stocking mask and gloves and counted his loot. A hundred and forty dollars. He was disappointed. He had hoped for more.

Later Wayne went fishing along the Cedar River with an old man he had befriended. He told the man, "I don't have a license, so if they come and check, say that I am with you." He was thinking, he later wrote, that if the cops did come, "I would have to shoot the cop first and then shoot my friend in the kneecap so I could get away." It troubled Wayne that he would have to shoot his friend just as Schwarzenegger had in one of his films.

Though Wayne tried to relax on the banks of the river, his paranoia got the better of him. He thought he saw cops hiding behind every bush, he heard them in every rustling of leaves. He couldn't take it, being out in the open for so long. It made him feel like a target. So, in the late afternoon he went back to his motel room. There, perhaps thinking that he could establish a new identity, he read the want ads in the newspaper. He even put in a call to one woman who was advertising for a tenant to share a trailer with her, but he got no answer.

That evening Wayne went to a country and western bar, but when a woman tried to make some time with him, he became suspicious and moved to another bar. There two men seemed to be staring at him, and he figured they were cops, so he left by a side entrance, thinking: "If they follow me I will have to blow them away."

That evening, having decided to commit another robbery, he wrote in his diary:

"I pray this one goes okay. I feel that this one will pay good and will be my last hit. I plan to party and fish for as long as the $$ lasts, and return to Des Plaines for my final stand. I pray that I don't shoot it out with these Iowa lawmen, and proceed with my death in D.P. If I can't pull this one off or another I'll have to return to Cedar Rapids for Pizza Hut. I had to do something. It's truly too early to go back now. I PRAY."

Though Wayne wanted to call home, he didn't know how he could do it. He imagined that the phones were tapped and that the house was being watched. And he was right. The Chaney house remained under constant surveillance.

Donna Chaney, fearing that she would miss a call from Wayne, had not gone back to work. For hours each day she sat in a chair facing the door. Staring at a picture of Wayne and Max, she prayed that her son would reach out to her. She wanted him to know that his family loved him, she wanted him to give himself up, to stay alive. Church friends came often and prayed with her.

Tom Chaney, shaken by the murder, did a good deal of soul searching during these days. He began to berate himself.

He had not been a good father, he said. He had been too preoccupied with career, he had not given Wayne enough attention.

Steve and Ken continued to search for Wayne. They visited the homes of Wayne's friends, leaving Steve's pager number in case he made contact.

There were some dreadful scenes. One morning Ken had a run-in with a friend of Connie's, who screamed at him for being the brother of a murderer. Steve had problems, too. He went back to work as a carpenter, but some of his customers, spooked by the Chaney name, canceled their work orders.

A few days after the funeral Steve was driving by a lake when he was pulled over by the police. He had been going five miles over the speed limit.

"Where are you off to?" one officer asked him. "Going to meet your brother?"

Steve blew his stack.

"That does it," he said. "You see that lake? Well I'm getting out of my truck and I'm going to walk over to that lake and sit and think."

"You are not going anywhere," the officer told him. "Do you hear me. I will have you arrested."

"I don't care," Steve said. "Go ahead and arrest me. I don't care anymore. I just need to sit and think."

He pushed his way out of the vehicle and began walking toward the lake. The officer grabbed him from behind, yanked his arms behind his back, and clamped cuffs on him. Suddenly all the tension of the past weeks caught up with Steve. He began to panic. Anxiety overwhelmed him. He felt as if he couldn't breathe. "I'm having a heart attack," he screamed.

The officer uncuffed him and called for an ambulance. By the time help arrived Steve was calming down. He had been hyperventilating. The officer sent him home.

Wayne drove to Waterloo, Iowa. There he cased a gas station. He planned the robbery in his mind. He even drove over his escape route, counting the minutes it took him to get away. In the evening, when he returned to the gas station, he found it bathed in much more light than he had imagined and he canceled his plan. But depression had been gaining on him and finally brought him down when he returned to the motel. He had accepted the fact that he would die soon. He no longer loved life, and he was becoming reckless.

He noted in his diary that seeing Sally Field, Connie's favorite actress, on television, had plunged him into a deep depression of memories of Connie and Max. He drove back to the gas station. It was a one-stop spot, with a small store. Wayne had no disguise this time, but he was beyond caring. He filled his gas tank, then walked into the store and grabbed a few items off the shelves. He placed his groceries on the small counter in front. He waited for another customer to leave, then he pulled out his gun and placed it against the head of the young woman who was on duty.

"I want all the money that's in the register," he told her. The clerk gave him the money and he left. He returned to his motel room.

The next morning Wayne rifled through the local newspapers, hoping for some story about the robbery. A small story noted that the robbery had occurred, that the police had no leads, and that they were looking for a man who was armed and considered dangerous. In his diary, Wayne wrote, "I've got to stay away. Do they know the make of my car? Do they have a sketch of me? Why wasn't it printed in the newspaper?"

In his diary he wrote, "Since it is close to the end of the month, I feel that Connie's boyfriend may be preparing to move out of his apartment at Wellington/Kimball in Chicago. This would give me the opportunity to give him what he's been asking for. Besides, he is the reason my wife got more distant, due to him dating her after five weeks of my wife leaving. Just before that time she was saying that maybe she's made a mistake and that she misses me. So I am off to Chicago for a quick stay and maybe an attack on D.P. or travel? But I realize if I stay loose or alive longer ... it would be that much longer for my son to start with his new mommy and daddy, so maybe it's better to go for it."

March 27, 1992

On the evening of March twenty-seventh, Wayne, distraught, lonely, and fatalistic, drove to a gas station near the

Arlington Heights apartment building where his brother Ken lived. He placed his diary on the front seat of the car, cleared away some empty soda cans, and left the car at the gas station, asking the attendant to give it an oil change and a tune-up. He pulled the hood of his gray sweatshirt up over his head, slipped on a pair of wire-rimmed eyeglasses, and began to walk to his brother's apartment building. By this time Wayne had grown a full beard, so he felt that he was thoroughly disguised.

In the dark he found his way to the apartment complex, County Glen Apartments, a massive multiwinged building that houses more than five hundred people and stood across from a building of similar size. He moved quickly into the vestibule of the building, glancing about for signs of surveillance, and rang Ken's bell. No answer. He rang again. Still, no answer. Jittery now, and feeling trapped in the small hallway, he rang other bells, hoping that somebody would at least buzz him into the building. But there was no response.

Wayne stepped outside and looked up at the face of the building. There were small balconies attached to the buildings and when he figured out which one was Ken's he told himself he could scale the building, break into Ken's apartment, and wait for his brother to get home.

He grabbed onto the side of the building and hoisted himself up. He knew he was taking a big chance. He could easily be caught doing this. But he was desperate for the company of friends and family, for news of his mother, and so he pulled himself forward. He worked his way, spiderlike, onto Ken's balcony. But Ken's door, like most of the doors in the neighborhood, was bolted, and Wayne could not make it budge. He climbed back down the side of the building.

Though he did not know it, irony was about to enter his life. Though he had been on the run for days, with half the cops in the suburbs searching for him, and Wayne spottings coming in by the dozens, the police were about to arrive without even knowing that he was there.

It happened that a loud party was occurring in one of the buildings, and one resident had been alarmed by the sight of a gang of kids, some of whom were carrying baseball bats. So he had called the cops. The officers who responded to the call were Dan Marshall, Paul Cagle, Bob Arrigo, and officer

Mark Caridei, and they were about to encounter a good deal more trouble than they had anticipated.

By the time the police arrived, Wayne had huddled in the vestibule in the apartment building across the street. Less exposed there, he had a good view of his brother's building and would know when Ken came home. He heard the police before he saw them. He held his spot in the small hallway, clutching the gun in his pocket. He knew that if they came after him he would have to shoot. Just outside of the building he could hear the officers stopping kids, asking to see I.D. He knew the cops hadn't come for him. But still—what if they spotted him and asked for identification? When one officer came into view Wayne pressed himself against the wall, trying to hide in the shadows. But it was too late. He saw two officers talking. One pointed toward him. His heart pounded. This could be it, he thought.

Three police officers moved closer to the building. Marshall stepped into the hallway with Wayne while the others stood outside and watched.

Marshall had grown up on the south side of Chicago and had an instinctive suspicion of strangers, especially strangers lurking in hallways. Keep your eye on his hands, Marshall thought, never take your eyes off his hands. Having no idea that he was confronting the area's most wanted criminal, Marshall stood before Wayne at a safe distance.

"What are you doing here?" he asked.

"I'm waiting for my brother," Wayne said. He pointed to the building across the way. "He lives over there."

Cagle, who stood behind Marshall, looked over his shoulder to where Wayne was pointing. Marshall's eyes never left Wayne.

"What are you doing here, if your brother lives over there?" Marshall asked.

"I'm waiting for him to get home," Wayne said.

Keep your eyes on his hands, Marshall thought. Wayne's hand slid into his pocket.

"Take your hands out of your pocket," Marshall ordered. Wayne did not respond.

"Take your hand out of your pocket," Marshall ordered again.

Wayne yanked his hand out, carrying his pistol. "Gun,"

Caridei shouted. But Wayne had already begun firing. Marshall, catching the bullets in the chest, bolted backwards and fell to the concrete. His flashlight bounced off the pavement.

Wayne flung open the door and rushed out, holding his gun in both hands. The officers moved back, grappling for covered positions. Cagle, rushing for the side of the building, slipped in the mud, twisting his ankle. Caridei took cover behind a corner of the building. He drew his pistol and prepared for battle. With one hand he called into his radio, "Shots fired, officer down." Cagle, barely able to move on his twisted ankle, hopped to the other side of the building, hoping to head off the gunman.

Arrigo did not get cover quickly enough. Wayne, dashing sideways and firing wildly, put two bullets into Arrigo's right knee. His legs went from under him and he landed on his back on the pavement, thinking he would be killed by this madman. He twisted onto his side, managed to get his gun steadied in his hands, and fired at Wayne. Wayne ran in the direction of the other building, then turned and fired again at Arrigo. Another bullet tore into the officer, this one severing an artery in his leg. Arrigo dropped his gun, now empty, and grabbed the new wound. Blood was spurting out of it. He was growing weak. He knew he would pass out soon, then he would die. In a moment he felt Caridei hunched over him, trying to comfort him. He quickly called out to dispatch that he had two officers down.

"Never mind me," Arrigo said. "Chase the man."

Marshall, in the hallway, knew that he would have died if he hadn't been wearing a bulletproof vest. As it was, the impact of the bullets, landing in the vest, just inches from his heart, had stunned him and knocked him over. Now he sat up and called in a description of the man who had shot him. Then he rushed to Arrigo and tried to help him stop the bleeding. A tenant from the building asked if he could help. Marshall yelled for him to bring a towel. He showed the man how to apply pressure to the wound area. Marshall then ran towards where he heard shots being fired.

Caridei, crouching behind a car, spotted Wayne dashing around the side of one of the apartment buildings. "In pursuit of the offender," he radioed in, not knowing if his message got through or not in all the radio traffic that was occurring.

He moved quickly but carefully, weaving in and out of cars in the dark parking lot. Suddenly the shadowy figure of the man dashed out from behind the wall. Caridei glanced behind him to see if other officers had joined the chase. No one had caught up with him yet.

"Freeze, motherfucker," Caridei called. "Throw down your gun."

By now Wayne had taken cover behind a van. "Fuck you," came the reply. Then suddenly Wayne came up, shooting. Six bullets rang out, all of them aimed at Caridei. Caridei, keeping himself as low as possible in the parking lot, returned the fire. One of his bullets caught Wayne in the left knee. Wayne, feeling vulnerable in the parking lot, where he could be surrounded, worked his way to the vestibule of the apartment building. Caridei moved in. He could see Wayne across the way. Wayne flung open the outer glass door of the building and tried to pull open the inner security door. But the door was locked. Wayne fired his gun madly at the lock, succeeding only in shattering the glass. Caridei could hear him screaming, "Shit, shit, shit."

Caridei took a position, pressed against a brick wall, with a narrow rain pipe for additional cover. From there he could see into the dim hallways, he could hear Wayne talking to himself, but his view of Wayne was partially obstructed by the branches of a birch tree. He lowered himself to his knees, held his gun steady. He could see that Wayne was pacing back and forth in the small hallway, like an animal in a cage, still frantically trying to break the lock on the security door.

Above him, Caridei could see that people had gathered at their windows to see what was going on. He shouted to them to get back. By now he had a clear shot at Wayne, but he wasn't ready to take it if he didn't have to.

"Police," he yelled. "Throw out your weapon."

Wayne turned suddenly, and stared out at the night. His eyes narrowed as he tried to spot the police but all he saw, apparently, was his own reflection in the glass of the door.

"Fuck you," he yelled. He jammed a fresh clip of ammunition into his pistol, then he kicked open the door and started shooting. "Come and get me," he yelled. The door flew open then bounced back shut. Wayne's bullets crashed through the glass, shattering it. Caridei shouted into his radio, "This is thirty-one. I have the offender cornered." Then, steadying his aim by pressing his arms against the drain pipe, Caridei pulled the trigger, firing twice.

His bullets went into Wayne's back. He cried out in pain and fell forward onto the floor of the hallway. But the fight had not left Wayne. He gasped for breath. He tried to roll over, tried to reach around for bullets that were in the pack around his waist. But he couldn't. He had another clip of bullets in his breast pocket, and he pulled those out instead, and filled his weapon again. Wayne then shot through a three-foot-high window by the door. The bullets crashed through the glass. Still lying on the floor, he bashed the barrel of his gun against the bottom of the glass in the door. Already there were two bullets in his spine and one in his leg, but he kept shouting at the police and kept firing his gun. He got off another ten shots. Now Cagle rushed in behind Caridei and fired a shot from the side of the building as Marshall moved close to a tree in front of the door.

Caridei yelled for Marshall to take cover, but Marshall took aim at the door and began firing. Then all the officers opened fire. Finally, one of the police bullets ripped straight into Wayne Chaney's nose, shattered his brain, and came out through the other side of his skull. It had taken fourteen bullets to kill him.

By the time they had moved in safely and rolled over the body of the mysterious gunman, a detective had arrived from Cook County.

"That man," he told them, "is Wayne Chaney, the guy who killed his wife and threatened to kill cops."

It was only minutes later that Ken Chaney pulled into the parking lot. As soon as he saw the flashing police lights and all the commotion, Ken knew what had happened.

"Where is my brother," he cried, pushing himself through the police lines. "I know they killed my brother."

When the police questioned him, Ken said he knew nothing about his brother being there. Still shocked and enraged over his brother's death, Ken was defiant. "That bitch, Connie, deserved to die," he said. "I would have killed her, too. None of this would have happened if you guys didn't arrest my brother last July."

Officer Arrigo was rushed to Northwest Hospital. By the

time he arrived, all feeling had gone from his legs. Doctors tried to stop the bleeding but the job seemed hopeless. It seemed for a while as if Wayne Chaney had been able to kill a cop before he died.

Arrigo, however, would live despite Chaney's best efforts. In a marathon fifteen hours of surgery, Northwest doctors were able to save Arrigo's life, and his legs, but they knew it would be months before he would recover and be able to go back on duty.

At the safehouse the Krausers heard reports of a man being gunned down by police. They listened eagerly to O'Connell's police radio, praying that it would be Wayne. When word came that Wayne Chaney had been killed, no tears were shed. The only thing that flowed was champagne. The family, jubilant, drank and celebrated the end of their ordeal.

In Wisconsin Prandini got the news from Freitage. Prandini's first question: Were any officers hurt? It was late when he hung up the phone and he was anxious to go home. He wanted to leave right away, but his wife convinced him to let the kids sleep through the night. Prandini did not sleep that night. Though he was immensely relieved, there was something oddly unfinished about it all. Wayne Chaney had been killed in a shootout with police, just as everyone had imagined. But Prandini had not been there, as he had imagined, he had not pulled the fatal trigger, he had not somehow avenged the death of Connie Krauser Chaney. In his mind he replayed the scene, but now it was he who put an end to Wayne. He knew that the fantasy was all that he would ever have. But, at least it was over, and he could finally return to normal life.

Tammy was at a bar when she heard the news. She immediately got on the pay phone and started calling friends of Connie.

Steve Chaney was sleeping at his girlfriend's house when Ken arrived to wake him up with the dreadful news.

"They killed Wayne," Ken said, and Steve could imagine the scene that had occurred. The brothers cried together, then pulled themselves together for the difficult task of informing their mother.

When Ken and Steve arrived at Donna Chaney's house late at night, they didn't need to speak at all. Their presence spoke tragic volumes. Wayne was gone, it was as simple as that. Donna woke her husband, and the Chaney family spent the night grieving together. In the morning Ken, Steve, and Tom Chaney went to identify the body. What they saw was their brother, dead, naked, wet from being washed down, his body devastated by the damage of fourteen police bullets. Steve Chaney took Wayne's hand, put his hands around the body, and wept.

While the Chaneys made plans for a wake and funeral, the Krausers had a new ordeal. Max had to be told. Chris dreaded the moment, but her anxiety was tempered by the knowledge that at least, with Wayne dead, she could take Max out of the foster home.

In the morning Chris and Patrick drove to the foster home. There they found Max, happy to see them, anxious to see his mother. Rushing into Chris's arms he asked, "Is Mommy coming home on Wednesday?"

Chris held him close. Would he ever really understand, she wondered. Would anybody ever really understand. "Yes," she said, hating to say it, yet unable to say anything else. "Yes, Wednesday. Mommy will be home." It had already been decided that Chris would not be the person to tell Max the truth. That job would fall to Kate Couris.

By the time Wayne Chaney's body was released and laid out in wake, the Krausers had gathered in Couris' office. They sat in a circle, most of them on the floor, and listened to the poignant letter that Connie had left behind. When the letter had been read, Kate asked each of them in turn to talk about what it meant to them.

There were tears. There was anger. There was self-recrimination.

"I should have forced Connie to leave the state and take Max," Chris said.

"She stayed here because all of you were here," Kate said. "You were her family, her support. Chris, Connie was a grown woman. She had to make her own decisions."

The family, with Kate leading them gently along, did as much emotional healing work as can be done in one session, until finally they all knew that they had reached the moment they were dreading. It was time to tell Max that his mother was dead.

Kate knew that it would not be easy. She had been down this road before with other children whose parents had died. While the Krausers were certain that Max did not know his mother was dead, Kate was not so sure. Children, she had learned, have instincts about these things. They pick up emotions, they piece together information in ways that are not obvious to the adults around them.

Chris and Patrick brought the small, blue-eyed boy into the room. Chris was feeling particularly tense. She could see that even beyond this ordeal, storm clouds were brewing. She knew there would be legal battles. She and Al would petition the court for temporary custody of Max, but the Chaneys would also want custody of Max. Donna Chaney would certainly want to see her grandson regularly. And she was sure there would be difficulty with Patrick over the insurance policy, and over Patrick's role in Max's life.

They brought Max into Kate's office. He looked about. So many people were there, but Mommy was not.

"Max, this is Kate," Chris said.

Max looked at the psychologist. "Do you have toys at your house?" he asked. "Do you have kids?" Apparently, he thought he was being introduced to someone new who would take care of him. He reached out to a small table and picked up a glass paperweight that held a small boat floating in water. Fascinated, he held the paperweight in front of his eyes and shook it.

"There are bullets in this boat," he said. "This boat is going to sink with bullets in it."

Chris and Patrick looked at each other.

"Max, why did you say that?" Kate asked.

Max, still staring at the paperweight, said, "Because there are bullets in the boat and the boat is going to sink and everyone is going to die."

Kate, carrying a can of soda, came around from her desk now and sat on the carpet, next to the boy. "Max," she said, "do you know where your mother is?"

"Mommy will be home on Wednesday," Max said.

Chris fought back the tears. Don't cry, she thought, it will only upset him more.

Kate leaned forward. She stared into the boy's deep blue eyes. Again she asked, "Do you know where your mommy is?"

Max said nothing. He carefully placed the paperweight on the floor and crawled away from Kate. He climbed onto Patrick's lap, then, changing his mind, he left Patrick and crawled onto Chris's lap.

"Max, where is your mommy?" Kate said.

Max still would not answer.

Now Kate went to a drawer where she kept toys and art supplies for the children of her clients. She pulled out a big sheet of paper and a crayon. She gave them to Max.

"Max, draw anything you want. Draw whatever you are feeling."

Max turned to Chris. "Go ahead," she told him, "draw a picture for Kate."

Now Max made his way over to Kate. He burrowed into her arms until he was securely settled on her lap, and he began to draw. First he drew the barrel of a gun. Then, extending the lines, he drew an entire pistol, filling the page with it. The family looked on. He knows, they thought. He knows. When he was done, he handed the picture to Kate. The room was silent.

"Max," Kate said, "why did you draw a gun?"

"Daddy has guns," Max said.

Realizing now that progress was not being made, that the painful moment was just being dragged out, Kate took away the paper and crayon. She sat the small boy on the floor. He looked so vulnerable. Max, as if sensing that awful words were coming, tried to crawl away from her, but she held him gently by the arms.

"Max, Mommy is not here because she is dead," Kate said.

Max, his eyes suddenly wide and filled with hate, glared back at Kate. He grabbed the can of soda she had been drinking and hurled it at her. The can smashed into Kate's head. Max stood up, fierce and defiant. "Mommy is not dead," he shouted. "Mommy is coming home on Wednesday. Mommy is on business."

It was a dreadful moment for everybody. Chris pulled Max into her arms and he fell into her lap, weeping uncontrollably.

"No," she said to him, patting his head, trying to hug all of him at once, "no," and she spoke the words she had always known she would have to say. "Mommy is not coming home. Mommy is in heaven. Mommy is dead."

In the days that followed Max was a whirlwind of emotions and confusion. For hours at a time he would be silent, and then suddenly he would begin to talk about his mother, saying that she was in heaven. He would look up through a skylight in the kitchen and say that Mommy had talked to him from heaven. Kate arranged for Max to see a child psychiatrist, but she continued to have her own sessions with him.

On his third visit to Kate she asked him if he knew where Daddy was. He replied, "Daddy is at Grandma and Grandpa's."

When Kate told him that Daddy was dead, he cried out, "Daddy is not dead. Daddy is not dead because Daddy has a gun and is a good guy and you can't kill somebody who has guns. Daddy is not dead."

By this time Max was living with Chris and Al and when he asked questions at home he was told that Kate would tell him whatever he wanted to know. It was best not to have the pain of these revelations coming from the people Max was supposed to bond with. Nonetheless, Chris and Patrick were present in Kate's office when Max asked the toughest question: What happened to Mommy?

"Mommy and Daddy had a fight," Kate said. "They weren't getting along and Daddy got very angry and he shot Mommy."

"No," Max screamed. His body shook from side to side. His face got red. "No, no, no. Daddies don't shoot mommies. That doesn't happen, no no, no."

"Max," Kate said, "It is not supposed to happen. But sometimes it does."

The legal battles that Chris had feared did come. The rift between Patrick and the Krausers grew deeper, as Patrick held to his claim that Connie intended him to have the hundred thousand dollars to take care of Max. Eventually an out-of-court settlement was reached in which $40,000 of the insurance money went to Max. The rest was divided up between Patrick Carlson and Connie's lawyers. Carlson, who dropped all claims for custody of Max, met another woman with a young son, and moved out of the area. Tom Krauser was given permanent custody of Max William Chaney and began the process of adoption.

On the first anniversary of Connie's death Tom Krauser filed a wrongful death lawsuit against a number of people, including the Cook County state attorney, Toni Winninger, Jim Kissel, the Cook County jail, Fred Musser, and Donna Chaney.

The newspaper and television stories continued long after Connie and Wayne Chaney were both under ground. Orders of protection were dissected. Stalking murders around the country were highlighted. Battered women became a common topic on talk radio. Investigations were begun.

And the publicity surrounding the death of Connie Chaney inspired the state legislature to hold hearings on a proposed antistalking law. Reports of women being killed by male stalkers had been coming in from every state in the country. In Illinois there had been at least five cases since the beginning of the year, including Connie Chaney's murder.

The hearings drew reporters from every medium. Police testified. Relatives of victims pleaded with the legislatures. Stalking, it seemed, had become the epidemic crime of the nineties.

The proposed law was not without teeth. Under it, if a threat was made, a report could be filed immediately. If the threatening person called or followed his victim twice, he would be regarded as a stalker and could be charged with stalking. Stalking would be considered a felony and it would be a nonbondable crime.

One woman who came forward in the publicity was a woman Connie's age, Dawn Wilson, a young, red-headed mother of a three-year-old daughter. Dawn, who had been beaten almost to death a year earlier by her stalking husband, had heard about Connie. At the hearing she told lawmakers that her husband, who now was in jail for beating her, was stalking her even from the jail by writing to her, despite an order of protection. Her husband was scheduled to leave jail in a few months and Dawn was afraid for her life, and worried that he might try to kidnap their daughter.

At the hearing Dawn showed blown-up photos of her

bruises. She described the many beatings she had suffered at the hands of her husband. She went through his lists of arrests, the orders of protection, the court dates, the complaints, all the accumulated legal maneuvers that had not stopped the abuse until the day he was put in jail. Dawn was, in the words of one police chief who attended, "Another Connie Chaney waiting to happen."

A few months later the Illinois stalking law went into effect. Connie Chaney's life and death had made a difference.

Afterword

Dawn Wilson's husband, Christopher, was taken back into custody on the day he was released from jail. Because he had written to Dawn from jail, he was charged with violation of protective orders. In a jury trial he was found innocent. Wilson, who spent a year wearing an electronic monitoring device, did not contact Dawn or their daughter, Christie. Eventually, he began a relationship with another woman.

Dawn appeared on a number of syndicated talk shows, and was the focus of an article in *Family Circle* magazine.

Donna Chaney was awarded the ten thousand dollars bond she had put up for Wayne. A Cook County circuit court judge ruled that "in the interest of fairness the money should be returned to Chaney's family."

However, the state attorney appealed, and the decision was reversed. Appeals court Justice Carl McCormick wrote, "Donna Chaney's hardship in having to repay borrowed funds does not ameliorate the risk she knowingly assumed, nor is it a legal justification to divest the state of its right to judgement mandated by the bail bond."

As for the lawsuit filed by Connie's family against Donna Chaney and the state attorney's office, all counts were denied by Judge Kathy Flanagan.

Thomas and Sarah Krauser are still in the process of adopting Max, who often talks of the moments he enjoyed with his mother and father, saying "I remember when Mommy did that with me," or "Daddy used to take me there."

When Max is old enough they feel that a book about what happened and how it happened will help Max to better understand his parents and to know that Connie and Wayne loved him.

GERA-LIND KOLARIK has been a journalist in Chicago since 1976 where she was a police reporter with City News Bureau and a freelance reporter with the former *Chicago Daily News*. She has also worked as a news assignment editor for the CBS and ABC television affiliates for ten years. She received an Emmy Award in 1984 for Best Spot News Reporting and was nominated in 1985 for an Emmy as a producer in an investigative reporting series. She is a member of the American Society of Journalists and Authors; Sisters in Crime; Association for Women Journalists; International Crime Writers Association; Mystery Writers of America; Society for Professional Journalists; International Press Club; and the Chicago Newspaper Reporters Association.

Kolarik is also a contributor to *Family Circle, Ladies' Home Journal, Chicago Magazine,* and the *American Bar Association Journal*. She is a frequent speaker concerning the role of journalists in reporting women-related crime stories. *Prisoners of Fear* is Kolarik's third book. She has previously written *Freed to Kill* (1992) and *"I Am Cain"* (1994), both published by Avon Books. Kolarik lives in Chicago.